The Advantage of Disadvantage

Does protest influence political representation? If so, which groups are most likely to benefit from collective action? *The Advantage of Disadvantage* makes a provocative claim: protests are most effective for disadvantaged groups. According to author LaGina Gause, legislators are more responsive to protesters than non-protesters, and after protesting, racial and ethnic minorities, people with low incomes, and other low-resource groups are more likely than white and affluent protesters to gain representation. Gause also demonstrates that online protests are less effective than in-person protests. Drawing on literature from across the social sciences as well as formal theory, a survey of policymakers, quantitative data, and vivid examples of protests throughout US history, *The Advantage of Disadvantage* provides invaluable insights for scholars and activists seeking to understand how groups gain representation through protesting.

LaGina Gause is Assistant Professor of Political Science at the University of California, San Diego. Her research explores US political institutions and behavior with a focus on racial and ethnic politics, inequality, and representation.

D1565848

Cambridge Studies in Contentious Politics

General Editor

Doug McAdam *Stanford University and Center for Advanced Study in the Behavioral Sciences*

Editors

Rina Agarwala, *Informal Labor, Formal Politics, and Dignified Discontent in India*

Ronald Aminzade, *Race, Nation, and Citizenship in Post-Colonial Africa: The Case of Tanzania*

Ronald Aminzade et al., *Silence and Voice in the Study of Contentious Politics*

Javier Auyero, *Routine Politics and Violence in Argentina: The Gray Zone of State Power*

Phillip M. Ayoub, *When States Come Out: Europe's Sexual Minorities and the Politics of Visibility*

Amrita Basu, *Violent Conjunctures in Democratic India*

W. Lance Bennett and Alexandra Segerberg, *The Logic of Connective Action: Digital Media and the Personalization of Contentious Politics*

Nancy Bermeo and Deborah J. Yashar, editors, *Parties, Movements, and Democracy in the Developing World*

Clifford Bob, *The Global Right Wing and the Clash of World Politics*

Clifford Bob, *The Marketing of Rebellion: Insurgents, Media, and International Activism*

Abel Bojar et al., *Contentious Episodes in the Age of Austerity: Studying the Dynamics of Government-Challenger Interactions*

(*continued after index*)

The Advantage of Disadvantage

Costly Protest and Political Representation for Marginalized Groups

LAGINA GAUSE

University of California, San Diego

CAMBRIDGE
UNIVERSITY PRESS

University Printing House, Cambridge CB2 8BS, United Kingdom

One Liberty Plaza, 20th Floor, New York, NY 10006, USA

477 Williamstown Road, Port Melbourne, VIC 3207, Australia

314–321, 3rd Floor, Plot 3, Splendor Forum, Jasola District Centre,
New Delhi – 110025, India

103 Penang Road, #05–06/07, Visioncrest Commercial, Singapore 238467

Cambridge University Press is part of the University of Cambridge.

It furthers the University's mission by disseminating knowledge in the pursuit of
education, learning, and research at the highest international levels of excellence.

www.cambridge.org
Information on this title: www.cambridge.org/9781316513576
DOI: 10.1017/9781009070171

© LaGina Gause 2022

First published 2022

A catalogue record for this publication is available from the British Library.

Library of Congress Cataloging-in-Publication Data
Names: Gause, LaGina, author.
Title: The advantage of disadvantage : costly protest and political
representation for marginalized groups / LaGina Gause.
Description: New York : Cambridge University Press, [2022] | Series:
Cambridge studies in contentious politics | Includes index.
Identifiers: LCCN 2021052919 (print) | LCCN 2021052920 (ebook) | ISBN
9781316513576 (hardback) | ISBN 9781009074322 (paperback) | ISBN
9781009070171 (ebook)
Subjects: LCSH: Representative government and representation. |
Minorities–Political activity–United States–History–20th century. |
Riots–California–Los Angeles–History–20th century. | Bush, George W.
(George Walker), 1946–Political and social views. | King, Rodney,
1965-2012. | Police brutality–California–Los Angeles–History–20th
century. | United States–Race relations–Psychological
aspects–History–20th century. | BISAC: POLITICAL SCIENCE / American
Government / General
Classification: LCC JF1051 .G38 2022 (print) | LCC JF1051 (ebook) | DDC
320.473–dc23/eng/20211120
LC record available at https://lccn.loc.gov/2021052919
LC ebook record available at https://lccn.loc.gov/2021052920

ISBN 978-1-316-51357-6 Hardback
ISBN 978-1-009-07432-2 Paperback

For my brother, LoJarric,
and all those who continue to fight for
justice and equality

Contents

Figures

Tables

Acknowledgments

I am grateful to the many people who have helped me complete this book. I will acknowledge some here, but many others have nourished me on the journey to publishing it.

This book started as a paper for Rick Hall's Legislative Behavior and Institutions graduate seminar. Rick introduced us to a rich literature on legislative institutions, particularly the US Congress. It was one of my favorite graduate courses because it focused on how legislators make decisions as imperfect beings in an imperfect world. If I wanted to understand the policies that affect ordinary people, then I needed to understand the incentives and institutions that influence legislative behavior.

One reading, in particular, stood out in Rick's course – Ken Kollman's *Outside Lobbying: Public Opinion and Interest Group Strategies*. The book focuses on how interest group leaders sometimes appeal to the public to influence legislators' actions. I thought the book was brilliant, except for one thing: it did not account for interest group inequalities. My intuition was that resources mattered for the way legislators respond to interest groups' outside lobbying. Also, those resources might encourage legislators to support low-resource groups more often than high-resource groups.

Rick was excited about the idea. Furthermore, he encouraged me to continue working on it as a potential project for my prospectus. Over the years, Rick has provided invaluable feedback and advice on the nascent research idea that would eventually become a published book.

One of the many advantages of being a University of Michigan graduate student is its faculty. The author of the book that inspired my dissertation was walking the same halls that I walked daily. Ken's research agenda had moved well beyond his first book on outside lobbying. Still, he was generous to meet with me to discuss my intuition to incorporate interest groups' resources into his formal theory. And he encouraged me to continue working on the theory to see whether the results would align with my intuition.

Heeding the advice of Ken and Rick, I continued to work on the formal theory. Eventually, I took it to Vincent Hutchings. Vince is not a formal theorist, but I was aware of his reputation of mentoring and advising graduate students. Vince's mentees informed me that he invests a lot of time and energy into his graduate students. He also has high standards and rarely, if ever, rubber-stamps research. Vince has definitely lived up to that reputation.

When I described my research idea to Vince, he was excited. He did not immediately agree with my intuition, but he told me that the project could make a substantial contribution whether I was right or wrong. I was a little deflated. How could he not think that my intuition was genius? I respected the advice, however. I knew that Vince was skeptical, not because he disagreed with me but because he wanted me to prove it. I left feeling that if I could convince Vince, then I could convince almost anyone. He helped me turn an idea for a class paper into a dissertation that would eventually become this book.

There are so many hidden rules to publishing books. Marisa Abrajano has exposed many of them to me. She has also protected me from the many service requests that would take time away from researching and writing.

I am also grateful to peer mentors who have provided professional and emotional support as I wrote, revised, and rewrote this book. I found my first group of peer mentors in Political Scientists of Color (PSOC) at Michigan. I shared with them not-very-fleshed-out ideas, and I built friendships over home-cooked meals and easy conversation during potlucks and coffee breaks. PSOC provided a safe and nourishing community. I especially thank PSOC members, including Chinbo Chong, Lashonda Brenson, Portia Hemphill, Vanessa Cruz Nichols, Hakeem Jefferson, Jennifer Chudy, Lafleur Stephens-Dougan, Bai Linh Hong, Steven Moore, and the many PSOC members from before, during, and after my Michigan days. In addition, Nicole Yadon and Princess Williams have spent countless hours providing words of wisdom and commenting on various drafts.

I am also thankful for Angie Bautista-Chavez. Angie has provided comments on chapters, abstracts, cover letters, and emails that assisted this publication.

My coauthors have graciously understood as I sometimes prioritized this book over our shared projects: Vanessa Cruz Nichols, Spencer Piston, Vince Hutchings, Mara Ostfeld, Steven Moore, Geoff Lorenz, Jennifer Garcia, Christopher Stout, and Maneesh Arora.

Teevrat Garg and Nico Ravanilla provided much-needed study breaks, writing partners, advice, and ears for those moments when I just needed to vent. I also thank Teevrat Garg, Meera Mahadevan, and Gaurav Khanna for their guidance and encouragement as I figured out how to negotiate with publishers.

Spencer Piston, Ashley Jardina, Davin Phoenix, and Nazita Lajevardi have recently written and published trailblazing books. They were kind to share with me their book proposals and publishing experiences.

While a postdoc at Harvard Kennedy School's Ash Center for Democratic Governance and Innovation, I benefited from the feedback and support of colleagues including Nisreen Ahmad, Marshall Ganz, Melissa Williams, Archon Fung, Quinton Mayne, Hannah Hilligoss, Tim Burke, Kai Thaler, Sean Gray, Brian Palmer-Rubin, Muriel Rouyer, Hilary Silver, and Julian Urrutia.

At UCSD, I have benefited from a remarkable group of fellow assistant professors: Pamela Ban, Kirk Bansak, Jasper Cooper, Sean Ingram, Federica Izzo, Garreth Nellis, Agustina Paglayan, and Yiqing Xu. During our workshops, they provided feedback on this book's drafts, advice, and encouragement. Stephen Haggard also provided extensive comments on the survey chapter of this book.

I'd be remiss if I did not acknowledge the people who provided their survey responses or the various random conversations I had with elected officials and activists who helped inform this project. I was pleasantly surprised that their opinions of protests, protesters, and legislative responsiveness aligned with my argument.

This book would not be possible without Michigan's Undergraduate Research Opportunity Program (UROP), UCSD's Faculty Mentorship Program (FMP), and the research assistance provided by Lejla Bajgoric, Nitya Gupta, Areeba Haider, Nadia Hartvigsen, Michele Laarman, Patrick Miller, Conor Rockhill, Brie Starks, Madeleine Tayer, and Shana Toor.

I am also thankful for the generous financial support of the Rackham Graduate School, Political Science Department, the Gerald R. School of Public Policy, the Gerald R. Ford Fellowship, and the Center for Public Policy and Diverse Societies. I would also like to thank the staff in the Political Science Department, Ford School, and Center for Political Studies – particularly Michelle Spornhauer, Mim Jones, Kathryn Cardenas, Elise Bodei, Cornelius Wright, and Nancy Herlocher.

I have benefited immensely from the Faculty Career Development grant at UCSD, which provided course releases to finish writing the book. I also profited from the Center for Faculty Diversity and Inclusion, particularly the writing retreats sponsored by Associate Vice Chancellor Frances Contreras and MarDestinee Perez. In addition, the Writing Hub's Matthew Nelson is an incredible facilitator and helped me drastically improve my writing process.

UCSD's Center for Faculty Diversity and Inclusion also funded my participation in the National Center for Faculty Development and Diversity's Faculty Success Program. The Faculty Success Program imparted valuable productivity tips that aided the book writing process. They also assisted in juggling the challenges of being an assistant professor while being a human being with responsibilities to myself and my community.

I participated in writing retreats sponsored by Dayo Gore and the Black Studies Project at UCSD. I also benefited from the financial support provided by UCSD's Political Science Department, Center for American Politics, and the Division of Social Sciences Special Initiatives grants. With their help, I financed a book conference, research assistance, and other activities that facilitated the completion of this book.

I also acknowledge Sara Doskow, David Meyer, and the anonymous reviewers at Cambridge University Press for recommending this book's publication and providing constructive feedback. Maya McCombs is the artist of the book's fantastic cover image. J. C. Flores has kept me mentally and physically in shape during this entire process.

Last and most importantly, I need to thank my family and closest friends for always showering me with their love and support. I am indebted to my parents, who, from a young age, have taught me the value of working hard, believing in myself, and never accepting mediocrity. In particular, my mom is my role model, friend, counselor, and teacher. I don't know where I'd be without her.

My sister, Makailah, has been there to celebrate every step in this process. And when I had creative blocks, she was eager to come up with ideas. Her enthusiasm pushes me to carry on.

My niece, Zaniyah, is my sunshine on any rainy day. The joy in her eyes, her determination, curiosity, and belief that she can do anything she puts her mind to encourage me never to settle.

My grandparents and many aunts, uncles, cousins, and friends who have become family inspire me daily. My family grounds me with their love, honesty, and mere existence, and they motivate me to persevere.

I dedicate this book to my brother. He was always my biggest champion. He bragged about my accomplishments and reminded me not to undervalue myself. He was so proud of this book, and he'd be excited to see it in print finally. I'm grateful for his kind heart, curiosity, and creativity. The book title was his idea.

I also dedicate this book to the people who courageously protest for justice and equality. It is often a tireless, exhausting, and thankless battle. I hope that this book reflects your experiences and can remind you that, while challenging, protest can and does change things for the better.

1

The Promise of Protest

On the cold, wintery night of December 16, 1773, a swarm of roughly 100 American colonists stormed aboard three ships docked in Boston Harbor.[1] The trespassing colonists were filled with anger and frustration. The British Parliament had once again imposed a tax without any representation of the colonists' interests in Parliament. To add insult to injury, the recently enacted Tea Act of 1773 gave the East India Company a virtual monopoly over tea imports. It also hurt the economic interests of Boston's wealthy merchants and tea smugglers, including the infamous Samuel Adams and John Hancock. In protest, the colonists demanded that the East India Company ships leave the harbor without paying the Townshend duty.[2] When the Massachusetts governor denied their request, the protesters proceeded to dump all 340 chests of tea aboard the East India Company ships into Boston Harbor.

The American colonists boarded the East India Company ships united by a popular grievance: "taxation without representation is tyranny." The colonists demanded that their government grant their right to a local, representative government. They believed that any taxes levied against them were illegal without representation. In response to the Boston Tea Party, the British Parliament implemented more punitive policies, including closing the Boston port and replacing any self-governance that Massachusetts had with the governor, Parliament, and the king's authority. The decision to discipline the colonists only intensified the conflict between the American colonists and Great Britain. As time went on, the

---

[1] For more on what would later be called the Boston Tea Party, see Carp (2010).

[2] The Townshend duty was essentially a tax paid by tea merchants in the colonies on imported goods, including tea.

American colonists became so wary of the British government that they declared their independence and established their own government.

In defense of their decision to seek independence from Great Britain, the American colonists wrote the Declaration of Independence. They asserted that "all men are created equal" with "unalienable rights," including the rights to "life, liberty, and the pursuit of happiness." They then proclaimed that it is the right and duty of men to "alter or to abolish" any government that does not acknowledge and protect their rights.

The American colonists reaffirmed the value and legal right to protest in the US Constitution. The First Amendment of the Bill of Rights insists that "Congress should create no law" abridging "the right of the people peaceably to assemble, and to petition the Government for a redress of grievances." Together, the Declaration of Independence and US Constitution establish the duty and legitimacy of collective action in the United States.

Collective action has a long tradition of challenging governments and institutions. In the United States, collective action was fundamental to the nation's founding. The American colonists who revolted against the British Empire championed equal representation and equality under the law. They declared that protest was crucial to realizing these ideals in a well-functioning democracy. This book assesses collective action's ability to promote democratic principles by evaluating the legislative representation of protest demands made by groups with different political, social, and economic power.

1.1 DEFINING PROTEST AND COLLECTIVE ACTION

Collective action occurs any time multiple participants publicly profess a grievance or concern.[3] Collective action can take on various forms, many commonly considered to be protest behaviors. Rallies, boycotts, sit-ins, and hunger strikes are all forms of protest. So too are the nonviolent acts of civil disobedience like those made famous by Mahatma Gandhi in South Africa and in the Indian Independence Movement, and by Martin Luther King Jr. and other activists during the US civil rights movements. Protest also characterizes the "violent, disorderly act of rebellion" known today as the Boston Tea Party.[4]

---

[3] For example, see McAdam and Su (2002).
[4] See Carp (2010, p. 219).

Popular understandings of the word "protest" overlook many of the tactics available for people to "alter or abolish" any government that does not protect the rights of the people.[5] Popular understandings of the word also ignore the many ways that people can exercise their First Amendment rights to peacefully assemble and "petition the Government for a redress of grievances." For example, protest is less often associated with the petitioning efforts to gain suffrage for women, letter-writing campaigns, or internet activism, like the infamous ALS Ice Bucket Challenge or *Kony 2012*.[6] Protest is also less often used to describe the mob violence and lynching campaigns targeting Black people in the United States throughout the end of the nineteenth century and the beginning of the twentieth century. Nevertheless, seemingly mundane petitioning, viral internet activism, and malicious mob violence are just as capable of communicating grievances and challenging institutions as marching in the street and participating in acts of civil disobedience.

In this book, I use the terms "collective action" and "protest" interchangeably to acknowledge the diversity of tactics used to make collective demands. The use of both terms also discourages potential misunderstandings. To be sure, one conventional definition of collective action refers to the provision of public goods by multiple people. This definition is often associated with the collective action problem, which describes how rational individuals will choose not to contribute toward a good if they believe that the good will be provided even without their participation.[7] The public expression of grievances by groups can involve collective action problems. I am more interested in understanding how elected officials represent demands that have already overcome collective action problems.

This book evaluates the political representation of protest demands. However, the arguments are not limited to collective action that targets politicians or policy. A key characteristic of many of the new social

---

[5] Recall this assertion in the Declaration of Independence.

[6] The ALS Ice Bucket Challenge encouraged participants to raise awareness and funds for amyotrophic lateral sclerosis (ALS) by filming themselves dumping a bucket of ice over their heads. They would then post the video on social media while challenging other people to do the same. *Kony 2012* was a short film produced by Invisible Children, Inc., to mobilize people all over the world to call for Joseph Kony's arrest. Kony is a Ugandan war criminal and the leader of the Lord's Resistance Army (LRA), a guerrilla organization notorious for kidnapping thousands of children to use as sex slaves or soldiers. The video was released on March 5, 2012, and within six days received more than 100 million views.

[7] Olson (1965) provides a comprehensive examination of the collective action problem.

movements that have emerged since the 1980s and persist well into the twenty-first century is that collective actions are primarily expressive behaviors. Sometimes they may demand institutional change, but they often occur as outlets for participants to express their identity-based grievances.[8] Collective action frequently concerns social or economic conditions, like obesity, alcoholism, or discrimination in the workplace.

Just because a protest does not confront elected officials or legislation does not mean that legislators can ignore it. Even apolitical protests can inform legislators about constituents' grievances on issues that demand representation. Moreover, apolitical protests can shift their target to elected officials if the concerns persist.

1.2 INSTITUTIONAL LIMITS ON EQUAL REPRESENTATION

The authors of the Declaration of Independence and the US Constitution endorsed collective action as a tool for people to make their demands known to their government. Once aware of the strength and direction of their constituents' preferences, the government could represent its constituents' interests. However, these authors did not want a government that addressed every collective action demand.

In Federalist Papers No. 10, James Madison warns that passions and self-interests incite groups.[9] He then insists on a large republic that could "refine and enlarge the public views, by passing them through the medium of a chosen body of citizens, whose wisdom may best discern the true interest of their country, and whose patriotism and love of justice will be least likely to sacrifice it to temporary or partial considerations." He and other authors of the Constitution designed a republic in which elected representatives would decide which collective action demands the government should represent.

---

[8] For more on New Social Movements, see Offe (1985); Johnston, Larana, and Gusfield (1994); Tillery (2019). For more on collective actions as expressive behaviors, see Chong (1991); Hamlin and Jennings (2011); Tillery (2019).

[9] James Madison was the fourth president of the United States. He was one of a group of men known as the Founding Fathers of the United States. He helped lead efforts by the American colonists to become independent from Great Britain. Once independence was achieved, Madison helped draft the US Constitution and the Bill of Rights. Madison also co-wrote the Federalist Papers – a collection of eighty-five articles and essays written to promote the US Constitution's ratification. The quotation comes from the Federalist Papers No. 10, where Madison argues for a large republic to defend against dangerous factions or groups of people guided by their passions and self-interests.

But as history and contemporary politics suggest, the representation of collective interests is biased. No matter the political party or government level, legislators are more likely to represent the interests of wealthier people than those who have less money.[10] Legislators are also more likely to represent the interests of White constituents than those of Black or Latino constituents, respectively.[11]

Perhaps this is by design. The people with the legally protected right to vote are the ones who select elected representatives. However, in no modern democracy is the right to vote given to every citizen subject to a government's rule. Democratic institutions have established voting rights based on citizenship status, where noncitizens cannot vote, or age, where people younger than a certain age are unable to vote. Democracies have also limited voting rights based on gender, race, ethnicity, and class. At the time of the first US presidential election in 1789, all but one state restricted the right to vote to White male property owners over the age of 21.[12]

Over time, collective action has granted more equality under the law. In fact, collective action was at least partially responsible for expanding voting rights to all White men, African American men, women, and then Native Americans. Still, collective action for greater equality and access to life, liberty, and the pursuit of happiness has also been met with

---

[10] Gilens (2005) demonstrates that national policy rarely reflects middle- and lower-income constituents' preferences across a wide range of policy issues. Meanwhile, more affluent citizens' preferences are often reflected in policy. Miler (2018) shows that legislators discuss the poor in political speeches and party platforms. Yet, they consistently underrepresent poor people's interests in legislation. Carnes (2013) contends that these disparities are explained by the numerical underrepresentation of congresspersons from working-class backgrounds. Moreover, Bartels (2008) finds that senators' own partisan preferences are more likely to predict their voting behavior than their constituents' preferences. When legislators' voting behavior does reflect constituents' preferences, only the interests of middle-class and affluent people seem to matter. Similarly, Ellis (2012) shows that legislators' voting behavior in the US House of Representatives better reflects their wealthier citizens' preferences than lower-income citizens' preferences. These differences in the legislative representation of constituents of different economic well-being do not disappear when accounting for differences in political knowledge or political engagement.

[11] Griffin and Newman (2007) argue that the preferences of White constituents are more likely to be reflected in legislative roll-call voting than the preferences of Latino constituents. In an original field experiment, Butler and Broockman (2011) demonstrate that legislators are more responsive to requests by White people than they are to requests by Black people.

[12] New Jersey allowed anyone who owned property the right to vote until 1807, when the state legislature restricted voting rights to tax-paying White men.

collective action in opposition to the same goals. Consider the fight over Black people's civil rights and civil liberties.

1.3 BLACK AND ANTI-BLACK COLLECTIVE ACTION

Since before the nation's founding, collective action has been a tool in a tug of war over Black people's civil rights and civil liberties. Black people's autonomy, humanity, and voting rights have been routinely contested. Over time, their collective action has also led to more civil rights and civil liberties. Collective actions negotiating Black liberation and equality raise questions about which protesters elected officials are most responsive to and which groups benefit the most from collective action efforts.

To begin, Thomas Jefferson is credited with the famous proclamation that "all men are created equal." Meanwhile, like other slave owners in the American colonies, Jefferson failed to acknowledge African slaves' equality and humanity. Jefferson and the authors of the Constitution enabled the coordinated theft of Africans from their countries for enslavement in the American colonies. With the Three-Fifths Compromise, they empowered slave owners to deny African slaves the right to represent their own interests in government – a collective action demand the colonists say incited their decision to seek independence from Great Britain – while simultaneously counting slaves as three-fifths of a human to increase the representation of slave owners' interests in government.

Slavery was a state-sanctioned, institutionalized collective action against Black bodies to advance the financial interests of White slave owners. The institution was brutal and uncompromising. But it did not progress unabated. From the oldest documented slave rebellion in 1663 to the emancipation of slaves in 1865, slave rebellions and revolts erupted throughout the American colonies and states.[13]

---

[13] For example, the 1739 Stono Rebellion was one of the largest and bloodiest recorded slave rebellions in the British colonies (Gates and Yacovone 2013). The revolt began with a gathering of about twenty enslaved men who were determined to find their freedom under Spanish law in St. Augustine, Florida. The fleeing slaves fought their way to Florida for more than a week. They killed numerous White people along the way, including store owners they attacked the first day of their journey. While they marched, they chanted in their native language, "Liberty" – a cry that men of the American Revolution would share in later decades. Many slaves joined the voyage, growing the number of fugitive slaves to about 100 people. Other slaves shunned the group. Some even hid

In response to the countless Black collective actions against forced servitude, White colonists imposed increasingly strict slave codes. The slave codes varied in nature depending on the colony or state; however, most slave codes made it illegal for slaves to free themselves from slave owners. Slave codes often required slaves to seek permission to move outside of their plantations. They also prohibited slaves from freely and legally marrying, and they criminalized any behavior seen as threatening the institution of slavery.

Slave patrols consisting of slave owners and other free White people enforced slave codes. They could punish slaves whenever they envisioned a violation of the slave code. In support of collective action by slave owners in Southern states, Congress passed the Fugitive Slave Act of 1850. The legislation required anyone who encountered an escaped slave to capture and return the fleeing person to their owner.

Still, Black collective action efforts boldly challenged the anti-Black collective actions for slave codes, slave patrols, and fugitive slave laws. The legends of Harriet Tubman, Charles Deslondes, Gabriel Prosser, Denmark Vesey, Sojourner Truth, Nat Turner, and many others tell the stories of extensive collective action efforts by Black people to dismantle slavery and acknowledge the value of Black lives. These stories demonstrate the agency of Black people who fought incessantly for their freedom and rights. They also recognize the Black activism that was at least partly responsible for building the moral consciousness that ended slavery in 1865 with the passage and ratification of the Thirteenth Amendment.

African descendants were emancipated from slavery in 1865, granted citizenship in 1868, and given the right to vote in 1870.[14] Yet, these collective action wins soon met staunch opposition, particularly in the South, where most former slaves lived. Jim Crow laws were implemented

their White slave owners to protect them from the rebelling slaves. Colonial forces eventually suppressed the uprising. Although some slaves found freedom in St. Augustine, most were captured or killed (Berlin 1998).

[14] The Thirteenth, Fourteenth, and Fifteenth Amendments to the US Constitution (also known as the Reconstruction Amendments) were passed and ratified after the American Civil War. The Thirteenth Amendment abolished slavery and involuntary servitude, except as a punishment for a crime. The Fourteenth Amendment grants citizenship to all persons born or naturalized in the United States, including freed slaves. It also gives all citizens equal protection under the law. Finally, the Fifteenth Amendment states that the right to vote cannot be denied or abridged based on race, color, or previous servitude. Women of all races would be legally denied the right to vote until Congress ratified the Nineteenth Amendment in 1920.

to control and suppress the agency of former slaves. In many places, White people used lynching to target Black people who threatened White economic power.[15] They also advanced poll taxes, voter identification laws, mob violence, and other forms of intimidation to keep Black people from exercising their legal right to vote.

Meanwhile, Black people continued to protest for their rights to life, liberty, and justice under the law. Ida B. Wells, and later the National Association for the Advancement of Colored People (NAACP), responded with collective action to end lynchings and counter the false narratives that extrajudicial lynchings were necessary to combat Black people's tendency toward violence and rape.[16] Protests for civil and voting rights coalesced into the 1950s and 1960s civil rights movement with prominent collective action events including the Montgomery bus boycott, the Greensboro sit-in, the March on Washington, Freedom Summer, Freedom Rides, and Bloody Sunday. Congress supported those collective actions with the Civil Rights Acts of 1957, 1960, 1964, and 1968; the passage of the Twenty-fourth Amendment; and the Voting Rights Act of 1965.

Well into the twenty-first century, marches, strikes, acts of civil disobedience, legal battles, uprisings, and demonstrations continue to negotiate civil rights and civil liberties in the United States. As the Black and anti-Black collective action examples demonstrate, groups of people with disparate levels of privilege and access engage in collective action to make demands on institutions. Elected officials occasionally represent those protest demands. For example, Congress supported slavery by enacting the Fugitive Slave Act but eventually abolished the institution with the Thirteenth Amendment. Anti-Black collective action resurfaced brazenly with mob violence and Jim Crow laws. Yet, when challenged by sustained collective action during the civil rights movement, Congress passed a series of laws to address Black collective action demands. Then again, many wins for Black collective action have faced backlash, retrenchment, and even reversion.

Of course, this is a simplistic overview of a long and complicated history of anti-Black and Black collective action. The purpose of this account is to demonstrate that legislators appear to be responsive to

---

[15] See Francis (2014, 2018) for examples.
[16] See Francis (2018).

collective action by different groups throughout US history. An open question remains: which groups are most likely to benefit legislatively from collective action efforts?

1.4 PROTEST'S INFLUENCE ON ELECTED OFFICIALS

This book makes a novel and perhaps provocative claim: whether elected officials support protesters' preferences depends on who is protesting. I argue that while elected officials are generally responsive to protest, they are exceptionally responsive to groups that protest despite high participation barriers. Collective action by groups who confront grave economic, political, social, or opportunity costs signals to elected officials that the grievance(s) instigating the protest truly matters for the group and could determine the group's electoral participation. Consequently, grievances expressed by low-resource protesters demand representation. Conversely, protest by groups with low participation costs is less informative for legislative behavior. High-resource groups can protest even when they place low value on policy support because they have ample resources to facilitate participation.[17] Legislators are, therefore, more likely to reward collective action by low-resource groups than that by high-resource groups.

1.4.1 Resources and Protest Costs

Protest is costly for all groups seeking to make collective demands. Participating in any collective action event means not devoting time to other activities, like work or school, spending time with family or friends, fulfilling childcare responsibilities, or completing household chores. Protest requires money to secure transportation or to purchase protest materials, like signs, clothing, or protective gear. Protest demands information about where to protest and the courage to publicly express grievances. It also requires the aggregation of individual skills, expertise, and experience.

Resources ease protest costs. Resources relate to the time, money, and labor available for collective action efforts. People without children or familial commitments have more discretionary time available for protest.

---

[17] See Banks, White, and McKenzie (2018) or Klandermans (1984).

Discretionary time is also present among college students, people early in their careers, and individuals employed in white-collar jobs.[18] A flexible schedule makes it easier to protest and still fulfill work, school, or familial responsibilities.

Monetary resources are also crucial for collective action. Discretionary income sustains leaders and formal interest groups who facilitate protests by informing and mobilizing protesters. It covers the costs of transportation and other expenses related to protest participation. Monetary resources can also compensate caregivers and personnel who can take care of household responsibilities. When more individuals have the financial resources to support collective action efforts, collective action is more likely to materialize.

Equally vital to protest efforts is the presence of labor and human capital. Good leaders have the expertise to provide the selective incentives necessary to confront collective action problems.[19] The 1950s and 1960s civil rights movement benefited greatly from charismatic leaders' ability to build solidarity and emphasize the importance of doing the right thing. Human capital also provides solidary incentives through the mutual participation of supportive friends and family members. Social networks help individuals process grievances and provide information on when and how to express those grievances in coordinated, collective efforts.

Some groups have fewer resources than others. People with less income and wealth tend to have fewer financial and political resources available for protesting than more affluent people. Income disparities also indicate less access for lower-income people to formal education and the social networks that motivate people toward political participation.[20] Additionally, members of the Black, Latino, and Asian American communities tend to have fewer political, social, and economic resources

---

[18] See McCarthy and Zald (1973).

[19] "Selective incentives" are exclusive reprimands or benefits provided to members based on their contribution to the common good (Olson 1965). Selective incentives could be material, like monetary payments given to or withheld from members. They could also be purposive or solidary. Purposive benefits arise from the personal satisfaction from doing what is good or moral. In contrast, solidary benefits result from the relationships and interactions that exist within a group.

[20] See Hansen (1993); Verba, Schlozman, and Brady (1995); Leighley and Nagler (2014). See also Corrigall-Brown (2010), who finds that income does not appear to have an independent influence on the likelihood of protest participation when measures associated with income, like gender, race, and education, are included in the empirical models.

than members of the White community. For example, the public, media, and state institutions are less likely to endorse protest by Black, Latino, and Asian American groups than they are to endorse protest by White groups.[21] Without resources, even people with salient grievances fail to engage in collective action.[22]

In this book, I engage various resource disparities to evaluate how who is protesting influences the legislative support of protest demands. I focus on protesters' race, ethnicity, and income levels. I also assess resource disparities based on protesters' organizational resources. Finally, I consider how digital technologies influence the resources available to protesters. I demonstrate that each of these resource disparities is important for legislators' ability to discern the salience of collective action demands among protest participants.

I evaluate each of these resource disparities separately to acknowledge that they are overlapping yet distinct contexts. For instance, Black and Latino community members are more likely to have less income and wealth than people who identify as White or Asian American. However, the resource disparities between racial and ethnic groups transcend economic differences. Social and political resource disparities determine differences in the protest costs facing groups of different racial and ethnic group identification. There are also resource disparities unique to lower-income people, regardless of their racial or ethnic group membership.

The resource disparities I explore in the ensuing pages may not be the only ones capable of communicating salient collective action demands and influencing legislative behavior. Inequalities exist across genders, sexualities, religions, ages, (dis)abilities, and many other characteristics. Some of these resource disparities have more implications for protest costs than others. For instance, women receive less income than men, but they are less likely than men to be subjected to aggressive police tactics. Whether a resource disparity matters for protest behavior depends on its implications for protest costs and, subsequently, its ability to communicate salient issue concerns.

---

[21] I elaborate more on differences in protest costs in Chapter 2. Also, see Davenport (2010); Davenport, Soule, and Armstrong (2011); Wright and Citrin (2011); Hooker (2016); Davenport, McDermott, and Armstrong (2018); Hooker (2016); Phoenix (2019).

[22] See McCarthy and Zald (1977).

1.5 CONTEXTUALIZING THE LEGISLATIVE SUPPORT
OF COSTLY PROTEST

Social movement and contentious politics scholars recognize protest as a rational effort by excluded and powerless groups to compel politicians to support their interests.[23] Protest can provide negative incentives that motivate politicians to engage in bargaining.[24] Yet, to date, little empirical evidence supports the belief that protest more frequently benefits the groups with the most to gain from representation. This book fills that void.

The United States was born out of protest. In principle, it legally protects and honors groups' duty and legitimacy to make demands on government institutions. At the same time, the United States advances institutions and practices that make collective action more costly for some groups than others. *The Advantage of Disadvantage* demonstrates that legislators are more likely to support collective demands made by groups that have overcome costly barriers to participation than they are to support grievances expressed by more resourced protesters.

The argument might seem counterintuitive. As I have already discussed, elected officials often limit the equal participation and representation of groups. Moreover, political scientists continue to demonstrate inequalities in legislative representation that disadvantage racial and ethnic minority groups and lower-income groups relative to their White and more affluent counterparts.[25] So, why should representation following protest be any different?

I theorize that the legislative support of protest demands begins with legislators' concerns about their reelection and their beliefs about protest costs. Collective action by low-resource groups sends a clear signal that the issue inciting the collective action is salient for protesters and will likely determine protesters' electoral participation. To be sure, protest can only happen when low-resource protesters are deeply invested in seeing their interests represented. When issue salience is low for low-resource groups, their protest costs prohibit collective action.

---

[23] See McAdam (1982).

[24] To be sure, Piven and Cloward (1977) demonstrate that grassroots collective action can effectively convince politicians to support policies that benefit low-income people, mainly when the mobilization is not led by leaders who tend to stifle the methods by which aggrieved populations can communicate their concerns. See also Gamson (1975) and Lipsky (1968).

[25] Refer again to Griffin and Newman (2007); Bartels (2008); Butler and Broockman (2011); Ellis (2012); Gilens (2012); Carnes (2013); Miler (2018).

Conversely, protest by high-resource groups sends an ambiguous signal about protesters' issue salience. High-resource groups can protest even without salient grievances since they have ready access to resources that reduce protest costs. Therefore, high-resource groups' protest may not indicate issues that will determine how they will participate in upcoming elections. I elaborate more on this theory in Chapter 2, but the bottom line is that costly protest effectively communicates that legislators who ignore their constituents' salient demands may do so at their peril.

I measure legislative support based on whether legislators vote in support of protest demands on protest-related bills. The focus on roll-call votes aligns with the assumption that legislators are motivated to support protest behavior out of concern for their reelection. Some legislators reluctantly support collective action out of concern that salient protest demands could translate into future electoral efforts to hold the legislator accountable for not addressing collective action demands. Other legislators support protesters' preferences because collective action helps them represent their constituents' concerns better. In either case, legislators represent costly protest to minimize threats to their reelection.

Legislators make concessions and create opportunities for credit claiming that might at least marginally benefit protesters. The more costly the protest, the more likely legislators will perceive the protesters' issues as intense. In addition, the more intense the preferences, the more substantial legislators believe the policy concessions will need to be to reduce reelection threats.

To make these arguments, I rely on a formal theory, an original survey of legislators and staffers conducted in 2018, and data on protests and legislative voting behavior from 1991 through 1995, and from 2012, exclusively. These analyses confirm that at least in some periods, the theoretical argument has empirical support.

The protest data from 1991 through 1995 assess legislative responsiveness in a period of relatively little protest activity. This period may make it more challenging to observe shifts in legislative behavior attributable to costly protest since few sustained social movements were operating then. Social movements comprised of collective action events that are larger, last longer, and have an identifiable issue framing and sustained organization are more likely to influence policymaking.[26]

---

[26] For examples, see McCarthy and Zald (1977); McAdam and Su (2002); Gillion (2013); Wouters and Walgrave (2017).

However, many of the collective action events in the early 1990s were limited in duration. They also received infrequent media attention, especially compared with the civil rights movements of the 1960s and 1970s or more recent protest efforts since 2014. Hence, assessing protests occurring from 1991 through 1995 enables a conservative empirical test of legislative behavior following collective action by protesters' resource capacity.

The original dataset assessing legislative behavior following collective action in 2012 helps discern how digital technologies, including social media and the Internet, might challenge the theoretical argument and the empirical findings of prior years. By 2012, internet technologies had developed sufficiently to provide new collective action opportunities on social media platforms and internet websites. Digital technologies also eased protest costs for collective action taking place in person. Does this mean that the ability of costly protest to communicate salient concerns to legislators is diminished? Or are legislators still responsive to costly protest even as participation costs are evolving? The analyses in Chapter 6 suggest an answer to these questions.

When marginalized populations, like racial and ethnic minorities or the poor, gain representation, it is often believed to be because of the actions of more privileged groups.[27] Indeed, this is a prominent narrative of the 1960s civil rights movement. Scholars argue that the movement was successful because of its ability to persuade Northern White liberals to support the efforts of Black activists in the South.[28] The influence of civil rights protests on White public opinion appears to persist. In places where civil rights activity was more significant, White constituents continue to support policies and politicians advanced by civil rights activists decades after activism ceased.[29]

The Advantage of Disadvantage demonstrates that the legislative behavior in favor of low-resource protesting groups occurs even beyond the influence of public opinion on legislative behavior. While collective action may influence the public opinion of more privileged populations, the empirical analyses demonstrate that legislators are more likely to support low-resource groups' preferences even as legislators consider the preferences and salience of other constituents in the district. Additionally, the amount of media attention dedicated to collective action does

---

[27] For examples, see Lipsky (1968, 1970).
[28] For example, see Garrow (1978).
[29] See Mazumder (2018).

not appear to negate the general argument. In this light, *The Advantage of Disadvantage* demonstrates the agency of marginalized groups who engage in collective action in the face of grave participation costs.

1.6 PLAN OF THE BOOK

Chapter 2 builds on social movement and collective action theories in sociology and theories established in political science on representation and inequality to create a theoretical model of legislators' responsiveness to protesters. I develop the theory with a formal model that evaluates a situation in which groups of different resource capacities signal to a legislator through their collective action that an issue is salient and, therefore, advantageous to support. The theory of costly protest and legislative behavior proposes that participation barriers are more prohibitive for those with fewer resources. As a result, reelection-minded legislators are more likely to discount higher-resource groups' collective action and reward lower-resource groups' collective action.

Chapter 2 also evaluates the limits of the theoretical argument. For example, are legislators responsive to nonvoters? What about the role of people who view collective action? Is issue salience only communicated by protest costs, or can it be conveyed by other protest characteristics? Should all legislators be responsive to costly protest, or are some legislators immune to the salient demands made during protest? What is the role of partisanship in the representation of protest concerns? Should Democrats be more supportive of protest demands than Republicans?

Chapter 3 presents the insights and perspectives of local, state, and national legislators and staffers who participated in an original survey that I fielded in 2018. I asked survey respondents about their views on collective action, whether they thought collective action was a legitimate form of political participation, and whether they believed collective action influenced their legislative behavior. I also asked them about their motivations to respond to collective action and whether they observed differences in the ability to protest based on the group protesting. The answers to these questions help clarify whether the people who determine legislative behavior believe they are acting in ways that align with the theoretical argument.

Chapter 4 includes empirical evaluations of legislators' roll-call voting behavior following collective action events reported in the *New York Times* from 1991 through 1995. This time frame enables the analysis of legislative responsiveness to specific collective action events without having to assess the spillover effects of larger social movements that have occurred in other periods. In some ways, this presents a more demanding test of the argument. Social movements suggest sustained pressure on political systems and perhaps a greater likelihood of responding to individual collective action events.

The focus on legislators' votes on final passage legislation presented before the US House of Representatives also represents a conservative test of the argument. Final passage roll-call votes are less likely to reveal a legislator's true preferences. Majority party leaders set the roll-call voting agenda. Therefore, few legislators have discretion over the content of the bills put before them for a vote. Still, roll-call votes are public. Regardless of how the roll-call vote came to be, it presents opportunities for constituents to observe their legislator's behavior. Constituents can then hold their legislator accountable for voting behavior that does not represent their salient interests. Therefore, legislators must be strategic in how they vote to avoid angering a group that has expressed its salient concerns during collective action.

Chapter 4 also conveys empirical results from analyses assessing whether legislators are more likely to support constituents' preferences communicated during protest than those not expressed during protest. The findings also reveal whether legislators respond more often to more (or less) costly protest based on whether the protesters are Black (relative to White), Latino (relative to White), Asian American (relative to White), low-income (relative to higher income), and grassroots (relative to formally organized) protests. The results evaluate legislators' representation of costly protest even while examining other legislative considerations, like the characteristics of the district and the legislator representing the district, and while considering other protest characteristics, including the size, disruptiveness, and media attention of collective action.

Chapter 5 explores how generalizable the theoretical argument is. Could variations in the legislator's race or partisanship or the composition of a legislator's district be responsible for the findings in Chapter 4? There are also some interesting coefficients on control variables in the empirical models presented in Chapter 4. Democrats are more likely than Republicans to support protest claims, perhaps because most demands are for progressive civil rights and civil liberties policy changes. At the same time, Black and Latino legislators are less likely than non-Black and non-Latino legislators, respectively, to support protest claims.

To address these questions, Chapter 5 evaluates legislative support of protest demands in different legislative contexts. The results focus exclusively on the differences in legislators' support of protest demands based on whether protesters are Black (compared with White) or Latino (compared with White). The results suggest that legislators are sometimes no more likely to support Black or Latino protesters than White protesters. Nevertheless, legislators are usually more responsive to costly protest and seldom more likely to support White collective action than Black or Latino collective action, regardless of the legislator's or congressional district's characteristics.

Chapters 4 and 5 focus on elected officials' responsiveness to protests occurring in the early 1990s. That period provides a conservative test of the influence of protest (that is, when national protests were less pervasive, and it was easier to assess when collective action had or had not influenced legislators' behavior). Yet, contemporary collective action is more pervasive and influenced more by the Internet and social media. Chapter 6 explores the evolution of digital technologies from the early 1990s and then presents a theory of collective action in the digital age. The theory suggests that online collective action is less costly than offline collective action and, therefore, less likely to communicate salient issue preferences. Consequently, legislators should be less likely to support collective actions occurring virtually than those in physical locations.

Furthermore, offline collective action enhanced by digital technologies should encourage legislators to remain more responsive to low-resource protesters. However, the ease of collective action for all online groups makes it difficult for legislators to discern the relative investment of protesters in online spaces. Online, formal interest groups' role in communicating the intensity of collective action participants' preferences becomes integral to legislators' responsiveness to protesters.

Chapter 6 empirically evaluates the theoretical implications of digitally enabled collective actions. The chapter uses a unique dataset of collective action events reported in 2012 in the newspaper with the highest circulation in the twenty largest US metropolitan areas. The data is aggregated based on the data collection methods used to create the Dynamics of Collective Action (DCA) dataset for the early 1990s. The chapter begins by comparing the original dataset of contemporary collective action with collective action events in the DCA. The comparisons suggest that while digital technologies have significantly evolved, the DCA provides an adequate representation of protest events for analysis.

Next, Chapter 6 explores costly protest by empirically evaluating the differences in legislative representation of costly protest occurring in person compared with less costly protest happening online. The chapter demonstrates whether the differences in resource capacities explored in the previous chapter remain in an environment with enhanced digital technologies. Together, the findings assess whether digital technologies impede legislators' ability to discern and represent salient constituency concerns revealed by protest costs.

In the concluding chapter, I consider what *The Advantage of Disadvantage* means in the context of democratic representation. Does costly protest challenge the persistent inequalities in representation, or does it only produce symbolic representation? The analyses in previous chapters demonstrate marginalized populations' agency to demand representation. They also highlight the extreme measures that low-resource groups must face to gain representation. Is this strategy sustainable or even an indication of a functioning democratic republic?

2

Costly Protest and Political Representation

The verdict was delivered around 3:15 p.m. on April 29, 1992. People were enraged. Despite video showing Sergeant Stacey Koon and Officers Laurence Powell, Timothy Wind, and Theodore Briseno beating an unarmed African American motorist, a mostly White jury failed to convict the officers of the assault and excessive use of force against Rodney King. Within minutes, large crowds mobilized in and around the city of Los Angeles. For the next several days, the Los Angeles metropolitan area was teeming with assaults, looting, arson, and even murder.

President H. W. Bush addressed the nation two days after the protests began.[1] He focused on the "incidents of random terror and lawlessness." He argued that what was taking place was "not about civil rights. . . . It's not a message of protest. It's been the brutality of a mob, pure and simple." President Bush's focus on the property damage and violence was an effort to delegitimize the protesters' grievances. It was an attempt to justify the mobilization of thousands of law enforcement agents to Los Angeles.[2] He gave an extensive description of the law and order measures that were being deployed in response to the protests, and he only briefly discussed how he planned to address the grievances that incited the protest. President Bush insisted that "[in] a civilized society, there can be no excuse – no excuse – for the murder, arson, theft, and vandalism that have terrorized the law-abiding citizens of Los Angeles."

---

[1] The transcript is available at www.c-span.org/video/?25847-1/reaction-los-angeles-police-trial.

[2] Weaver (2007) argues that after the civil rights movements of the 1960s, conservative elites and politicians coordinated efforts to associate Black civil rights demands with criminal behavior to justify punishment instead of social reform as the proper response to racial disorder.

His plea for a calm and peaceful reaction to the verdict is understandable, considering that most Americans object to violence and property destruction. But asking aggrieved populations not to express anger and outrage while confronting inhumane circumstances is unreasonable and perhaps undemocratic.[3] Moreover, the expectation of calm in response to injustice is not leveraged equally across populations.[4]

Congresswoman Maxine Waters represented the South Central Los Angeles district where the Rodney King events unfolded. She asked observers to concentrate less on the way people expressed their grievances and more on the reason behind the collective outrage. She insisted that people listen to her repeated appeals to invest in low-income and minority communities, like the one she represented. Congresswoman Waters explained, "[The problem] has been simmering because of a lack of attention to these inner cities for so long. The hopelessness, the unemployment, the frustration has been festering. The jury verdict was just the straw that broke the camel's back."[5] Congresswoman Waters's comments call attention to the disregard for Black communities, particularly in comparison with White communities.

When protesters took to the streets in the spring of 1992, they did so not only to express outrage over the lack of justice for Rodney King. They protested an entire system of oppression that regarded Black people as less than citizens. The uprisings demonstrated that African Americans would not quietly endure the status quo. Confronted with institutions, like the courts, that consistently failed to provide liberty and justice for all, Black people employed the only resource available to them: protest.

Members of the US Congress responded to the Rodney King protests with the Dire Emergency Supplemental Appropriations Act of 1992.[6] The legislation provided funds to rebuild businesses destroyed in the protests. It also funded a summer youth employment and training program sponsored by the Department of Justice's Employment Training

---

[3] See Hooker (2016).

[4] Phoenix (2019) argues that White people are more prone to anger than Black people. However, experiences and elite rhetoric encourage White people to act on their anger while encouraging Black people to suppress and redirect their anger into resignation.

[5] Quoted in Shuit (1992).

[6] The Dire Emergency Supplemental Appropriations Act, 1992, for Disaster Assistance to Meet Urgent Needs Because of Calamities Such as Those Which Occurred in Los Angeles and Chicago (H.R.5132) was enacted on June 22, 1992.

Administration. Most Republican members of Congress voted in opposition to the bill, but Republican Congressman Jerry Lewis deviated from his normal voting behavior to support the legislation.

I contend that Congressman Lewis's vote was likely motivated by the Rodney King uprisings that reached sixty miles east of Los Angeles to his congressional district representing San Bernardino, California. The protests revealed that Congressman Lewis's constituents were fed up with the lack of justice and welfare for Black people. They demanded that those grievances be addressed. Congressman Lewis responded to the protests by voting in support of H.R.5132 – his first opportunity to provide some legislative support to the issues raised during protest by constituents in his district.

This chapter presents a theory of costly protest and legislative behavior. The theory contributes to a growing literature on legislators' responsiveness to collective action demands.[7] The theory adds to the existing literature by answering an open question: are the groups with the most to gain from representation the most likely to benefit legislatively from protest efforts?

The theory suggests that it is not only likely but strategic for legislators to more frequently support the interests of protesters than non-protesters, especially when protesters have fewer resources to engage in collective action. Legislators are more likely to support low-resource groups' protest demands than higher resource groups' protest demands because costly protest is a stronger indication that protesters have a salient desire for their issues to be represented. Any legislator who ignores salient collective action demands risks electoral participation that could cost their reelection.

---

[7] Bailey, Mummolo, and Noel (2012) reveal that Republican legislators are more likely to vote in support of Tea Party–approved legislation as the number of Tea Party activists in their district increases. Gillion (2013) finds that increasingly salient protest for racial and ethnic minorities' interests leads to responsive roll-call voting by legislators representing districts in which collective action occurs. Gillion (2013) measures protest salience with an index of protest characteristics. He argues that protest increases in salience as the number of the following are present: more than one hundred people, lasts more than one day, supported by a political organization, results in property damage, draws a police presence, leads to arrest, protesters have weapons, injury, and death. Moreover, Wouters and Walgrave (2017) demonstrate that asylum-issue protests that are large and have a cohesive message are more likely to shape Belgian elected officials' interests, position-taking, and future actions concerning asylum policies. For other examples, refer to McAdam (1982); Gamson (1990); Cress and Snow (2000); Andrews (2001); Agnone (2007).

2.1 LEGISLATORS' INCENTIVES TO REPRESENT PROTEST DEMANDS

The theory begins with the understanding that legislators' primary, if not exclusive, goal is to win elections.[8] Legislators may have other objectives, like having power, prestige, or making public policy. Still, to achieve these goals, legislators must win elections.[9] Reelection is a concern for even the most experienced and popular legislators. In any election, "latent or unfocused opinions can quickly be transformed into intense and very real opinions with enormous political repercussions."[10] Consequently, all legislators are watchful for constituents who could become mobilized during elections.

Reelection-minded legislators want to respond to the concerns of constituents who are most likely to influence their reelection prospects. They want to respond to the people in their district willing to reward or punish legislators for their (in)actions. Therefore, reelection-minded legislators desire to support constituents with salient preferences who monitor and hold legislators accountable for their roll-call votes on issues important to them.[11] This desire is evident in legislative behavior. Legislators are more likely to represent constituents' issue preferences when the issue is salient to constituents.[12] Yet, how do legislators learn about the strength of their constituents' issue preferences?

Sometimes legislators rely on election returns, public opinion polls, and lobbying behavior for information about their constituents' preferences. They may also reference newspapers and media reports for signs that public opinion might be shifting. However, these sources do not adequately communicate issue salience. Elections occur infrequently and are more capable of revealing issue preferences than issue salience. The issues discussed in public opinion polls and media reports are limited to the survey designer's or editor's awareness of pressing issues. The way questions are framed restricts the information that surveys reveal about constituents. Relatedly, effective lobbying is more about access and networks than about communicating the intensity of issue preferences.[13] Where these conventional conveyers of constituents' preferences

---

[8] See Mayhew (1974); Fiorina (1977); Fenno (1978).

[9] See Fenno (1978).

[10] Arnold (1990), p. 68.

[11] See Ansolabehere and Jones (2010); Canes-Wrone, Minozzi, and Reveley (2011).

[12] For examples, see Kingdon (1977); Kollman (1998); Canes-Wrone (2001).

[13] For example, see Baumgartner et al. (2009).

inadequately reveal issue salience, protest is a fruitful alternative. Protest provides elected officials with valuable information about the direction and strength of their constituents' policy preferences.[14]

Early social movement and collective action scholars emphasize the role of grievances in encouraging protest mobilization. They contend that collective action is only possible when there is "an increase in the extent or intensity of grievances."[15] In other words, grievances motivate protest participation. Those same grievances could also motivate electoral participation.

Protesters are more likely than non-protesters to participate in elections.[16] They also influence the participation of third-party observers. For instance, observers – whether or not they would benefit from the representation of protest demands – might become so persuaded by protesters' grievances that they move from observing collective action to participating in it. Collective action by large groups signals a critical mass of people who share a concern, and it indicates a constituency with high issue salience.[17] The larger the protest, the more likely that a legislator will support protesters' demands.[18]

The disruptiveness of a protest event can also communicate issue salience and compel legislative behavior.[19] The more significant the grievance, the more willing individuals are to pursue disruptive tactics.[20] There is some evidence that disruptive collective action increases legislative support; however, most evidence suggests the opposite.[21]

---

[14] For examples, consult Lipsky (1968); Piven and Cloward (1977); Gamson (1990); Cress and Snow (2000); McAdam and Su (2002); Gillion (2013).

[15] McCarthy and Zald (1977), p. 1214. See also Gurr (1970).

[16] See Rosenstone and Hansen (1993).

[17] See Lohmann (1993), who demonstrates that protest size helps legislators discern their constituents' issue preferences. See Olson (1965) on the difficulty of protest for large groups. Also see Marwell and Oliver (1993, p. 7), who contend that "Olson's theory may be reinterpreted as saying that people will not engage in collective action solely from motives of isolated material self-interest in the collective good, but will also have solidary ties to other collective actors, have a sense of moral purpose, stand to gain personally from the very fact of acting, or any combination of these motives."

[18] Consider Bailey, Mummolo, and Noel (2012); Gillion (2013); Wouters and Walgrave (2017).

[19] Disruptive characteristics include property damage, arrests, injury, death, police, and weapons (Lipsky 1968, 1970; Piven and Cloward 1977; Browning, Marshall, and Tabb 1984; Cress and Snow 2000).

[20] For example, see Gurr (1970).

[21] For example, McAdam and Su (2002) suggests that disruptive antiwar protests during the Vietnam War positively shifted congressional voting behavior in favor of peace but decreased the pace of congressional action. And, Piven and Cloward (1977) suggests

Legislators are often wary of violent or disruptive collective action, especially those that lead to social unrest. Social unrest can disrupt the economy or challenge the legitimacy of governing institutions by exposing to the public issues that the government created or failed to address. To mitigate social unrest, legislators attempt to end disruptive protests with either repression tactics, concessions to protesters, or a strategy involving both repression and concessions.[22]

The fear of negative electoral repercussions is not the only reason that legislators support protest demands. Sometimes protest presents legislators with an opportunity to rebrand themselves or appeal to new constituencies that could increase the legislators' reelection chances.[23] Relatedly, collective action provides opportunities for legislators who

disruptive protest is essential for the legislative support of poor people's interests. Gamson (1990) performs a meta-analysis of fifty-three social movement organizations and finds that of the twenty-one groups that used violence two-thirds achieved their desired goal. Conversely, Browning, Marshall, and Tabb (1984) contends that contentious actions decreased the success of minority protest in Northern California cities in the 1960s and 1970s. Moreover, Chenoweth and Stephan (2011) argues that nonviolent protests are twice as effective as violent protests.

[22] See Piven and Cloward (1977); Gamson (1990); Andrews (2001). Repression tactics involve police or military actions, curfews, or new laws that make it difficult for people to congregate in public spaces. Concessions might include symbolic gestures, like giving collective action leaders positions in government institutions or creating commissions to diagnose the problems leading to social unrest. Examples of commissions include those following the uprisings in Chicago in 1919, Los Angeles in 1965 or 1992, or across the United States in 1967. Often, commissions are given little enforcement power to address the issues they identify (Lipsky and Olson 1977; Lupo 2010). Concessions could also provide substantive legislative support for protest goals. For example, legislators responded to the civil rights movement with the Civil Rights Act of 1964 and the Voting Rights Act of 1965.

[23] Consider the political incorporation of African Americans by the Democratic Party. Initially, African Americans were ardent supporters of the Republican Party. As the party of Lincoln, Republicans were responsible for freeing Black people from slavery and supporting Black people's collective demands for suffrage. The Democratic Party first attempted to incorporate Black voters in the early twentieth century, when Black people began fleeing the South's mob violence, Jim Crow laws, and poor economic conditions for cities in the North and West. The Democratic Party's efforts to mobilize Black voters were not successful until the 1960s when it incorporated civil rights demands into the Democratic Party platform. The civil rights movement communicated to legislators the intensity of the Black community's racial justice and equality concerns. The Democratic Party recognized the Republican Party's refusal to support those salient demands. Democrats successfully shifted their platform to gain a new voting block of Black supporters. See White and Laird (2020). Also, see Philpot (2007) on how the Republican Party has been unsuccessful in recapturing the support of Black voters due to the Republican Party's symbolic appeals aimed at addressing Black collective action demands.

are already sympathetic to protest demands to increase their representation of protesting groups.[24] Moreover, collective action can change the "hearts and minds" of legislators who may not have previously supported collective action demands. Legislators interested in making good public policy could look to protest to inform them of the issues in their district that are most critical for their attention.[25]

Legislators are concerned with goals, such as maintaining their image or making good public policy. They must simultaneously be mindful of how their legislative support of protest will influence their reelection.[26] To win elections, legislators must maintain an image that they are good at their job. They must win challenges by candidates who run against them, perhaps on a platform that appeals to collective action participants and observers. They are, therefore, attentive to collective action participants and observers who care enough about the issue to affect the legislator's probability of reelection. They make concessions out of their reelection concern. Legislators who do not support protest efforts risk mobilizing observers who might harm the legislator's reelection, even if those mobilized are uninterested in the specific protest demands.

Furthermore, legislators who respond to protest because they agree with the protest demands also do so out of reelection concerns. As the

---

[24] For example, Congresswoman Maxine Waters was in her first term as a member of Congress when the Rodney King protests occurred. Even before the collective action, she was vocal in her admonishment of a political system that enabled racial and ethnic minorities' inhumane living conditions in her Los Angeles district. The collective action following the Rodney King verdict helped her to be more vocal and insistent in her advocacy of Black, Brown, and low-income communities.

[25] This is likely the reason for the repeal of the Medicare Catastrophic Coverage Act in 1989. The bill was intended to improve medical benefits for the elderly. It passed in June 1988 with the support of the American Association of Retired Persons (AARP) and with bipartisan support in Congress and the White House (Tolchin 1989). However, once the bill was passed, grassroots organizations like the National Committee to Preserve Social Security and Medicare began to call attention to the catastrophic premiums and surtaxes that accompanied the legislation. The direct mail efforts led to elderly constituents overwhelming town meetings and campaign rallies in California, Florida, Nevada, and districts across the Southwest. In a viral video captured by a news crew, Ways and Means Committee chairman, Dan Rostenkowski, is seen fleeing his car after being swarmed by angry elderly constituents. Following the backlash, Senator John McCain, who was one of only eleven senators to vote against the legislation, commented, "Every member of Congress has been accosted at town meetings" (quoted in Tolchin 1989). These protest efforts resulted in a repeal of the Medicare Catastrophic Coverage Act and have convinced legislators that collective action demands for health care are not to be taken lightly.

[26] See Fenno (1973); Mayhew (1974); Arnold (1990).

survey of legislators and staffers in Chapter 3 suggests, legislators who champion protest demands seize the opportunity to communicate to constituents what they are doing to support protest demands. The reelection incentive is, therefore, the primary motivation for legislators' responsiveness to protesting constituents. The reelection incentive motivates the formal theory of legislative behavior following protest.

2.2 PROTESTERS' RESOURCE CAPACITY AND THE MOBILIZATION OF GRIEVANCES

While protest motivates legislators to support constituents' salient issues, protests' ability to communicate constituents' salient issue preferences depends on protesters' resource capacity. As I described in the previous chapter, resources (e.g., time, money, information, labor, and skills) make it possible for groups to afford protest costs.[27] Groups with flexible work schedules, discretionary income, and social and professional networks can easily aggregate the resources necessary for protest participation. For these high-resource groups, protest costs matter less for their ability to engage in collective action. They can take time off work to attend protests. They can afford the transportation costs required to travel to an event. They exist within networks that provide the information and social support that facilitate participation. Conversely, for groups with lower resource capacity, protest costs can prevent collective action even if constituents have a salient grievance that warrants representation.

Many variables can define high- and low-resource capacity groups. Differences in resources exist based on a group's race, ethnicity, and income levels. Resource differences are also defined based on a group's organizational capacity. Variations in resources exist based on a group's access to the Internet and other digital technologies. In the coming sections, I describe how each of these resource disparities influences whether or not a group can voice its grievances during protest.

2.2.1 Black and White Resource Disparities

Resource differences between Black and White people in the United States began with the institution of slavery. During slavery, Black people were considered subhuman and given little agency over their own lives.

---

[27] See McCarthy and Zald (1977).

Even poor White people could vote and were not subject to the slave codes that made it difficult for Black people to gather in public places. As members of slave patrols, White people had the legal authority to restrict the free movement of Black slaves in efforts to increase the costs and consequently decrease the likelihood of Black collective action. For instance, in many places, limits were set on the number of Black people who could congregate at one time.

The Reconstruction Amendments[28] ended the legal institution of slavery. Yet, considerable protest costs remain for Black people, especially when compared with their White counterparts. There is less investment in social welfare programs, including public education, gainful employment opportunities, and unemployment protections, in locations with more Black people.[29] Indeed, support for means-tested social welfare decreases substantially when the policies are associated with African Americans.[30] Racial animosity toward African Americans and race-based notions of deservingness are primarily responsible for the opposition to poverty-alleviating programs.[31] Whatever the explanation, Black people are less likely than White people to benefit from social welfare programs that provide economic and civic resources that could facilitate collective action.

Resource disparities between Black and White people are also evident in the public and elite support of protest demands. Elected officials, media, and other elite actors explicitly associate Black protest with criminal behavior to delegitimize protest demands.[32] Elites also create and perpetuate narratives that Black people are criminals and, therefore,

---

[28] The Reconstruction Amendments include the Thirteenth, Fourteenth, and Fifteenth Amendments to the United States Constitution. They were ratified after the American Civil War. The Thirteenth Amendment abolished slavery and involuntary servitude, except as a punishment for a crime. The Fourteenth Amendment granted citizenship to all persons born or naturalized in the United States, including freed slaves. It gave all citizens equal protection under the law. Finally, the 15th Amendment states that the right to vote could not be denied or abridged based on race, color, or previous servitude. At the time, the right to vote was denied based on sex. Women of all races could be legally denied the right to vote until the Nineteenth Amendment was ratified in 1920.

[29] See Alesina, Glaeser, and Sacerdote (2001); Luttmer (2001); Lee and Roemer (2006); Frymer (2008).

[30] See Gilens (1999).

[31] See Alesina, Glaeser, and Sacerdote (2001); Luttmer (2001); Williams (2003); Lee and Roemer (2006); Frymer (2008).

[32] Weaver (2007) describes coordinated efforts by conservative elites and politicians to associate Black civil rights demands with criminal behavior.

unworthy of having their collective action demands met.[33] These associations not only shape whether the public understands and supports protest demands; they also sway police interactions with protesters.

Police actions tend to be more aggressive in response to Black protest than White protest.[34] Aggressive police tactics increase participation costs for Black people who fear arrest or physical harm from their collective action participation. Repression tactics also dissuade other groups from joining or supporting collective action efforts.[35] Even if people agree with protest demands, they are less willing to join collective action events if they believe that arrest or violence at a protest is likely.

Aggressive police actions can potentially garner support for protest demands if observers believe that police actions were unjustifiable. However, beliefs about whether police or protesters are to blame for conflict between police and protesters depend on the race of the observer, the police, and the protesters.[36] Conflict between Black protesters and White police officers may mobilize Black people who did not participate to become active. It may simultaneously dissuade support for protest demands from White observers.[37]

As a whole, Black people have less political, economic, and social capital for collective action than their White counterparts. Due to notions of deservingness and racial animosity, Black people have less formal education and income than White people.[38] Black people are also more likely than White people to face physical and emotional protest costs due to

---

[33] For instance, Gilliam and Iyengar (2000) find that media overrepresents Black people as criminals in their local news coverage. Moreover, when the perpetrator of the crime is Black, White viewers (but not Black viewers) are more likely to support punitive policies, like the death penalty. Neither Black nor White respondents change their preferences on punitive policies when the perpetrator is White.

[34] Davenport, Soule, and Armstrong (2011) demonstrate that police arrest and presence are more likely when the protesters are Black than White, even while controlling for the protest's disruptiveness. However, this empirical finding is not consistent for all years of their analyses.

[35] See, for example, McCarthy and Zald, (1977 p. 1222).

[36] See Davenport, McDermott, and Armstrong (2018), who find that White protest observers are more likely to believe that police violence against protesters is justified when the police are White and protesters are Black. At the same time, Black observers are less likely to blame Black protesters for conflicts with White police. See also Jefferson, Neuner, and Pasek (2020).

[37] As I previously discussed, protest observers could be a valuable resource or an additional cost for protest's mobilization.

[38] Formal education provides civic skills, political efficacy, social networks, and trust in government, which all facilitate political participation.

state repression, delegitimization, and stigmatization. This does not mean that Black people never protest or that protest costs do not exist for White people. Instead, protest costs are typically higher for Black people than for White people.

2.2.2   White Groups Compared with Other Racial and Ethnic Groups

While there are considerable resource disparities between Black and White groups, Black people are not the only groups that face high participation costs. Kim (2000) demonstrates that the racialization of racial and ethnic minority groups in the United States is based on the racial ordering, or positioning, of groups relative to Black and White Americans. She argues that racial ordering is a process that occurs along two axes: (1) the superior/inferior axis, in which Black people are on the bottom and White people on the top, and (2) the insider/outsider axis, in which new immigrants are placed in relationship to Black and White people.

Some groups, like Korean Americans, are perceived to be superior to African Americans due to stereotypes of their greater intellect or work ethic. These stereotypes suggest that some methods of suppressing collective action, like rhetorical associations with criminality, may be less useful for some racial and ethnic groups than for others. Many Asian Americans in the United States have positive stereotypes that facilitate collective action, but they are simultaneously ostracized for being too foreign and unable to integrate into White culture and society. Other ethnic groups, like Irish immigrants, can lose their "outsider" or foreign status by assimilating into existing American racial groups.[39] Where racial and ethnic groups are in the racial ordering determines the resources available to them for collective action. Groups that can successfully integrate

---

[39] Roediger (1999) provides one example with the assimilation of Irish immigrants into White culture. In the years before the Civil War, White Americans referred to Irish immigrants as "low-browed and savage, grovelling [*sic*] and bestial, lazy and wild, simian and sensual" – stereotypes often associated with African Americans (p. 133). But in the years after the war, Irish immigrants were able to lose their inferior, outsider status. To reap the "wages of whiteness" and separate themselves from associations with African Americans, Irish immigrants exercised racial prejudice and hostility toward African Americans. They engaged in violence and intimidation against African Americans to keep African Americans out of jobs and associated themselves with White Americans. Irish immigrants' political incorporation into the Democratic Party and their social incorporation into the Catholic Church facilitated their successful incorporation into White America.

into White America enjoy the higher resources of White people. Otherwise, racial and ethnic groups lack the higher resources available to White people.

One resource available to White people but less likely among other racial and ethnic groups is the public's support. For example, the presence of foreign imagery, like another country's flag, at a protest is enough to increase adverse reactions to protest and decrease support for immigration.[40] As previously mentioned, public support can dissuade aggressive police tactics or encourage legislators to respond to protesters' demands.

Relatedly, Black, Latino, and Asian American community members tend to have lower levels of political efficacy and trust in government than their White counterparts.[41] Some of these differences in political orientations are due to individuals' experiences with government agents. Black and Brown communities are more likely to have negative experiences with government agencies, whether director or indirect, which decreases political participation.[42] They are also less likely to be engaged by political candidates and political campaigns.[43]

Moreover, descriptive representation can reduce feelings of alienation, increase trust and political efficacy, and in turn increase political participation.[44] At least in part, this is because legislators are more likely to fully understand and represent the interests of groups that share their race or ethnicity than those that do not.[45] However, legislators are disproportionately White, which decreases the likelihood of receiving the benefits of descriptive representation for groups that are not White.[46]

Whatever the case, public and elite support, political efficacy, and engagement are crucial resources for political participation. Protest is more likely among people who are politically active and believe their actions will make a difference.[47] These political and social resources are more likely found among White people than other racial and ethnic

---

[40] See Wright and Citrin (2011). Also, reference Tilly (1975); McAdam (1982); Davenport (2010).

[41] See Schlozman, Brady, and Verba (2018); Gay (2002).

[42] See Burch (2013); Michener (2018).

[43] See Rosenstone and Hansen (1993); Leighley (2005); Schlozman, Brady, and Verba (2018).

[44] See Gay (2002).

[45] See Mansbridge (1999) and Broockman (2013).

[46] For example, see Schaeffer (2021).

[47] See McAdam (1982).

groups. In other words, a lack of protest-related resources means that protest costs are more harmful for Black, Latino, Asian American, and other racial and ethnic groups than they are for White groups.

2.2.3 Economic Resource Disparities

Another relevant resource capacity for protest participation relates to protesters' economic resources. Economic resources mitigate the monetary costs of collective action. Economic resources supply high-speed internet access, reliable transportation, and funds for bail in the case of arrest during a protest. Throughout US history, African Americans and Latinos have been more likely to live in low-income households than White Americans, and African Americans have been more likely to live in poverty for longer stretches of time than other racial and ethnic groups in the United States.[48] Nevertheless, poverty is a persistent concern across and within all racial and ethnic groups. In general, groups with fewer economic resources face higher protest costs than other members of their racial or ethnic groups.

2.2.4 Other Resource Disparities

Beyond income, race, and ethnicity, resource disparities are also evident in the organizational capacity of collective action. Experienced organizers have the skills, familiarity, and knowledge to mobilize people to protest. They know which issue frames might get people to show up to an event. Experienced organizers tend to pay close attention to impending policy changes, and they have relationships with activists, media outlets, and policymakers who can effectively communicate protest demands.

Still, the resources that leaders provide can impede collective action's success.[49] Professional organizations may have the experience to instigate collective action, but that experience leads legislators to question whether issue salience is real or manufactured.[50] Well-financed organizations frequently subsidize participation to give the appearance of a grassroots effort in pursuit of their goals.[51] Experienced leaders can also

---

[48] See www.census.gov/prod/2/pop/p70/p70-55.pdf.
[49] See Piven and Cloward (1977).
[50] See McCarthy and Zald (1973, 1977).
[51] One such organization is Americans for Prosperity, which was funded in part by the affluent Koch brothers. During the Affordable Care Act debate, the organization was often reported masquerading as a grassroots group with salient interests opposed to policies like Medicaid expansion. See, for instance,

mobilize people to participate for issues that are not salient for them. So, while professional organizations can represent a valuable resource for constituents, they can also make it difficult for legislators and other observers to know whether the protesters are participating because they have a salient grievance or concern.

Lastly, digital technologies, including cellular phones and social media, enable groups to communicate their grievances and share information about how to mobilize. Digital technologies decrease the information, communication, and coordination costs associated with collective action. Consequently, groups with reliable access to digital technologies can protest more freely, that is, with fewer information, communication, and coordination costs, than groups without steady access.

In general, inequalities exist across genders, sexualities, religions, ages, (dis)abilities, and many other characteristics. Some of these resource disparities have greater implications for protest costs than others. Whether a resource disparity matters for the representation of protest demands depends on whether the resource disparity affects protest costs.

Protesters' resource capacities influence whether a group can aggregate its resources to mobilize collective action. The greater the resources, the easier a group can protest. Scarce resources do not mean that a group cannot protest. Instead, the ability to protest is more difficult. The theory that I present in the next section demonstrates that groups with lower resources can only protest when issue salience is high. Thus, legislators are more likely to support their protest demands than the protest demands of high-resource groups that can protest at will.

2.3 A FORMAL THEORY OF PROTEST AND LEGISLATIVE BEHAVIOR

To understand how protesters' resource capacities influence whether legislators support protest demands, I create a formal theory of legislative behavior following protest. The specifications of the theory appear in the Appendix. Here, I describe how the strategic behaviors of a legislator and a group of constituents lead to the central argument of this book – that after collective action, legislators are more likely to support the protest demands of low-resource groups than those of high-resource groups.

this Al Jazeera America article connecting the Koch brothers to Americans for Prosperity's grassroots efforts against Medicaid expansion and other policies: america. aljazeera.com/articles/2014/8/12/colorado-kochtopusamericansprosperity.html. See also Walker (2009).

I create the formal theory based on the canonical signaling model, which is a type of formal model that allows actors to communicate private information in situations of information asymmetry. As I previously discussed, legislators are eager to represent the salient interests of their constituents, but they do not know if or when issue salience is high for specific groups in their district. This is a situation of information asymmetry. The group knows whether the issue is salient for them but the legislator does not. A group could signal its issue salience via protest. What makes this situation more complicated is that protest imperfectly reveals issue salience. A group can protest with low issue salience. A group can also fail to protest with high issue salience.

In the signaling model, both the legislator and the group must consider the pros and cons of their decision to pursue a set of actions (i.e., protest or not; support the group or not). Both actors are aware of the actions and incentives available to the other. The formal model then provides expectations for what happens when the legislator and group independently work to achieve the best possible outcome for themselves.

As with any model, whether empirical or theoretical, this formal theory does not and cannot account for everything that might influence the decisions to protest or support protesters. However, I include the circumstances that weigh most heavily on those decisions. Indeed, while every collective action event is unique, collective action events are also interconnected with other events.

The set of strategies, or "repertoires of contention," available to actors is dependent on the awareness, experiences, and social networks of people with experience and knowledge of other collective actions.[52] Protesters test strategies over time, and they borrow the tactics they believe have been successful. Innovations are gradual, and those that seem to be sporadic or novel are usually an improvement on the success and failures of other protests.

Similarly, legislators rely on relatively stable indicators when making voting decisions. They make decisions about whom to represent based on their personal preferences, partisan pressures, and constituency demands. They avoid behaviors that could cost them their reelection.

If the repertoires of contention are generally stable or somewhat predictable, then the public and legislative responses to those actions should also be predictable. As Koopmans asserts, "change as a result of strategic anticipation is subject to strong equilibrating pressures: if

---

[52] See Tilly (1975).

A can anticipate pretty well what B will do, the reverse is usually true as well, and A [*sic*] and B's interactions will be highly routinized, save for limited oscillations and perhaps some gradual change."[53] Sure, there will be exceptions that challenge the ability to predict collective action and responses to collective action. Nevertheless, formal theories help evaluate how actors' strategic behaviors might interact *on average* to produce a set of outcomes. If actors can be reasonably confident in anticipating and updating responses to each other, then formal theories can determine how institutions, incentives, and goals might produce specific outcomes.

2.3.1   Formal Theory: Actors, Actions, and Beliefs

The theory builds upon Kollman's (1998) outside lobbying as costly signaling model. There is a group with private information about whether or not an issue is salient to constituents and a legislator who desires information about their constituents' issue salience. Both the legislator and the group know that the group has some probability of having high issue salience and a corresponding probability of having low issue salience. Only the group knows whether or not the issue is salient for them. The group must decide whether or not to protest. The legislator must decide whether or not to support the group's preferences. Each of their decisions is based on their knowledge of the incentives and actions of the other.

The group's decision to protest is influenced by its expectations of the legislator's behavior. The group prefers that the legislator support its policy interests even if the group's issue salience is low. The group only benefits from policy support when the legislator chooses to support the group. If the legislator votes against the group's preferences, then the group gets no utility from protesting.

The group prefers to get legislative support without having to protest because protest is costly. Even when legislative support is likely and the group's issue salience is high, protest costs could prohibit participation. Thus, the utility that the group receives from protesting is a function of the expected value obtained from participation and protest costs. The group will protest if it expects that the costs and benefits of protesting outweigh the costs and benefits of not protesting.

Protest costs are lower if the group has high issue salience. As an example, consider the protest cost relating to the resources necessary to

---

[53] Koopmans (2008), p. 30.

spark potential protesters' interests in an issue. When issue salience is high, there is little need for a leader or organizer to convince the group that a grievance is worthy of representation.

Protest costs also decrease as the group's resource levels increase. In general, previous scholarship does not adequately account for the resource levels of participants when seeking to understand legislative behavior following protest. Yet, a group's resource capacity could be as important for the decision to protest as it is for a legislator's decision to support constituency demands.

Based on the group's decision whether or not to protest, the legislator must decide about supporting the group's policy preferences. The legislator would prefer to support a group that provides more electoral support than electoral opposition. Groups with high issue salience are more likely to base their electoral participation on the legislator's representation of their issue preference. So the legislator would prefer to support a high-salience group over a low-salience group.

What makes this decision complicated is that the legislator does not know whether a high- or low-salience group is protesting. Higher levels of salience increase the probability of protest, but groups with lower levels of salience can also protest. To navigate this predicament, once the legislator observes whether or not the group protests, they update their beliefs about the probability of the group having high or low issue salience.[54]

When the group has high issue salience, the legislator receives a positive benefit for supporting the group. They receive no benefit if they do not support a group. Supporting the group may result in an electoral gain, but this decision is also costly. The legislator's costs from supporting the group could arise from writing and implementing legislation, convincing others to adopt the group's policy position, supporting the group instead of another constituency, or any other type of support that results in the legislator expending resources on behalf of the group. This cost is particularly high when participants' issue preferences diverge from other legislative considerations – that is, party pressures, other constituents' preferences, and the legislator's personal preferences.

A legislator will support a group if the expected utility of supporting the group is greater than the expected utility of not supporting the group. A legislator can support a group even if that group chooses not to

---

[54] Both the legislator and the group are aware of the legislator's updated beliefs about the group's issue salience.

protest. A legislator's support is possible regardless of whether or not the group decided to protest. The legislator's decision to support the group is based on the legislator's beliefs about the benefits and costs of supporting the group relative to the benefits and costs of not supporting the group. The benefits are greater when the group has high issue salience and when the legislative costs of supporting the group are minimal.

2.4 THEORETICAL EXPECTATIONS

To understand whether and how a group's resource capacity influences the decision of a legislator to support collective action demands, I evaluate the perfect Bayesian semi-pooling equilibrium in which the legislator supports a protesting group with some probability but never supports a group that does not protest, and the group always protests when issue salience is sufficiently high but protests with some probability when issue salience is low.[55] This equilibrium characterizes real-world phenomena in which some groups protest despite having low issue salience, while some high-salience groups do not receive legislative support for their issues.[56] It also reveals several theoretical implications relating to legislative behavior.

2.4.1 Legislative Support of Protesters

The first implication of the formal theory concerns the likelihood that legislators support protesters' interests compared with their support of non-protesting groups' interests. It suggests the following:

> **Protest Hypothesis**: A legislator is more likely to support a group that protests than a group that does not protest.

While legislators represent the preferences of constituents who do not protest, the strategy informing this hypothesis is based on the ability of protest to reveal constituents' issue salience to reelection-minded legislators. As I stated before, legislators are eager for information about

---

[55] The probability that the legislator supports a protesting group is separate from the probability that the group protests when issue salience is low.

[56] The discussion here focuses on the equilibrium most relevant for assessing legislators' responsiveness to protesters' resource capacities. Nevertheless, each of the equilibria from the formal theory is available in the Chapter 2 Appendix.

the salient preferences of their constituents. Protest is better at revealing constituents' issue salience than other communication channels, such as public opinion polls, focus groups, or election returns.

Moreover, protest demonstrates the political power of a group that might influence the legislator's reelection chances. A group that has mobilized to engage in collective action demonstrates that it can mobilize again during an upcoming election. Indeed, protesters are more likely than non-protesters to pay attention to legislators' voting behavior, and they are more likely than non-protesters to participate politically to hold their legislators accountable if the legislator does not address collective action demands.

2.4.2 Resources and Legislative Support

Constituents are more likely to hold their legislator accountable when their issue salience is high, but issue salience is private information. Legislators are often uninformed about it. The decision to protest can provide information about the group's issue salience since protest is motivated by grievances. However, grievances have different levels of salience. Some issues are more important to constituents than others. Protesters' resource capacity provides valuable information that can help legislators become more informed about their constituents' issue salience.

Result 5 of the perfect Bayesian semi-pooling equilibrium describes the probability of legislative support given the resource capacity of protesters.[57] This result yields the following hypothesis:

> **Resource Constraint Hypothesis**: A legislator is more likely to support protesters' preferences as the resource capacity of the group decreases.

Figure 2.1 is a graphical representation of the *Resource Constraint Hypothesis*. The figure depicts the probability of collective action for a high-resource group and a low-resource group. For both groups, the likelihood that each group protests increases as the group's issue salience increases. In other words, groups with high issue salience are more likely to protest than groups with low issue salience since the benefits of

---

[57] The derivation of this result is in the Chapter 2 Appendix.

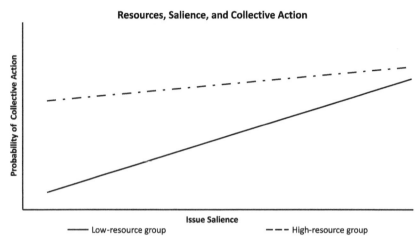

FIGURE 2.1 Expectations for the likelihood of protest by low- and
high-resource groups

Note: This is a hypothetical depiction of the relationship between resources, salience, and
the likelihood of protest based on the expected utility of protest (Eq.1 in the Chapter 2
Appendix. The semi-pooling perfect Bayseian equilibrium are also delineated in the
Appendix and described in text.) and the implications of the semi-pooling perfect Bayesian
equilibrium. The solid and dashed lines denote how increasing costs (based on protesters'
resource capacities) and issue salience interact to influence the likelihood of protest for
low- and high-resource groups, respectively.

legislative support increase with issue salience.[58] What differs for high-
and low-resource groups is the ability to protest when issue salience is
low. High-resource groups can protest regardless of their issue salience,
but groups with low-resource capacity are typically unable and unwilling to afford protest costs unless they have intense issue preferences.[59]
When issue salience is low for low-resource groups, protest costs prohibit
participation.

The theory posits that legislators are aware of the differences in protest
costs for high- and low-resource groups.[60] When legislators see protest by low-resource groups, they can be confident that issue salience
is high for the group. Since high-resource groups can protest regardless
of the group's issue salience, legislators are uncertain of the group's issue
salience even after observing protest.

---

[58] Also see Results 3 and 4 in the Chapter 2 Appendix.
[59] For example, see Klandermans (1984); Banks, White, and McKenzie (2018).
[60] The survey results in Chapter 3 provide some evidence that legislators recognize
differences in protest costs for high- and low-resource groups.

2.5 LEGISLATIVE SUPPORT

Legislators can support protest demands in many ways. They can make a speech or issue a public statement recognizing protesters' grievances. They can directly communicate their acknowledgment of protesters' preferences in private meetings, mailed flyers, or email communications. They can also write a bill or cosponsor legislation to support protest demands. In this book, I focus on legislative support apparent in legislators' votes on protest-related legislation.

Roll-call voting is essential to lawmaking. Legislators write many bills, but if the legislation does not receive an affirmative vote by the legislative body, then it cannot become law. Roll-call votes also enable legislators to claim credit for representing constituent concerns. Most important for the task of this book, roll-call votes are public and easily traceable, which means that constituents can effortlessly monitor or become aware of their legislator's actions in support of or in opposition to protest demands. Indeed, it is the recognition that constituents will vote against a legislator once they are made aware of a roll-call vote on an issue important to them that incites legislators to be strategic in casting roll-call votes.[61] Still, various dynamics undermine the purity of roll-call votes as a measure of legislative support.

Political parties often disallow issues on the agenda that will potentially divide or hurt the party, particularly in more professional legislatures like the US Congress.[62] Consequently, legislators' roll-call voting behavior may not reflect issues important to collective action participants because the opportunity to represent constituents' interests does not present itself. Even when the opportunity arises, a yea or nay on a roll-call vote cannot differentiate between a legislator who reluctantly supports a protest demand and a legislator who is an ardent supporter.[63] In fact, a legislator who regularly votes in support of a protest demand might not appear supportive of protest since they would have supported the issue even if the collective action had not occurred. Moreover, a legislator's true preferences are concealed if they prefer to support a group on a roll-call vote, but party leaders entice them to cast an alternative vote to advance the interests of the party.[64]

---

[61] Consider, for instance, Arnold (1990); Hutchings (2003); Ansolabehere and Jones (2010).

[62] See Cox and McCubbins (1993).

[63] See Hall (1996).

[64] See Cox and McCubbins (1993). The likelihood of party pressure varies with the type of roll-call vote. Procedural roll-call votes are the most likely to be subject to pressures

That there is a significant relationship between collective action and legislative behavior during strategic roll-call voting suggests that representation following collective action might be stronger using a different measure of legislative behavior capable of revealing true preferences. However, this investigation does not seek to discover whether legislators *prefer* to support collective action participants but whether legislators' behavior responds more favorably to collective action participants with fewer resources. Roll-call voting presents a good yet conservative test of a legislator's strategic support of protest demands.

2.6 PUBLIC OPINION, PARTISANSHIP, AND LEGISLATORS' PREFERENCES

Legislators do not decide to support protest demands in a vacuum. They are not passive actors but rather strategic decision-makers who must weigh the costs and benefits of their actions. Legislators support protest demands when they believe that the net electoral benefit of supporting costly protesters' demands outweighs the net electoral benefit of not supporting their demands. Protesters are only one of many constituencies that could influence a legislator's reelection. Also important are the preferences and issue salience of other constituents in the legislator's district, the legislator's political party, and the legislator's personal preferences.

Protest observers who agree with protest demands may provide a supportive legislator with positive electoral participation, including conventional voting behavior.[65] When public opinion shifts in favor of protesters' preferences, legislators are less concerned that their support of protest demands might mobilize non-protesters to oppose their reelection.[66] Even then, legislators could still face negative threats to their reelection from people who oppose protest demands.

---

that entice members to vote with their party (Cox and McCubbins 2005; Crespin 2010). Members of Congress are given more freedom on amendment and final passage roll-call votes, but there is a large variation in whether legislative votes on amendments will be controlled by party leaders (Whitby 1997; Jenkins, Crespin, and Carson 2005). Some amendments, like the Social Security Amendments of 1965, which established Medicaid and Medicare, are highly visible and not likely to be subject to party pressures, but others are inundated with party-line votes.

[65] See Lipsky (1968, 1970); Giugni (2004).

[66] Mazumder (2018) finds that people living in counties where civil rights protests occurred are more likely to support policies benefiting the African American community in the decades following the civil rights protests.

The extent of the backlash that a legislator might expect depends on their district. Most collective action demands are for more liberal policies.[67] Liberal protest demands are more likely to be accepted and supported in districts with the highest levels of formal education, although constituents with higher levels of formal education are often more economically conservative than those with lower educational attainment.[68] Affluent constituents are more socially liberal but economically conservative than the rest of the American population,[69] so they might be more supportive of policies like abortion or same-sex marriage and less supportive of government interventions in the economy, including social welfare programs to address social inequalities. Relatedly, the greater the percentage of racial and ethnic minority groups in a congressional district, the greater the electoral incentives for legislators to support protest demands that benefit racial and ethnic minority groups.[70]

The cost-benefit analysis that legislators conduct does not mean that legislators *only* support protest demands when protesters' preferences align with public opinion within the legislator's district. While it is easier for legislators to support protest demands when public opinion agrees with protesters' preferences, public opinion is generally less likely to be supportive of low-resource groups' protest demands than of high-resource groups' protest demands.[71] Legislators should still support low-resource groups more often than high-resource groups because they are concerned about representing issues that are salient for constituents and therefore likely to translate into electoral participation.

If protest observers do not have salient interests concerning protest demands, then whether their legislator supports those demands may not

---

[67] My data show that in the 1990s, 76 percent of collective action demands for civil rights, civil liberties, and minority issue claims were liberal, 21 percent were conservative, and 3 percent had no clear ideology. The ideologies were roughly coded based on whether coders for the Dynamics of Collective Action (DCA) dataset indicated that protesters were for or against mostly liberal claims. A more accurate measure of the ideology of protest claims is present for the original dataset of protests in 2012. Coders specifically categorized collective action demands as liberal, moderate, conservative, or having no clear ideology. The majority (46 percent) of protest claims were for liberal policies. About 44 percent of claims had no clear ideology. Only about 10 percent of claims were for conservative policies. And virtually no protest demands were for moderate policies.

[68] See McCall and Manza (2011).

[69] See Gilens (2012); Page, Bartels, and Seawright (2013).

[70] See Lublin (1997); Whitby (1997); Hutchings (1998).

[71] Recall Cohen (1999); Gilens (1999); Davenport (2010); Wright and Citrin (2011).

shape protest observers' electoral participation. Protest observers are unlikely to base their electoral participation on how legislators respond to issues that are not important to them. When the public's issue salience is low, legislators are more concerned about the opinions and electoral participation of constituents who have demonstrated with their protest that they have high issue salience. Consequently, legislators are more likely to support protest demands, particularly by low-resource groups, even if public opinion does not align with protest demands.

When issue salience is high for protesters and protest observers, observers' preferences weigh more on a legislator's decision to support protest demands. Legislators will only support protest demands if the benefits outweigh the costs. The costs may be high if there is social unrest. Protest observers may be more opposed to the social unrest caused by the protest than by the protesters' specific demands for representation. Thus, legislators may provide concessions to protesters or employ repression tactics to decrease the social unrest caused by disruptive protest in hopes of decreasing issue salience for protest observers. They may also make use of concessions or repression tactics to dissuade future protests or to keep the issue from becoming salient for more constituents who may respond in unpredictable ways to their legislator's support or lack of support for protest demands.

Typically, Democratic legislators are more likely than Republican legislators to support protest demands since the Democratic Party platform is more liberal on civil rights, civil liberties, and minority issues. As such, Democrats are also more likely to benefit from their representation of protest demands for these issues. To be sure, Canes-Wrone, Minozzi, and Reveley (2011) contend that when a party that rarely represents a salient issue increases its representation of that issue, constituents believe both parties (even the one that does demonstrate renewed legislative support) support the issue. However, when a party that normally represents a salient issue legislatively supports the issue, voters only attribute legislative support to that party. This may encourage Republican legislators to support salient demands communicated during protest since constituents only recognize Republicans' representation of salient issues when Republicans actively support those concerns, compared with Democrats who might not represent salient concerns but still would be perceived as responsive. However, Republicans must believe that protesters pose enough of an electoral threat to warrant the representation of protest demands. Communicating a credible electoral threat is difficult (but not impossible) when the legislator is opposed to the protest demands and protesters are unable to directly or indirectly threaten the legislator's reelection.

While Republican legislators may have motivation to support protests out of the fear of looking unresponsive to constituents willing to punish or reward legislators for their representation, Democrats cannot be complacent in their representation. Any vote against a salient constituent demand could motivate groups with salient interests to shift their electoral participation in ways that threaten a legislator's reelection. Protesters may become more enraged when they observe a legislator who is supposed to represent their interests not being responsive to protest demands. Accordingly, legislators must seriously consider representing protest demands made by salient constituencies.

In sum, legislators must consider many constituencies when trying to decide whether to support protest demands, particularly when protest demands are made by low-resource groups. Legislators must consider how their actions might influence the behavior of protesters, protesters' supporters, and protesters' opponents. They must take into account what resources their political parties can provide and how their legislative support might challenge their personal opinions on the best policies for their constituents. The formal theory includes all of these considerations. Even while accounting for the many pressures on legislators' voting decisions, the theory suggests that legislators are more likely to support constituent demands communicated during protest than those that are not communicated during protest. They are also more likely to legislatively support protest demands by low-resource groups rather than those of high-resource because low-resource protesters, relative to their counterparts, are more likely to have salient demands that could influence the legislators' reelection prospects.

2.7 EXTENSIONS OF THE THEORY

I developed the theory evaluating legislators' support of costly protest with the US House of Representatives in mind, but the theory is not exclusive to that legislature nor to the eligible citizens who can hold legislators accountable with their votes. The theory can apply to any elected official who has incentives to strategically support collective action demands. To be sure, consider the characteristics of the US House of Representatives that motivate the theoretical model.

2.7.1 Legislators and Legislatures

The US House of Representatives consists of 435 legislators representing roughly equal numbers of constituents residing within the same state but across city and county boundaries. Legislators serve two-year terms. They face reelection at the end of each two-year term but can serve as many terms as their constituents allow them. This electoral structure ensures that representatives are accountable to their constituents via elections.[72] Nevertheless, the reelection incentive may not be the only mechanism for accountability.

Legislators could represent constituents out of their desire to make good public policy or gain more prestige in Congress. A female legislator could support protest demands for gender equality in the workplace because she believes in the issue and in representing issues that would benefit women. She might support protest demands for better environmental regulations to support her political party's efforts to emphasize its environmental policy position. While the reelection incentive may be the primary reason that elected officials support protest demands, they could support them to achieve other goals.

Supporting protest demands is costly for legislators. I have described costs related to crafting legislation, party pressures, personal preferences, and the opinions of protest observers. These costs exist for many representatives and elected officials. Other costs may also be relevant. Regardless, when applying the theory to other elected officials, they must incur some cost for supporting protest demands. Otherwise, legislators would always support constituent demands even in the absence of salience-revealing protest.

Another feature underlying the theory is the professional nature of the US House of Representatives. Professional legislatures provide legislators with the resources to discover their constituents' salient interests and strategically represent those interests. Legislators are paid a full-time salary. Not having to secure other income sources means that legislators can devote their full attention to the representation of their constituents. In this professional legislature, legislators are also supported by paid and volunteer staff who advise and coordinate their fundraising, legislating, and roll-call voting behaviors. Moreover, legislators have offices in Washington, DC, where the entire chamber meets to cast their roll-call votes,

---

[72] See Federalist Paper No. 39.

as well as offices in their home districts, where legislators cultivate trust with their constituents and explain their DC actions.[73]

Resources are also provided by actors hoping to support the ever-present reelection concerns that confront legislators facing reelection every two years. Legislators meet with campaign donors and lobbyists who financially support reelection campaigns. Legislators depend on the expertise and skills of interest groups and lobbyists who help them craft legislation and inform roll-call voting behavior. They rely on their political party, which provides a policy platform and resolves coordination and collective action problems. Legislators understand that each of these actors could withhold or redirect resources if the legislator supports a protest demand their supporter disagrees with.

Extending the theory to less professional governing bodies and to representatives with fewer resources requires an understanding of elected officials' capacity to strategically represent protest demands. It also requires an awareness of threats to legislators who support protest demands that do not align with resource contributors. This does not mean that legislators with fewer resources do not have an incentive to strategically represent protest demands, but there is a possibility that resource constraints may not permit legislators to represent protest demands. Resource constraints could also lead legislators to respond differently to protesters.

The theory requires that legislators perform some action to support constituents. I evaluate roll-call votes because they are public, visible, and easily traceable, but other forms of legislative support could also address constituents' collective action demands. Legislators could make a public statement in support of protest demands. They could (co)sponsor legislation that addresses protesters' grievances. They could also create committees or commissions to evaluate grievances and provide solutions to collective action concerns. Whether alternative types of legislative support are applicable depends on their ability to be observable by constituents who could become aware of whether and how legislators support collective action demands.

Next, the US House of Representation, like most legislatures in the United States, has a winner-takes-all electoral system. The legislator who acquires a plurality of the votes wins the office and the losing candidate(s) receives no position in government. This results in a two-party system,

---

[73] See Fenno (1978).

where only members of two major political parties are likely to win elections. The number of political parties has implications for the number of issues that are represented in government. In a two-party system, there are fewer issue cleavages than in a multiparty system. For example, no one party primarily represents the interests of the working class. Compared with two-party systems, legislatures in multiparty systems may face different reelection incentives, which could make the strategic representation of protest demands more or less complicated. Legislators may believe themselves accountable to more constituencies or they may have fewer constituencies that might oppose the representation of protest demands.

2.7.2   Relevant Constituencies

The theory may not only extend to different legislatures. It could also extend to different types of constituencies. In Chapters 4–6, I define constituents as members who reside within the legislator's district. Theoretically, the group could be any constituency that a legislator desires to represent or could hold the legislator accountable for their representation of protest demands. Perhaps, a group believes that a legislator should represent the group's interest because they share a similar, salient identity. Black voters might expect a Black legislator to represent their interests even if they do not live in the legislator's district. The Black voters could still support the legislator's reelection with campaign donations, policy proposals, volunteering for the legislator's campaign, or advertising on behalf of the legislator. Providing any type of support could free the legislator to appeal to other constituencies and still represent their salient concerns.

Legislators are not exclusively accountable to their voting constituents. Non-voting constituents can also provide threats or rewards to a legislator's reelection. Legislators are often concerned about nonvoters who decide to become active in elections.[74] But even nonvoters who choose never to vote or who cannot legally vote can incentivize legislators to support their protest demands. Youth who have not reached the legal voting age, noncitizens, and people who have been disenfranchised due to criminal offenses or mental incapacity can hold their legislators accountable through other forms of electoral participation, including financial contributions, campaign volunteering, and

---

[74] Recall Arnold (1990); Hutchings (2003); Ansolabehere and Jones (2010).

advertising for the candidate with yard signs or bumper stickers. They can also target protest observers to encourage them to act on protesters' behalf.

Legislators may also receive electoral benefits from representing nonvoting protesters. Legislators could legislatively support nonvoters' protest demands in hopes of politically mobilizing and incorporating a new voting constituency.[75] Alternatively, they could use their legislative support of protest demands to claim credit for representing a constituency that is important to voters. Indeed, supporting the naturalization of undocumented immigrants is a salient policy for undocumented immigrants and their voting family members.

The formal theory extends to any group meeting the following characteristics: first, the group must be able to assist or challenge the legislator's goals. In most cases, this is the reelection goal but other goals may apply. Second, the group must have some private information that the legislator desires. I contend that the private information concerns issue salience, which relates to electoral participation, but there might be other types of private information that are meaningful for legislative behavior. The private information must vary over time, across groups, or in some type of way that makes legislators uncertain about its exact nature. Third, the group must have some means for holding a legislator accountable for their support of protest demands. Again, the accountability mechanism does not have to be from their voting behavior. Fourth, the group must incur some participation costs that could prevent its participation. Otherwise, protest would not be a credible signal of private information.

Fifth and finally, the theory incorporates protesters' resource capacity since resources influence protest costs and the group's ability to protest. Throughout this book, I define resource capacities based on the group's race, ethnicity, income, organizational characteristics, and access to digital technologies. Other resource disparities may also differentiate protesting groups. For a resource type to be relevant for a legislator's decision to support protest demands, it must influence a group's ability to protest.

---

[75] Admittedly, this is rare. Legislators and parties tend to focus their mobilizing on groups that are already party supporters and will vote in predictable ways. See Rosenstone and Hansen (1993) and Leighley (2005). Still, the political incorporation of Irish immigrants (Roediger 1999) and Black people into the Democratic Party (Philpot 2007; White and Laird 2020) demonstrates that political parties do mobilize nonvoters for electoral gains.

2.7.3 Conclusion

I motivate the theory by focusing on the legislator's reelection incentive within a representative democracy. In this context, the legislator is not only concerned about reelection threats from protesting groups but also from protest observers, including the legislator's political party. Applying the theory to other legislatures, legislators, and constituencies means paying attention to the costs, benefits, and strategies available to groups choosing whether to protest and legislators deciding whether to support collective demands. For the group, we must consider how the protest costs and resource disparities might differ. For the legislator, we must consider what costs they are facing when deciding to support constituency demands. How much flexibility does the legislator have in supporting constituency demands? How strong are party pressures? What resources constrain their ability to strategically represent protest demands?

The survey responses from a convenience sample of elected officials and staffers from local, state, and national legislative offices throughout the United States presented in the next chapter provides some evidence that the theory is not limited to the US House of Representatives. It also provides some evidence that elected officials think about protest in ways that align with the theory's mechanisms and implications. The people who determine legislative behavior following protest say that they support protest demands. They say that they recognize differences in protest costs based on the protesting group. They also say that their support of protesters' preferences is based on reelection concerns.

3

How Legislators Perceive Collective Action

In high school, I interned at a legislator's office. I remember there was a debate around school funding and this one district in South Jersey literally flooded our office with tens of thousands of post cards detailing the fiscal challenges they were facing. It was incredible. It was over 15 years ago but I can still remember it .... [I remember it because] it was massive and it showed coordination .... I was an intern [at the time] but I believe it swayed the Assemblyman.

(City Council Member, Democrat, New Jersey)

This chapter presents the results from an original survey of local, state, and national elected officials and their staffers. I created the survey to empower the people who determine whether collective action demands influence legislative behavior to describe their views on collective action voluntarily. And they could do so without the fear of backlash or the promise of reward for their participation. The survey responses provide meaning, context, and understanding of the theoretical argument made throughout this book.

As a reminder, the central argument here is that legislative voting behavior is more likely to support protesters' interests than non-protesters' interests, especially as participants' protest costs increase. The previous chapter explained the theory supporting the argument. In brief, the theory suggests that legislators are concerned about getting reelected and are therefore watchful for indications that their constituents have salient issues that warrant representation. Protest has the potential to reveal constituents' issue salience to legislators. It is most likely to do so when participants face high costs to participation because of their low resource capacity. Only when issue salience is high are low-resource groups willing and able to endure the participation costs that typically prevent their participation. In contrast, high-resource groups can afford to protest regardless of their issue salience because their participation costs are relatively low. Reelection-minded legislators interested in representing the salient interests of their constituents are consequently more likely to represent interests conveyed during collective action by low-resource groups than by high-resource groups.

For this theory to be correct, several necessary conditions must be present. First, legislators must be aware of collective action events. If they are not, then collective action cannot reasonably influence their legislative voting behavior. Second, legislators must believe that protest has value for their legislative behavior. Otherwise, legislators will simply ignore the collective action that they observe. The third condition is that collective action – any collective action – must influence legislative behavior. Fourth, the theory requires that legislators are strategic actors who are more likely to respond to some collective action events than others. Finally, legislators must observe differences in protest costs and act upon those differences.

Chapter 2 includes a well-developed literature review and a formal, theoretical argument that support each of these conditions. Yet, an open question remains: do the people tasked with representing protesters' demands see themselves acting in ways that align with the theory? To answer this question, this chapter reveals the survey responses of the people who determine whether to support collective action demands legislatively.[1]

Since I am interested in the opinions of the actors who determine legislative behavior, I intentionally sent surveys to legislators and the people who staff legislative offices. Legislators are elected to cast votes on bills, craft legislation, and publicly represent constituents. Nevertheless, the efforts of legislative staff members are integral to the ability of elected officials to perform these duties. Legislative staffers are the ones who read constituents' emails and answer constituents' phone calls. Staffers decide who gets a meeting with a legislator. Staffers are also responsible for analyzing information, crafting legislation, and helping the legislator determine which issues are worthy of their attention. When I asked survey respondents about how legislators respond to collective action, one former staff member freely described the role of staffers:

---

[1] The survey questionnaire is available in the Chapter 3 Appendix.

As an office we were expected to reach out to the organizers of the events and collect information on its credibility. Those who were lobbying [or] protesting about fringe issues like breaking up California were politely ignored. We acted as a screen for the Senator, sifting to the ones that were serious and did not have terrible risk of embarrassment or backlash.

(Former Staff Member, California State Senate, Democrat)

This former staff member from the California State Senate detailed how staffers in the senator's office were expected to communicate with protesters. They, not the legislator, made the initial decisions about which collective actions were credible and which events their office should ignore. The staffers determined how much information to collect and which events were worthy of their legislators' response.

In most legislative offices, staffers have an incredible amount of decision-making power and influence on their boss's legislative behavior. So, while this book focuses on legislative behavior following protest, it is not simply legislators' perceptions that matter for whether and how legislators support collective action demands. These decisions depend on the perceptions of legislators *and* their staffers. Consequently, I employ the survey responses from legislators and staffers to assess whether policymakers behave in ways that comport with the theoretical argument.

I asked elected officials and staffers closed- and open-ended questions concerning their perceptions of and responses to collective action and collective action participants. The vast majority of survey responses provide strong support for the conditions necessary for the theoretical argument to be valid. I discuss the survey responses that less clearly support the theoretical argument throughout this chapter. Even the theoretically inconsistent responses provide valuable insight into how legislators understand and respond to collective action.

As a whole, the survey responses reveal that policymakers are aware of collective action, and they think that collective action influences legislative decision-making. As expected, they do not believe that they can and should represent all collective action. They view themselves as strategic actors who are motivated by reelection concerns. These views also align with the theoretical argument.

Moreover, policymakers observe differences in the costliness of protest based on the group protesting, also in alignment with the theory. They do not make any statements suggesting whether those differences in protest costs influence whether they support protest demands. This omission is likely more a function of the survey design than an indication of how the legislators and staffers view the influence of costly protest on legislative behavior. Nevertheless, the survey responses suggest that the people who determine legislative behavior understand themselves to act in ways that align with the theoretical argument.

The survey responses uncover other information as well. When deciding how and whether to respond to collective action, legislators and staffers say they also consider the tactics, grievances, and potential political repercussions, like those relating to reelection concerns, partisan politics, or ideological alignment with the protesters' goals. While policymakers say that their legislative behavior is motivated by protesters' resource capacities, they also mention the disruptiveness and size of events as determining factors. These insights are not surprising. They align with literature on protest influence,[2] and they inform the quantitative analyses in subsequent chapters. More importantly, they do not invalidate the theoretical argument I propose. Instead, the survey responses demonstrate that legislators consider many things when determining whether and how to respond to protest. Prominent among these considerations are the reelection incentives that motivate legislators to support low-resource groups' protest demands more often than claims made by high-resource groups.

3.1 DESCRIPTION OF SURVEY, RESPONDENTS, AND RESPONSES

Representative surveys of elites are notoriously difficult to accomplish.[3] Policymakers are busy. Responding to a survey inquiry is low on their list of priorities. There is also no readily available list of every individual involved in making legislative decisions. Legislators and some key staffers are publicly known, but seldom is a list of every staffer publicly available. Legislators and staffers who are mentioned on websites or in databases can be hard to contact. In addition, a sample of the target population will always refuse to complete the survey. The difficulty in acquiring a representative survey of elites does not preclude sampling techniques that can provide information about legislator's decision-making.

In this chapter, I present the results of a survey employing convenience and snowball sampling techniques. Both of these types of sampling are forms of non-probability sampling techniques that can contact hard-to-

---

[2] For example, Lohmann 1993; Bailey, Mummolo, and Noel 2012; Gillion 2013; Wouters and Walgrave 2017.

[3] See Goldstein (2002).

reach individuals.[4] Non-probability sampling is susceptible to selection bias. It is also limited in its ability to generalize to the larger population of legislators, but the purpose here is not causal identification. This chapter employs convenience and snowball sampling techniques to capture elite perspectives on collective action and demonstrate whether these perspectives comport with the logic of the theoretical argument outlined earlier.

3.1.1 Survey Design

I created an internet-based survey questionnaire of legislators and legislative staffers that I distributed via email. Internet-based surveys have gained popularity for their efficiency, costlessness, accessibility, convenience, adaptability, and ability to reach large and diverse populations.[5] Moreover, internet surveys distributed via email are as representative of elected officials as mail surveys.[6]

In summer 2018, a research assistant collected the publicly available email addresses of the staff members for every member of the US House of Representatives.[7] She also aggregated the publicly available emails of city council members and their staff members in a semi-random selection of cities in New Jersey, Florida, Maryland, Nebraska, and South Carolina. I chose the city councils for their regional diversity and to provide some variation in city size. The publicly available emails for the staff of congressional representatives and city council members varied, but titles included the chief of staff, legislative director, legislative assistant, legislative aide, press secretary, communications director, and scheduler.

A personalized email was sent from Qualtrics from a dedicated account using the ucsd.edu domain to help reduce the chances that the email would be blocked or end up in a junk folder. Additionally, the university domain could potentially provide legitimacy to the request for information about elites. The subject of the email was "Representatives' Perceptions of Constituents." In the email invitation, I asked elected officials and their staffers to consent to their voluntary participation in a ten- to twelve-minute research survey seeking to understand representation

---

[4] See Tansey (2007) and Goldstein (2002).

[5] See Orr (2005).

[6] See Fisher and Herrick (2013).

[7] Representatives' email addresses are not publicly available. Constituents can often contact their representatives via contact forms posted on their websites. A staffer is more likely than an elected official to collect and respond to those contact requests.

and the perceptions of elected officials. The email invitation included a personalized link to the Qualtrics survey, which opened in a new window. The invitation also contained a request for the contact information of other people interested in participating in the survey. The invitation concluded with my name and university affiliation. Two weeks after the initial email, I sent a reminder email to email addresses that had not bounced back or opted out of the survey. I fielded the survey from July 29 through October 31, 2018.

After clicking on the link in the email invitation, a new window appeared with a consent form providing further details about the survey, researcher, and the respondent's consent to participate in a voluntary, anonymous survey. Once respondents consented to the survey, the survey proceeded with questions gauging the respondents' gender, race and ethnicity, party affiliation, ideology, and information about their service in a legislative office. I asked about their position title, how current the experience was, and the state and type of the legislative office where they served. Then, respondents answered a series of original, closed-ended questions about their perceptions of the relative costliness of collective action for participants, their perceptions of various groups and individuals, their beliefs about the legitimacy of specific forms of participation, and their likelihood of responding to different forms of participation.

Finally, I asked respondents to answer a series of original, open-ended questions about collective action. Before beginning to answer these open-ended questions, respondents received the following prompt:

Now we'd like to ask you a series of questions about collective action, which includes anything from people calling their legislators or signing petitions to boycotts, marches, and acts of civil disobedience. Other examples include letter-writing campaigns, advocacy, strikes, media appeals, marches, and riots. These don't have to target an elected official.

They were also reminded of these examples in the prompt for each open-ended question.

3.1.2 Descriptive Statistics

The emailed invitations resulted in twenty-one responses of legislators and staffers in local, state, and national offices across the United States.[8]

---

[8] Only about 1 percent (14 of 1,505) of people invited to participate in the survey using publicly available email addresses responded to the survey. I acquired seven additional respondents via email invitations sent to personal contacts with current or previous

The survey respondents communicated the perspectives of five current city council members and a current party official. Additionally, nine current legislative staffers responded to the survey. The current staffers include three chiefs of staff, five senior staff members, and one fellow. They served in offices in Colorado, Georgia, Massachusetts, New Jersey, Louisiana, Maryland, or the District of Columbia. These staff members support legislators in national and state houses of representatives, city councils, and a county council office. Respondents also include six former staffers of state senate, US Senate, and US House of Representative offices in California, Missouri, and the District of Columbia.

In addition to the geographical, position type, and office level variation of survey respondents, there is also variation in respondents' ideology and party affiliation. One-third of the legislators identify as ideologically liberal, another third as moderate, and the final third as conservative. The majority (twelve) of staffers identify as ideologically liberal, while one staffer identifies as conservative and two others as moderate. Three city council members and one senior staff member identify as Republican. Another senior staff member and a former intern either have no party affiliation or identify as Independent. The remaining respondents say they are members of the Democratic Party.

All twenty-one respondents answered at least two closed-ended questions. Fifteen respondents completed both closed-ended and open-ended survey questions. A few surveys took more than 100 minutes to complete. This likely occurred because the respondent did not finish all of the survey questions in one sitting. Excluding those extraordinarily lengthy completion times, the average respondent completed the survey in twelve minutes.

In the remainder of this chapter, I consider all responses relating to the theoretical argument recapped in the initial paragraphs of this chapter.[9] Again, the purpose of these responses is not to draw generalizable conclusions about legislative behavior following protest. These responses demonstrate whether the people who decide how to support protest think in ways that align with the theoretical argument. This chapter reveals that

experience in legislative offices and to people referred to in response to initial survey invitations. These personal contacts and referrals increased the diversity of the sample with additional survey responses from a current party official, a current chief of staff in a Maryland county council member's office, and staff members with prior experience in the US Senate, the US House of Representatives, and the California State Senate.

[9] Any responses that I excluded are either represented by included responses or unrelated to the theoretical argument.

there are policymakers of various positions, office types, partisanships, and ideologies across the United States who understand collective action the way my theoretical argument suggests they should. The responses show that legislators and their staffers are aware of collective action events. Legislators and staffers believe collective action is meaningful for their legislative behaviors. They are strategic actors who are motivated by reelection concerns, and they view collective action differently depending on who is protesting.

3.2 CONDITION 1: AWARENESS OF COLLECTIVE ACTION EVENTS

The first necessary condition for the theoretical argument is that legislators are aware of collective action events. This condition is critical to the central argument of the book. If legislators are not conscious of collective action, their legislative behavior following collective action may not be attributable to collective action or collective action participants. Accordingly, I asked legislators and staffers to *"Discuss any memorable collective action events"* and answer this question: *"Why were those collective action events memorable?"*

Eleven out of the fourteen legislators and staffers who responded to at least one open-ended question discussed collective action events that were memorable. On average, these eleven legislators and staffers mentioned at least two specific collective action events. The most willing respondents noted as many as six specific collective action events.

The events referenced vary considerably. Several respondents referenced protests relating to Donald Trump and his presidency. They listed trade, gay marriage, breaking up California into multiple states, Ebola, and education. Respondents brought up social movements such as Me Too, anti–Iraq War, gay rights, pro-life, anti-immigration, and gun rights. Some even mentioned specific groups like Indivisible, Black Lives Matter, unions, Dreamers, and DACA recipients. They also noted the LGBTQ, Filipino, and Jewish communities. Respondents even cited collective action on specific legislation, including the Affordable Care Act of 2010, the Stop Online Piracy Act (SOPA), and the PROTECT IP Act (PIPA). Some of the responses to the survey prompt to discuss any memorable collective action event(s) follow:

Calls and protests re DREAM Act in 2018; women's march and other Trump-focused marches from 2017–; ongoing impeachment calls; episodic tech focused collective action events like net neutrality and the SOPA/PIPA bills. [These were

memorable due to the fact that] some generated notable and sustained uptick in calls [and] emails to the office, others were very visible in person events that garnered media coverage.
(Chief of Staff, US House of Representatives, Democrat)

Protests in Charlottesville, Va that resulted in the death of Heather Heyer. Various protests against the 45th President. These protests were memorable because of the number of people who were involved, and in one instance, a person died. In my opinion, these protests led to a greater number of women and racial and ethnic minorities running for office. Progressives and minorities have recently won primaries in states and congressional districts where they have not [before]. This movement may lead to Democrats taking back the House of Representatives.
(Former Intern, Missouri, Independent)

Social media movements for Eric Garner; view media campaigns for Ebola; frequent calls from constituents about a particular issue. [They were memorable because of] the number of people involved and invested in the conversation.
(Former Staff Member, US House of Representatives, Democrat)

Memories of collective action appear to inundate the chief of staff in the House of Representatives. The majority of protests he discusses seem to coincide with the candidacy and election of Donald Trump. Others relate to internet technology, like the Stop Online Piracy Act (SOPA) and the Preventing Real Online Threats to Economic Creativity and Theft of Intellectual Property Act (PIPA). He believes these events were memorable because of the increase in the number of people contacting his office on those issues.

Other events were significant to him because they garnered media attention and the protesters participated in person. I assume the chief of staff mentions the in-person protests in contrast to less costly virtual participation on internet platforms. For instance, consider the 2012 collective action of Wikipedia, Google, Reddit, and other organizations that shut down their websites or blacked out their website content to oppose the proposed SOPA and PIPA legislation. I explore legislative behavior following in-person and online collective action in greater detail in Chapter 3. For now, at least one survey respondent believes collective action is more memorable and perhaps more likely to receive legislative support when performed in person than online.

In the second quote, the former intern from a legislator's Missouri office also mentioned protests related to Donald Trump. Additionally, he recalled the Unite the Right, white supremacist rally in Charlottesville, Virginia, on August 12, 2017, that resulted in the death of counter-protester Heather Heyer. He believes Heyer's death made that particular event memorable. He also believes that bigger events are more likely than smaller events to make an impression on him.

Beyond describing memorable events and explaining why they stuck out for him, the former intern gave his opinions on the implications of collective action. He believes that protest can encourage new elected officials to run for office and could even create a critical mass in the Democratic Party in the US House of Representatives. New elected officials, especially when they increase the capacity of Democrats in legislative bodies, can provide better representation for the interests of progressive and racial and ethnic minority constituents.

The third quote also mentions a variety of collective actions, from protests surrounding the deaths of Eric Garner to campaigns about Ebola outbreaks to calls to the legislator's office on various issues. This staffer believes these particular events were memorable because of the number of people involved in the collective action. Indeed, the size of the event was a common consideration for many policymakers in this survey. She also says they are memorable because the participants seemed invested in the conversation on those policy issues, which reinforces my argument that legislators are wary of constituents with salient issue preferences who are likely to electorally punish or reward their legislator based on whether that legislator supports the salient issue.

In sum, when I asked legislators and staffers to discuss memorable collective action, their responses mentioned collective action events employing a wide range of tactics. The memorable events concerned issues across the ideological spectrum. Some of them occurred more recently than others. The legislators and staffers also mentioned why they believe collective action events were memorable. Some discussed the size, frequency, and media attention attributed to collective action. Others said that the commitment of the participants to the issue determined whether the protest was memorable. The primary insight from this question is that the responses align with the first necessary condition of the theoretical argument: collective action appears to be on the minds of elected officials and staff members.

3.3 CONDITION 2: PERCEPTION OF PROTEST'S VALUE

The second necessary condition of the theoretical argument is that legislators and staffers believe that protest has some value that warrants representation. If they do not value collective action, they have no incentive to respond to collective action demands. Legislators and staffers may value and desire to represent collective action because they believe collective action is a legitimate means for constituents to voice their opinions. Additionally, legislators and staffers may believe collective action can help legislators better represent their constituents. I explore each of these potential reasons that collective action is valuable in turn.

3.3.1 Legitimacy

To discern whether legislators and staffers think that collective action is legitimate and therefore worthy of representation, I asked respondents, *"How legitimate is each form of participation?"* I then randomly showed them each of the following participation types: voting, volunteering, contacting elected officials, protesting, lobbying, running for office, voicing opinions. The survey responses reveal that the people who create and determine votes on legislation believe that protest is a legitimate way for constituents to communicate their concerns.

Figure 3.1 shows that almost all respondents (14 out of 15) believe that protest is a legitimate form of political participation. Relatedly, nearly all respondents believe that contacting elected officials and voicing opinions are very or extremely legitimate forms of political participation. Each of these methods can be perceived as collective action. On average, legislators and staffers perceive lobbying to be the least legitimate form of participation, and, unsurprisingly, they perceive voting as the most legitimate form of participation.

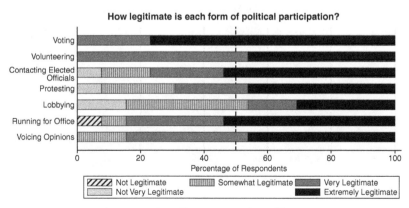

FIGURE 3.1 Legislators' and staffers' perceptions of legitimate participation

These responses suggest that legislators and staffers may not value collective action as much as they do voting. Still, collective action has qualities that could lead to the representation of protest demands. A communications director in the US House of Representatives stated that "legislators should be more engaged with collective action and less engaged with lobbying." Perhaps this is because of the ability of collective action to convey the truly salient concerns of constituents.

Some of the open-ended survey responses are also revealing regarding whether and how legislators value protest. Some of the legitimacy for collective action as a means for communicating constituency concerns arises from beliefs in rights guaranteed in the First Amendment of the US Constitution:

The member has a very strong view on 1st amendment rights and believes people ought to be heard. Collective action, in his view, is a first step towards getting their representatives' attention.

(Former Staff Member, US Senate, Democrat)

In this view, collective action is a constitutionally supported channel to help constituents get their representatives' attention and facilitate representation. This perspective aligns with the principles expressed by the authors of the US Constitution. However, some legislators are concerned about whether protest is the best way for constituents to communicate their interests:

When we see mis-targeted & disruptive protests, or aggressive callers, it makes us pause and consider whether we should "reward" those actions with the result they're calling for – for example, if they're calling for something we might already be considering.

(Chief of Staff, US House of Representatives, Democrat)

This chief of staff voices concern about rewarding unruly behaviors with policy support even on issues his office was already planning to represent. His anxiety suggests that how protesters express their grievances could influence whether legislators and staffers believe the protest is legitimate. Despite these concerns, Figure 3.1 indicates that most legislators believe that collective action is generally a legitimate and valuable form of political participation.

3.3.2 Informative Value

Some policymakers express concern about supporting aggressive or disruptive collective action. Yet, most respondents suggest that collective action can reveal information about their constituents that they previously did not have. One former staff member described how the congressman that she worked for was constantly searching for information about his constituents' preferences:

> The elected (Congressman) that I worked for usually agreed with the majority position of the voters in his district. He followed public opinion closely, monitoring opinion pieces, public opinion polling, call logs and correspondence to his office, and anything that was said by popular news anchors, etc. When collective action indicated that public opinion was changing, I think he would change his opinion.
>
> (Former Staff Member, US House of Representatives, Democrat)

Public opinion polls, constituency contact, and media outlets are essential sources for legislators. Still, they do not always contain the most up-to-date information about what constituents care about and how opinions may be shifting. The former staff member from an office in the US House of Representatives suggests that collective action can be a valuable source of information on fluctuating public sentiments. Another staff member also suggests that collective action can be informative:

> Collective action can have influence when it calls attention to an issue or argument that we hadn't previously focused on.
>
> (Chief of Staff, US House of Representatives, Democrat)

This quote demonstrates that legislators and staffers value the information protest can reveal about their constituents' preferences. Indeed, the chief of staff sounds grateful for collective action because it can communicate new information and new arguments that the legislators had not considered. Legislators and staffers do not simply believe that collective action is normatively valuable because it is a legitimate form of political participation. They also believe that collective action is beneficial because it can provide information that helps them perform their jobs better.

3.4 CONDITION 3: COLLECTIVE ACTION AND LEGISLATIVE BEHAVIOR

The third condition of the theoretical argument is that collective action influences legislative behavior. The theory does not require that collective action always influence legislative behavior, but collective action does need to influence legislative behavior at least sometimes. The responses

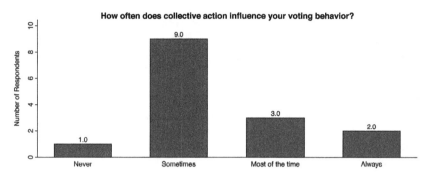

FIGURE 3.2 Legislators' and staffers' perceptions of collective action influence

that follow suggest that legislators and staffers do believe that collective action influences legislative behavior. They believe collective action influences the way legislators sponsor bills, issue public statements, and communicate with their constituents. Legislators and staffers also think that collective action influences the way that legislators vote on legislation, which is the outcome variable of statistical analyses in later chapters.

3.4.1 Legislative Voting Behavior

I asked survey respondents, *"How often does collective action influence your vote on legislation or a bill?"* Figure 3.2 displays the distribution of responses to this closed-ended question. The survey results indicate legislators and their staffers agree that collective action influences legislative behavior. The average response is 2.85, suggesting that the average policymaker believes that collective action influences voting behavior almost half the time. Nine survey respondents believe collective action influences their voting behavior *sometimes*. Three think collective action influences legislative voting behavior *most of the time*. Two respondents believe collective action *always* influences their legislative voting behavior.

I did not include any open-ended questions about whether collective action influences legislative voting behavior. But survey responses to other open-ended questions reveal that legislators and staffers believe that collective action influences legislators' voting decisions. For example, consider the following:

When collective action indicated that public opinion was changing, I think he would change his position. For instance, while I worked for the Congressman, it became much more acceptable to support gay rights and gay marriage. Although I think the Congressman always held these views, he was able to be more vocal about them when he had the public's support.

(Former Staff Member, US House of Representatives, Democrat)

This former staff member suggests that collective action can be an indicator of shifting public opinion in the legislator's district. She thinks the legislator's position on legislation would change when he observed public opinion changing due to collective action. She also believes that the new information on public opinion shifts might have led the legislator she worked for to increase the representation of issues that the legislator already supported. This is an important point. A legislator who already votes in support of an issue cannot look responsive to protest by continuing to vote in support of that issue. They may need to demonstrate their support in other legislative behaviors, like bill (co)sponsorship, public statements, or private communications sent to constituents.

Only one person indicated that collective action *never* influences legislative voting behavior. While this staffer does not believe collective action influences legislative voting behavior, he does believe collective action influences legislative behavior more generally. This US House of Representatives fellow indicates that collective action *sometimes* influences a legislator's bill (co)sponsorship and public statements. He also states that collective action influences the likelihood of legislators joining or engaging in collective action *about half the time*. Open-ended responses reveal that this policymaker believes collective action influences legislative behavior when protesters employ various tactics. In answering the question, *"When (or why) is collective action more likely to influence your behavior?"* he states:

When multiple forms are pursued concurrently: petitions alone aren't enough, but a bevy of calls and media/social action might focus the attention of staff or the official to produce, at the very least, time spent analyzing the issue at hand.

(Current Fellow, US House of Representatives, Democrat)

This respondent states that collective action never influences legislative voting behavior. Yet, his responses to other questions suggest that he believes collective action does influence legislative behavior. He thinks that collective action, particularly that involving multiple tactics, influences the bills legislators (co)sponsor, the speeches they make, and the likelihood that the legislator he worked for will participate in collective action. He just does not believe collective action is enough to change his boss's vote on legislation.

Another respondent stated that collective action was simply an annoy-ance. He believes that collective action has little influence on how his boss votes on legislation related to an issue raised during collective action:

Whenever there'd be a trade vote in the House, unions would flood the phones with calls to the point of shutting down our phone lines. It wouldn't change my bosses [*sic*] view of the bill (he was a free trader), but he knew that the unions were strongly opposed . . . . The unions jamming our phone lines were memorable only because it was such a pain. The others don't really stick out in my memory . . . . Another issue that I can recall was slaughtering horses on federal land. My boss represented an urban district in Los Angeles with no federal land, let along [*sic*] wild horses roaming. However his district had a number of very vocal people passionate about animal rights. They were vehemently against allowing the slaughter of horses, so my boss voted for horse slaughter bans. We all knew it was bad policy, but the animal rights people were passionate and we weren't going to fall on our sword with them over an issue as inconsequential as horse slaughter.

(Former Staff Member, US House of Representatives, Democrat)

This former staff member describes two collective action events: one regarding trade and the other the slaughtering of horses on federal land. In both descriptions, the staffer seems to be irritated by the protests. Still, one campaign influences the legislator's voting behavior while the other does not. He does not provide a clear explanation for the dif-ference in responsiveness. The former staffer describes the legislator as opposed to both issues. He reports both collective action events as being executed by zealous protesters. What stands out about this former staffer's response is that the legislator he worked for voted in support of a house slaughter ban even though the legislator and staffers disagreed with the policy.[10] This suggests that even legislators reluctant to support an issue may represent collective action participants' concerns at least sometimes.

The open- and closed-ended responses to whether collective action influences voting behavior broadly align with the necessary condition that collective action influences legislative behavior. All but one respond-ent believe that collective action influences legislators' voting behavior at least sometimes. What is more impressive is that all of the policymak-ers who responded to this survey agree that collective action influences legislative behavior more generally.

---

[10] To be sure, this staff member did indicate on the closed-ended question that collective action influences the voting behavior of his boss *sometimes*.

3.4.2 Legislative Behavior More Generally

Several open-ended responses illustrate how policymakers perceive the influence of collective action on legislative behavior beyond voting behavior. In addition to the potential collective action has for changing a legislator's vote, collective action intensifies the legislators' attention to protest demands. Collective action can also increase the communication constituents receive about what their legislator was already doing. To be sure, consider the opinions of these staffers:

In most of these cases, the calls [and emails] supported a position our office was already taking, but the intensity of the action spurred us to be more visible/vocal [*sic*] in our work to make sure constituents were more aware.

(Chief of Staff, US House of Representatives, Democrat)

Collective action was more influential when the member's views already aligned with that group (e.g., a union) or the group was active electorally (e.g., business groups in the state). Generally speaking, the outcome from most collective action was a meeting to make the group's case and from there sometimes that lead to more action.

(Former Staff Member, US Senate, Democrat)

These open-ended responses suggest that ideology and issue preferences are on the minds of many legislators and staffers when considering how collective action influences legislative behavior. Even legislators and staffers who believe collective action influences legislative behavior at least sometimes think that it influences legislative behavior when protesters' demands align with legislators' policy positions. In those cases, collective action influences behavior by altering how legislators communicate with their constituents who engage in collective action.

For the theoretical argument to be valid, legislators must first be aware of collective action. These responses reveal that legislators and their staffers believe that collective action is clearly on the minds of policymakers. The argument also demands that collective action influences legislative voting behavior. What it does not require is that policymakers be aware that collective action influences legislative behavior. Indeed, humans can respond to stimuli (e.g., blinking when their eyes are dry) even if they are unaware of the stimulus (e.g., dry air). Remarkably, these responses reveal that legislators and staffers do believe that collective action influences their legislative voting behavior. The policymakers mention changing their voting behavior on legislation relevant to the issue after becoming aware of their constituents' salient concerns during collective action.

The responses also provide other insights. Sometimes the shift in legislative voting behavior is motivated by collective action participants with concerns aligning with the legislator's preferences. Other times the collective action seems to alter the behavior of reluctant legislators. Even more, policymakers believe collective action is influential beyond voting behavior. Legislators and staffers speak of having meetings with constituents who have engaged in collective action. They describe messaging done to communicate with constituents the measures the legislator has been or will be taking on the issues raised during collective action. Each of these insights supports the presence of the necessary condition that collective action influences legislative behavior. Some of them even support the condition that collective action influences legislative voting behavior, specifically.

3.5 CONDITION 4: LEGISLATORS' STRATEGIC SUPPORT OF COLLECTIVE ACTION DEMANDS

To this point, I have demonstrated that legislators are aware of collective action. They value collective action as a legitimate and informative form of participation, and they believe collective action influences their behavior. Another essential component of the theoretical argument is that legislators are strategic actors who prefer to support some collective action demands over others. I argue that legislators are concerned about their reelection and often look for information to discern which constituents they should represent. In this section, I reveal survey responses that support this contention. I begin with the perception that legislators strategically decide which collective action issues they should represent.

3.5.1 Differential Collective Action Influence

Supporting collective action demands is not costless. Legislators privately respond to some collective action by meeting with collective action participants or sending letters responding to mass emails or phone calls. Other legislative behavior in response to protest is quite visible. Voting on or (co)sponsoring legislation, making public statements, and participating in collective action events are all part of the public record. Even the private support of collective action could be costly to a legislator who diverts time from addressing the concerns of other constituents.

The theory suggests that some collective action events should be more likely than others to influence legislative behavior. Legislators' differential responsiveness to collective action is also a common finding in the contentious politics and social movements literatures. Scholars often find that a protest's size, frequency, framing, organizational strength, context, tactics, and disruptiveness are important factors determining whether protest demands are supported in public policy.[11] I find support for legislators' differential responsiveness to collective action in the survey responses.

In the survey, I asked elected officials and legislative staffers whether they responded equally to all collective action events. Specifically, I asked, *"Which forms of participation are likely to receive a positive response from you?"* I inquired about their responsiveness to lobbying, financial contributions, acts of civil disobedience, petitions, marches or rallies, constituency contact, and social media posts. I randomized the order in which survey respondents saw each participation type.

Figure 3.3 reveals that the mean legislator's office is almost *slightly likely* to respond favorably to most forms of political participation. The exception is for demands communicated during acts of civil disobedience. Elected officials and their staffers say that they are least likely to respond positively to acts of civil disobedience. Figure 3.3 demonstrates that a third of legislative offices are *slightly likely* or *moderately likely* to respond positively to acts of civil disobedience. The majority are *unlikely* to give a positive response.

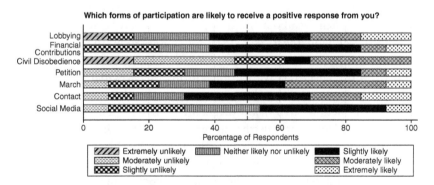

FIGURE 3.3 Likelihood of positive legislative response

---

[11] See, for instance, Lipsky (1968); Lipsky (1970); Piven and Cloward (1977); Cress and Snow (2000); McAdam and Su (2002); Bailey, Mummolo, and Noel (2012); Wouters and Walgrave (2017); Gillion (2013).

Two former staff members provide some insights about why acts of civil disobedience are *unlikely* to receive a positive response from legislators' offices:

My boss also is highly sensitive to certain types of collective action, especially those that are more dramatic or [have] more "flair." He wants to be associated with those big collective action events (large marches and strikes) if it fits his legislative brand. But he will stay away or distance himself from events that have a capacity for violence or look bad, like riots or fights.

(Former Staff Member, California State Senate, Democrat)

I always found marches and acts of civil disobedience to be the least effective. First off, I have no idea if they're constituents or not. However when we heard from individual constituents who took time to write a letter or email, we'd take time to craft a thoughtful response. We'd also take an internal tally of the mail (not just form letters, which are easier to ignore). If you dropped a stack of petitions at our office, I would have no idea if someone actually signed them or you just printed your name. But a thoughtful individual call, email or letter would warrant far more attention.

(Former Staff Member, US House of Representatives, Democrat)

The former staff member from the California State Senate is not necessarily opposed to acts of civil disobedience. He states that his boss appreciated events with "flair" because they helped the legislator's brand, but he is concerned that violent or disruptive collective action might look bad for the legislator. This response mirrors the concern articulated by the chief of staff, whose comments helped inform whether legislators value collective action as a legitimate means of participation: the chief of staff was apprehensive about rewarding violent collective action events.

On the other hand, the former US House of Representatives staff member contends that the reason his office was less likely to respond to acts of civil disobedience, relative to other forms of participation, was the reelection incentive. Policymakers do not know whether the people who participate in acts of civil disobedience or even sign petitions are constituents of the legislator's district. Instead, he says that his office prefers thoughtful calls, letters, or emails that can verify whether the person making contact is a constituent. Perhaps this is why legislators are most likely to respond positively to direct constituency contact rather than other forms of participation (see Figure 3.3).

Figure 3.3 displays the results of a closed-ended question that only asked policymakers about their likelihood of supporting specific tactics. The open-ended responses reveal that policymakers do not consider these tactics in isolation. Remember the current US House of Representatives fellow who responded to this question, *"When (or why) is collective action more likely to influence your behavior?"* He replied that collective action is more likely to influence his behavior "[w]hen multiple forms [of collective action] are pursued concurrently: petitions alone aren't enough, but a bevy of calls and media/social action might focus the attention of staff or the official to produce, at the very least, time spent analyzing the issue at hand." Multiple types of collective action increase the odds that the legislator's office is aware of the issue and that participants communicate their preferences effectively. It also increases the number of people who might participate in collective action. Someone may not be aware of a petition to express their support. However, they may have seen a social media post or a call to participate in a letter-writing campaign. Therefore, multiple forms of participation increase the number of voices available to communicate a salient concern effectively.

The number of collective action participants is a reliable indicator of successful collective action efforts.[12] Collective action events that are larger are more likely to include constituents who are invested in the issue enough to support, oppose, or abstain from supporting the elected official in the next election. Several policymakers say that the size of a particular collective event is vital to whether legislators respond to participants:

> If organizers can demonstrate [there] are a large number of constituents that share a specific view or opinion, my old boss would certainly take note. It completely depends on the issue. It won't be enough to sway a vote on its own. There are a large number of factors that go into that decision. However, if we hear from a large number of constituents on any issue, it certainly puts that issue on our radar.
>
> (Former Staff Member, US House of Representatives, Democrat)

> A collection of people coming together to respond to a particular issue.
>
> (Former staff member, US House of Representatives, Democrat)

These quotes indicate that size (i.e., a large number or collection) matters for legislative behavior. The last comment suggests that legislators are also motivated by constituents who have coordinated grievances. If people can come together to respond to a particular issue, then they can come together to support (or not) an elected official who favorably (or not) responds to their concerns.

Still, legislators are not simply strategically responding to the size or cohesiveness of protest efforts. They are also motivated by constituency

---

[12] For examples, see Lohmann (1993); McAdam and Su (2002); Gillion (2013).

concerns that are communicated effectively. It is difficult for legislators to respond to collective action demands that are not on their radar. A former intern from Missouri states, "When participating as a group, your voice about an issue is magnified compared to one person calling their member of Congress, for example." Extending this example, when there are constant calls on the same issue, the issue is more likely to be remembered during policy discussions.

An issue preference is also more likely to be remembered and supported when it is thoughtful and compelling. Several policymakers discussed the need for collective action to deliver a clear and relevant message:

> Showing an understanding of the issue and why the action that's being called for is necessary and strategic. As opposed to calling for something that would be "counter-productive", or showy without being effective.
>
> (Chief of Staff, US House of Representatives, Democrat)

In a similar vein, policymakers expressed a preference for supporting events that were well organized and strategic:

> The number of people; if there were injuries; the duration of the protest; the reputation of the groups involved that is, is the group seen as an expert on the topic; can the group provide evidence-based solutions concerning the issue.
>
> (Former Intern, Missouri, Independent)

> Often times, we are invited to the events ahead of time so there was planning involved. Spontaneous actions are looked down upon and generally tried to be avoided.
>
> (Former staff member, California State Senate, Democrat)

The former staff member from the California State Senate suggests that they look down on spontaneous actions. There is some concern about whether the message communicated during collective action is credible. Just as groups can use collective action to communicate salient constituency preferences, they can also use collective action to convince a policymaker that an issue is salient when it is not. Thus, legislators and staffers look for information that can help them determine which events they should support.

When asked *"What things make you more likely to respond to collective action?"* a fellow in the US House of Representatives responds, "Constituent involvement. Ideological alignment with the cause. A credible reputational impact from lack of action." Suppose a group is constantly engaging in collective action. In that case, there is more uncertainty about whether the issue is presently salient for constituents.

To summarize, the survey responses suggest the necessary condition of the theoretical argument that policymakers prefer to respond to some collective action events and not others. They say they prefer to represent collective action events that are large, civil, and with a clearly articulated message. They are also strategic in their efforts. They seek evidence to determine whether the collective action event provides credible information about the salient interests of their constituents.

In alignment with the theory, many survey respondents express a preference for responding to collective action events that facilitate their reelection goals. They desire to support protests that will improve, and certainly not worsen, the legislator's public image. They want to support events containing many people with a clearly articulated protest demand. Representing cogent interests important to a lot of people means appeasing a voting bloc that could be consequential on Election Day. The reelection concern is a central mechanism of the theoretical argument. I argue that legislators support costlier protest more often than less costly protest because legislators are concerned about their reelection. Several of the previous quotes stress collective action characteristics that facilitate strategic reelection efforts. In the next section, I explore the reelection incentive in greater detail. I reveal survey responses that emphasize the role of reelection in legislators' strategic responsiveness to collective action.

3.5.2 Reelection Concerns

The theory contends that legislators support some protests more than others, particularly costly protest because legislators are motivated by their concerns for reelection. This concern is more of a mechanism motivating legislative behavior than a necessary condition for the theoretical argument. Indeed, some other mechanisms, like pressure from the legislator's party or the legislator's convictions about the issue preference communicated during collective action, could be responsible for the strategic legislative behavior that supports collective action by low-resource groups more often than collective action by high-resource groups. Legislators and staffers do mention other motivations for legislative behavior. They at times discuss ideology, (dis)agreement with the protest goals, and partisan considerations when discussing whether and how they respond to protest. Nevertheless, the reelection concern is the most common explanation that legislators and staffers give for their legislative behavior in response to collective action.

One former intern was even explicit in stating that reelection was the primary reason for whether and how legislators respond to collective action:

First, they are concerned about reelection and … they do not want to be seen as unresponsive. Second, they can use these incidents to advance their legislative proposals or ambitions.

(Former Intern, Missouri, Independent)

Collective action may follow other motivations, like furthering a legislator's policy goals, but the foremost reason for legislative behavior following collective action is the reelection incentive. The former intern from a Missouri office declares that reelection concerns are the first motivation for responding to collective action. The second motivation is the desire to use collective action to create legislation and further the legislator's career ambitions. Both these efforts facilitate reelection, and they require a legislator to be in office to perform them.

Another motivation that the former intern discusses is not wanting to appear unresponsive. He mentions this motivation in tandem with the reelection concern, which suggests that a legislator who ignores collective action participants risks losing reelection. The fact that a legislator or staffer fears appearing unresponsive does not mean that collective action will necessarily result in positive legislative behavior. As this staffer describes:

We could always justify our votes. If it was collective action for a vote or issue that my boss didn't agree with (lets [sic] say the handful of gun rights, pro-life, or anti-immigrant advocates in our district), we weren't afraid to politely disagree. They knew we didn't agree, and we knew they probably weren't going to vote for us anyway.

(Former Staff Member, US House of Representatives, Democrat)

As this statement suggests, reelection concerns do not mean that legislators support every protest. Again, legislators are strategic actors. They try only to represent collective action participants who affect the legislator's reelection by swaying votes for or against the legislator. They are also careful and measured in their responsiveness.

A District of Columbia fellow in the House of Representatives argues that "[s]ome officials respond too quickly to collective actions – they require some analysis before issuing [a] response. An official who jumps too quickly may come to regret it later." As suggested in previous quotes, the reactions that this fellow mentions could relate to some moral conviction or costs to the legislator's image. "Regret" likely relates to reelection concerns. Many legislators are concerned that some previously silent constituency will observe how their legislator voted on legislation important to them and mobilize to hold that legislator accountable.[13]

The timing of collective action events and the issue salience of protesters are vital considerations for reelection minded elected officials. A New Jersey city council member expressed during the survey that he is more likely to be influenced by collective action occurring "around election time [or] at a council meeting." When an event happens around election time, constituents are likely to recall it easily and consider the legislator's actions (or lack thereof), particularly on issues salient to them. Similarly, events that occur at a council meeting are more visible to the legislator (i.e., they cannot deny being made aware of the issue) and to constituents who are more likely than the average citizen to monitor their elected officials' behavior. As such, legislators are intent upon responding to attentive constituents who are most likely to influence legislators' reelection prospects.

To satisfy the reelection concern, many legislators prioritize the preferences and participation of people in their geographic constituency – people who are residents of a legislator's district. It is this population that can vote in support of or opposition to the elected official. Other constituents are also important. People outside the geographic district boundaries can volunteer or contribute money to a campaign. They can publicly or privately voice their support or opposition to the elected official's actions. They can even participate in collective action concerning the elected official's behavior. However, only constituents in the geographic boundaries of a district can directly influence a legislator's reelection with their vote during elections:

[Collective action w]orks best when the people engaging in collective action are from my boss's district. He tends to pay more attention when his constituents are out there rallying.
(Former Staff Member, California State Senate, Democrat)

Whether those engaged were in his geographic constituency and then he gave much more attention to those who supported him or the party.
(Former Staff Member, US Senate, Democrat)

Legislators are also concerned with how supporting collective action participants will benefit or disadvantage their relationship with their political party or reelection constituency. The previous quote suggests

[13] See, for instance, Arnold (1990).

that whether protesters' preferences align with legislator's preferences or the legislator's political party's preferences is imperative for whether the legislator supports protest demands. A New Jersey city council member expresses a similar concern: "I was concerned about how [my response] would impact a group that supported me." Legislators must therefore be strategic in whether and how they respond to collective action demands. They consider the preferences of collective action participants and other members of their reelection constituency.

Elected officials need to run on a brand or platform so that constituents have a better idea of how the legislator will perform in the future. If a legislator is constantly changing their position or consistently voting against the party, then constituents tend to lack confidence in the likelihood that the elected official will act on their behalf in the future. Likewise, elected officials are interested in keeping the support of constituents who supported them in past elections. However, as the survey responses indicate, maintaining a reelection constituency is not easy. Public opinion changes. Some issues that were not salient to constituents in the previous election become salient before the next election.

The theoretical argument is grounded in the assumption that elected officials' reelection concerns are a primary motivation for why legislators respond to collective action participants. The survey responses support this assumption. As the survey responses reveal, many elected officials respond to collective action participants, especially those who live in their districts, because they are concerned about reelection. The theory and survey responses also confirm that legislators respond to collective action participants even while considering their personal ambitions, party pressures, and other constituents' preferences.

3.6 CONDITION 5: PERCEPTIONS OF COLLECTIVE ACTION PARTICIPANTS

I argue that legislators are more likely to support the interests of low-resource protesters than high-resource protesters because low-resource groups face more significant barriers to participation. For this relationship to be accurate, it is not enough for groups to have differences in their ability to protest. The people who create and vote on legislation must also perceive and act upon these differences. To understand legislators' perceptions of the costliness of collective action for disparate groups, I created a series of survey questions assessing whether legislators and legislators' staff believe that some groups face greater difficulty than others when politically participating.

Specifically, I presented survey respondents with this prompt: *"Think about the difficulties people face when participating politically. Move the slider towards the group (GROUP COMPARISON RANDOMIZED) that you believe encounters greater difficulty when engaging in each form of political participation listed below."* The question was repeated for each of the following group comparisons: women compared with men, individuals compared with organizations, Black people compared with White people, youth compared with adults, and poor people compared with rich people. The forms of political participation included voting, contributing financially to campaigns, contacting their elected official, lobbying, running for office, voicing their opinions, and most vital for the theoretical argument protesting. I randomized the order in which the survey presented the groups and the forms of political participation to the survey respondents.

Figure 3.4 displays the results of the question for protest behavior. The majority of respondents do appear to view collective action as more difficult for some groups than others. The mean responses are that when engaging in protest, poor people face greater difficulty than rich people, Black people face greater difficulty than White people, and individuals face greater difficulty than groups. These survey results support the contention that low-resource groups face more significant barriers to

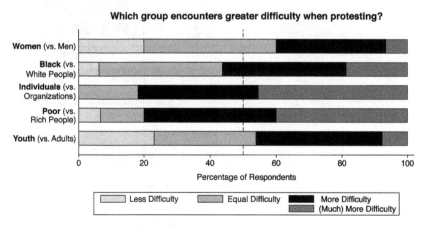

FIGURE 3.4 Legislators' and staffers' perceptions of costly protest

participation than high-resource groups. In alignment with the theory, legislators do observe the differences in the ability of groups to protest.

Figure 3.4 also suggests that survey respondents are not simply identifying differences in participation because I am asking them to make a comparison. Indeed, some respondents perceive no group differences in barriers to participation. The average and median respondents believe Black people face *more difficulty* than White people when protesting. However, the modal response choice for comparisons between Black and White protesters is that the two groups face *equal difficulty* when protesting. Additionally, the modal response for women versus men is that men and women face *equal difficulty* when protesting. However, unlike race, the average survey respondent does not appear to perceive differences in the ability to protest based on gender, nor do they perceive differences based on age.

As further confirmation of the reliability of these survey results, I also asked respondents about differences in the difficulties groups face when voting. In line with conventional expectations,[14] Figure 3.5 demonstrates that legislators and their staffers view voting as a more difficult activity for poor people than rich people, youth compared with adults, and Black people compared with White people. They do not perceive any group differences in the ability to vote based on gender or whether individuals or groups are voting. Consequently, it does not appear that these responses are spurious.

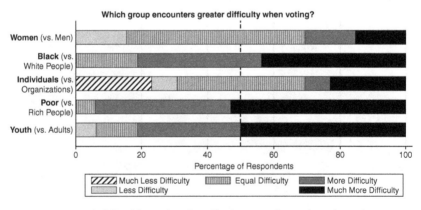

FIGURE 3.5 Legislators' and staffers' perceptions of costly voting

---

[14] For examples, see Verba, Schlozman, and Brady (1995) or Leighley and Nagler (2014).

One survey respondent implicitly acknowledged the protest costs that some groups face:

We participated and responded to every example of collective action. . .. The Congressman marched in the anti–Iraq War protests, the Pride parade, the Veterans Day parade, etc. He responded to every letter and call from his constituents. We also organized round tables with public opinion leaders in certain constituencies, for example LGBTQ, the Filipino community, the Jewish community, etc., to actively encourage people to undertake collective action events.

(Former Staff Member, US House of Representatives, Democrat)

In her response to my prompt to *"Discuss any memorable collective action event(s)"*, this former staff member describes how the congressman that she worked for valued collective action so much that he often participated in collective action events. The congressman also responded to every collective action event that targeted their office. She even notes that their office would encourage collective action from low-resource groups, including the LGBTQ members, the Filipino community, and the Jewish community. Of course, some of these groups have greater resource capacity than others. Still, each has disadvantages based on their sex or sexuality, ethnicity, or religion. Recognizing that these groups were not engaging in collective action as much as the legislator would have liked, their office attempted to ease some of their participation costs.[15]

The closed-ended responses demonstrate that the people who legislate perceive protest to be more difficult for low-resource groups, namely low-income people, Black people, and individuals, than for their higher-resource counterparts. The open-ended response suggests that legislators also observe protest costs relating to protesters' sex, sexuality, ethnicity,

---

[15] Another possibility is that the legislator and staffer encouraged participation for groups who aligned ideologically with the legislator. Collective action can help legislators justify their votes on issues they already desire to cast. For example, the same former staff member who said that the congressman she worked for was more vocal in his support of gay rights and gay marriage when those issues became more popular. However, she also reports that the legislator attended Veteran's Day parades. But the legislator's participation was not motivated by the fact that the veterans shared the legislator's ideology. She wrote, "I think the military and veterans events were the most memorable because they were organized by people who generally wouldn't support a democrat politically, but they were happy that the Congressman [*sic*] attended. 'He may be an SOB, but he's our SOB.'" The legislator's behavior in response to collective action does not appear to be motivated by ideological or partisan concerns. Therefore, the legislator's attempt to mobilize groups with lower resource capacity than their counterparts could be because the legislator recognizes the costliness of protest for those groups.

or religion. Protest requires resources that are scarcer for some groups than for others. Securing transportation to attend a collective action event is difficult without a car or when an event does not occur on a reliable public transportation route. Economic hardships can emerge from contributing financially to a cause or getting arrested during an act of civil disobedience. Paying for child care can be virtually impossible for someone with an inflexible income. Similarly, the civic skills and expertise required for coordinating events are less likely to exist among groups with lower levels of formal education or those detached from civic-minded social and professional networks. Individuals who participate in groups, like social or professional networks, gain information about policies and who can affect change and a sense of solidarity in their shared experiences. This sense of solidarity often facilitates political participation.

While racial and ethnic minorities have less income and education than their White counterparts, the resource capacities relating to race and ethnicity are more than just socioeconomic. Physical and emotional costs resulting from state repression and stigmatization are more likely to occur for Black protesters[16] and other marginalized groups, especially when events diverge from mainstream narratives.[17] For example, Black protesters are more likely than White protesters to be arrested at a protest event.[18] The presence of flags of other countries at a protest is enough to increase adverse reactions to protest and decrease support for more immigration.[19]

These participation costs are evident in participation rates. Political participation increases with income and education and is more likely among White constituents than racial and ethnic minorities.[20] The recognition of these participation barriers in the survey responses suggests that the people who create policies are aware of the burdens some groups overcome to voice their concerns during collective action. This recognition is essential for demonstrating the legislative representation of collective action participants' salient issue preferences.

[16] See Davenport, Soule, and Armstrong (2011).
[17] See Davenport (2010).
[18] See Davenport, Soule, and Armstrong (2011).
[19] See Wright and Citrin (2011).
[20] See Verba, Schlozman, and Brady (1995); Abrajano and Alvarez (2010); Leighley and Nagler (2014).

3.7 CONCLUDING THOUGHTS ON POLICYMAKER'S INSIGHTS

Do legislators and staffers think of themselves behaving in ways that align with the theory presented in the previous chapters? A convenience sample of current and past local, state, and national legislators and legislative staffers suggests that they might. The survey responses are not definitive proof of the conditions necessary for the theoretical argument to be valid. For one, legislators and staffers can behave in ways that align with the theory without being aware of that behavior. Second, this sample is far from representative. The survey responses are valuable in providing more evidence that can be useful in assessing the validity of the theoretical claims.

To be sure, I argue that legislators vote in support of issues expressed during collective action, and they are more likely to do so as participation costs increase. I theorize that legislators are motivated to support costly protest because it is a clearer signal of constituents' issue salience than less costly protest.

For this theory to be accurate, the people who determine whether and how to vote on legislation relevant to collective action demands must first be aware of collective action. Some respondents readily listed several collective action events while others provided vivid descriptions of collective action, like the one concerning horse slaughter bans. These survey responses suggest that legislators and staffers are aware of collective action. They also indicate that at least some collective action events have made a lasting impression on the people who determine legislative behavior.

The awareness of collective action by itself does not lead to legislative responsiveness to collective action. Legislators and staffers must also believe that collective action warrants representation. The people who completed my survey appear to think that collective action is a legitimate way for constituents to communicate their preferences. Even so, a few survey respondents did express concerns about the legitimacy of violent or disruptive protest. Their apprehensions did not prevent them from valuing the information that collective action could provide about the protests. Indeed, many respondents stated that they appreciate protest because it can provide new information about the opinions and preferences of their constituents.

The third necessary condition of the theory is that protest influences legislative behavior. Again, protest could influence legislative behavior even without legislators being conscious of its influence. Nevertheless, the survey responses indicate that all but one survey respondent who answered the question believe that protest influences legislative voting behavior. All survey respondents indicated that collective action influences legislative behavior more generally. These results do not provide definitive proof of the influence of collective action on legislative behavior. Legislators and staffers may simply want to believe that they are responsive to collective action demands. However, the fact that legislators and staffers believe that their behavior is influenced by collective action does provide some evidence of this necessary condition.

Next, for the theory to be valid, legislators must support some collective action events over others. Once again, the survey responses comport with the theory. Legislators and staffers say that some collective actions are more likely than others to influence their behavior. Moreover, their responses suggest that reelection concerns are primary explanations for their strategic behavior in supporting protesters. The results align with the theoretical assumption presented in the previous chapter that legislative behavior is motivated by reelection concerns.

The final necessary condition that legislators observe differences in protest costs based on the group protesting also finds some support in the survey responses. As expected, legislators and staffers indicate that they perceive protest to be more difficult for Black people than for White people, poor people compared with rich people, and individuals compared with organizations. They do not observe differences in protests based on the gender or age of protesters.

Overall, the survey responses suggest that legislators think and behave in ways that the theory suggests. Although the survey is based on only twenty-one responses, the legislators' and staffers' voices provide insight into how legislators incorporate the information they encounter from collective action. The survey responses support the theoretical argument. They also demonstrate the breadth of the relationship. Legislators across national, state, and local offices appear to be influenced by and responsive to costly protest.

Another benefit of these survey responses is that they allow for consideration mechanisms and perspectives not suggested by the theory. For example, I contend that legislative behavior is influenced by the protest costs that groups face. Yet, survey respondents expressed that their strategic legislative behavior in response to collective action was motivated by protest characteristics, including size, frequency, novelty, and tactics. Many of these characteristics were implicitly and sometimes explicitly discussed relative to the legislators' reelection incentive. Nevertheless, the empirical results in Chapter 5 suggest that even while legislators consider protest characteristics, they are still responsive to protesters' participation costs.

Additionally, survey respondents discuss how the characteristics of the participants influenced them. For instance, some survey respondents expressed a preference for supporting partisans and issues aligned with the legislator's platform. Other respondents described cases where they represented protest demands made by constituents who were not partisans or ideologically aligned with the legislators.

The survey responses suggest that the party affiliation of the protesters may be essential for legislative responsiveness to collective action. Equally important may be the partisan affiliation of the survey respondents. As I previously disclosed, more than two-thirds of survey respondents identified as members of the Democratic Party. A look at some of the responses suggests that the opinions of legislators and staffers may not be entirely dependent on their partisanship or ideology.

All three of the Republicans in this survey did indicate that collective action influences their legislative behavior *at least sometimes*. They also appear to perceive some differences in the costliness of protests across groups. Republican respondents observe that Black people face more difficulty when protesting than White people. However, they are equally distributed across answer choices for other potential resource disparities based on gender, organizational capacity, income, or age. Still, we should not make too many inferences from these few Republican survey respondents. The key takeaway here is that at least some Republicans and most Democrats believe that protest is more costly for low-resource groups than for high-resource groups.

Chapter 5 evaluates how these perceptions based on legislators' partisanship influence legislative roll-call voting behavior. The empirical results in that chapter suggest that Republican and conservative legislators may be equally likely to support Black and White protesters' concerns. That is, Republican legislators demonstrate no statistically significant difference in their legislative support of Black people's protest demands relative to White people's protest demands. However, legislative voting behavior is more likely to support the preferences of Latino protesters than White protesters. These findings suggest that Republican and conservative legislators may be influenced by costly participation, even though collective action on the liberal protests that I analyze infrequently aligns with Republican and conservative agendas.

The fact that legislators and legislative staffers all over the United States and across the political spectrum say they are aware of protests and are influenced by them is an essential empirical finding. Research demonstrates the influence of protest on legislative behavior. There are also examples of legislators stating publically that they support protest efforts. Some legislators even attend collective action events to demonstrate their support for their constituents' concerns.

An added benefit of this survey is that what we learn is not based on any public or performative behavior. The responses arise from the voluntary participation of elected officials and staffers, to whom I provided an opportunity to express their opinions without any political consequences. Their answers are anonymous and not subject to any electoral pressures to appear responsive to any particular constituency.

So far, Chapter 2 established that it is logical for legislators to support costly collective action. This chapter demonstrates that legislators and their staffers believe they behave in the way the theoretical argument suggests they should. The next chapter describes the data that I use to evaluate the theoretical argument with statistical models.

4

How the Average Legislator Responds

On April 14, 1991, a coalition of legal-rights organizations including the NAACP Legal Defense and Educational Fund, the Legal Aid Society, and the Puerto Rican Legal Defense and Education Fund, filed a federal lawsuit to "block a $500 million renovation of St. Luke's–Roosevelt Hospital Center and to stop the center from reducing services relied on by the poor at its Morningside Heights campus" in New York City.[1] The coalition also charged that the center was "discriminating against black and Hispanic patients and people without health insurance and ignoring its community-service obligations under Federal law."[2] When the lawsuit was filed, Republican Congresswoman Susan Molinari represented the New York City plaintiffs in the US House of Representatives. Congresswoman Molinari supported her Black, Latino, and lower-income constituents' collective action demands when she voted to pass the Civil Rights and Women's Equity in Employment Act of 1991 (H.R.1).[3]

Nearly a year later, another federal lawsuit was filed to protest civil rights violations against some of Congresswoman Molinari's constituents. The Ancient Order of Hibernians rejected the Irish Lesbian and Gay Organization's application to participate in New York City's annual St. Patrick's Day parade. The organizers asserted that "the group [was] excluded because the parade is a Catholic celebration and in the teachings of the church, homosexuality is impermissible; and that the gay marchers [were] unwelcome because of 'outrageous behavior' by some

---

[1] Shipp (1991).

[2] Shipp (1991).

[3] H.R.1 amended the Civil Rights Act of 1964 to restore and strengthen civil rights laws that ban employment discrimination and for other purposes.

homosexuals during [the previous] year's parade."[4] In protest of their exclusion, the Irish Lesbian and Gay Organization filed a lawsuit arguing that the parade sponsor's rejection of the group's participation due to the sexual orientation of its members was a civil rights violation. This time, Congresswoman Molinari cast a roll-call vote in opposition to her constituents' protest demands.

Congresswoman Molinari voted with 59 percent of House of Representatives members to approve the District of Columbia Appropriations Act, 1993 (H.R.6056). The bill included a Republican Party–sponsored rider that prohibited federal or local funds to implement the District of Columbia's Health Benefits Expansion Act. The rider stated that "[n]one of the Federal funds appropriated under this Act shall be used to implement or enforce any system of registration of unmarried, cohabiting couples whether they are homosexual, lesbian, heterosexual, including ... extending employment, health, or governmental benefits to such couples on the same basis that such benefits are extended to legally married couples."

The bill only applied to District of Columbia residents. However, it presented an opportunity for Congresswoman Molinari to represent the protest demands of her constituents. Both the decision by the Ancient Order of Hibernians to ban the Irish Lesbian and Gay Organization from the 1992 parade and the appropriations bill were explicit in excluding members of the LGBT community because of their sexual orientation. As such, the roll-call vote by Congresswoman Molinari in support of H.R.6056 was a vote in opposition to the preferences of LGBT community members protesting their exclusion from the St. Patrick's Day Parade.

Why did Congresswoman Molinari choose to legislatively support the protest claims of Black, Latino, and low-income protesters who filed the civil rights lawsuit in 1991 but not the Irish lesbian and gay protesters who filed a similar lawsuit in 1992? The theory of costly protest and legislative behavior that I presented in Chapter 2 suggests that the answer lies in who is protesting. People with low incomes and members of the Black and Latino communities tend to have less political, social, and economic resources than members of the Irish LGBT community. These resource disparities are evident in the fight against the HIV/AIDS epidemic in the United States in the 1980s and 1990s.[5]

---

[4] Weber (1992).
[5] See Cohen (1999) and Stockdill (2003).

While members of the Irish LGBT community certainly faced stigma and discrimination due to their sexual orientation, their experiences with HIV/AIDS paled in comparison with the experiences of Black and Latino people who contracted HIV/AIDS. White LGBT community members could leverage their political connections, economic resources, and social status to collective action for policies and practices that addressed HIV/AIDS in their community. Meanwhile, Black and Latino people with HIV/AIDS, including members of the LGBT community, women, and drug users, were ignored by elites outside and within the Black and Latino communities because of sexism, classism, and homophobia. They lacked the resources to organize collective action against HIV/AIDS.

The resource disparities between the Irish Gay and Lesbian Organization members and the plaintiffs seeking access to health care are also evident in the protesters' issues. The Irish Lesbian and Gay Organization protested their right to participate in a St. Patrick's Day parade and for protection against sexual orientation discrimination. Their protest demands were not trivial.

The Ancient Order of Hibernians is a conservative Irish Catholic fraternal organization. Suppose it had recognized the right of Irish Gay and Lesbian community members to march in the parade. That recognition might have reduced hate crimes against members of the LGBT community by people with similar opposition to homosexuality. The symbolic move might have even led to more public support for same-sex marriages or legal unions that would provide benefits to homosexual couples. Nevertheless, the protest demands made by the Irish Gay and Lesbian Organization were less critical for the group's survival relative to the collection action for access to health care and services that the Black, Latino, and lower-income community members were fighting for in the gentrifying Morningside Heights, New York City neighborhood.

St. Luke's–Roosevelt Hospital Center was one of the only places remaining in the medically underserved areas of Morningside Heights, Manhattan Valley, and Central and West Harlem.[6] If the hospital's initial plan was to succeed, residents would have to travel fifty-five blocks to receive obstetric, pediatric, and neonatal intensive care. The plan would primarily affect Black, Latino, and especially low-income patients who already faced high infant mortality rates and were unlikely to travel long distances to receive health care services. Consequently, an unsuccessful

---

[6] See Shipp (1991) for more details on the lawsuit.

lawsuit would reduce or even eliminate access to health care for an already resource-deprived community.

According to the theory of costly protest and legislative behavior, Congresswoman Molinari may have reached different conclusions after observing the Irish Lesbian and Gay Organization's collective action compared with the Black, Latino, and low-income groups' collective action. Both groups were represented by formal interest groups with the skills and experience to file federal lawsuits and mobilize collective action. The difference between the groups is in the resources of the constituents.

For instance, as members of the dominant racial group in the United States, Irish Gay and Lesbian Organization members are more likely than Black, Latino, and low-income community members to be mobilized by interest groups and political parties for electoral participation.[7] They are also more likely to have higher levels of formal education and white-collar occupations, which also facilitate political participation. Moreover, their social and political standing enables a greater array of issues that determine their voting participation. For example, Dawson's (1994) theory of linked fate posits that Black voters, particularly those with more formal education and income, prioritize their social interests over their economic interests because of their experiences with racial discrimination. This contrasts with White voters who have more freedom to pursue their preferences because they face fewer social and political constraints. Members of the Irish Gay and Lesbian Organization would be understandably upset by legislation that failed to address sexual orientation discrimination. However, Congresswoman Molinari could not be confident that her vote concerning sexual orientation discrimination would determine whether the group would support her reelection efforts.

In comparison, the legal-rights organizations coalition represented constituents with relatively few discretionary resources. The St. Luke's–Roosevelt Hospital Center plan posed a threat to health care access. It also signified the dangers posed by the gentrification of a neighborhood that was becoming too expensive for Black, Latino, and low-income residents. The collective action assured Congresswoman Molinari that the residents cared intensely about civil rights discrimination. The members did not have the resources to mobilize for any collective action unless the

---

[7] See Rosenstone and Hansen (1993).

group card deeply about the issue.[8] Even more, the lawsuit revealed the presence of formal interest groups that could mobilize their constituents during the next election if Congresswoman Molinari did not support their protest demands.

I argue that Congresswoman Molinari's decision to support some collective action participants and not others is predictable. Relative to high-resource protesters, legislators are more likely to represent the preferences of low-resource protesters who exhibit with their costly protest that they are deeply concerned about an issue and willing to base their electoral participation on how their elected officials represent their salient concerns. Moreover, legislators are generally more likely to represent the preferences of protesters than non-protesters. In this chapter, I conduct a series of empirical analyses to assess this costly protest and legislative behavior theory.

4.1 DATA ON DYNAMICS OF COLLECTIVE ACTION

I rely on the Dynamics of Collective Action (DCA) dataset to evaluate how legislators respond to protest demands. The DCA covers every protest reported in the *New York Times* from 1960 through 1995.[9] The DCA includes a wealth of information on the nature and frequency of protest. It contains the type of event, the reason for the collective action, and protester characteristics.

I confine the empirical analyses to the most recent collective action events available in the DCA, 1991 through 1995. This shorter period avoids the infamous social movement activity of the 1960s, 1970s, and 1980s in which many politically marginalized groups were involved in sustained social movement activity for radical change. Collective action was more frequent, media attention was more prevalent, and public issue salience for civil rights and civil liberties–related issues was relatively high. The prominence of social movement activity makes it difficult to determine the influence of individual collective action events on legislative behavior. Hence, assessing protests from 1991 through 1995 enables a more straightforward, albeit conservative, empirical test of legislative

---

[8] Recall Banks, White, and McKenzie (2018) and Klandermans (1984) who argue that groups with high participation costs can generally only protest when they have high issue salience because they have insufficient resources to facilitate participation.

[9] See McAdam and Su (2002) for more information on the DCA.

behavior given protesters' resource capacity. I revisit the generalizability of the empirical findings in Chapter 7.

4.2 LEGISLATIVE SUPPORT OF CONSTITUENCY PREFERENCES

In Chapter 2, I derived the *Protest Hypothesis*, which contends that legislators will be more likely to support constituents' preferences revealed during protest than preferences not communicated during protest. The hypothesis develops from the theory that legislators are more likely to support protest demands because protest demonstrates the salience of constituents' preferences. Other sources of information do not. To empirically evaluate this hypothesis, I create a variable, *Support*, which indicates whether a legislator votes in support of their constituents' preferences. In districts with protest, I measure constituents' preferences based on the demands expressed by protesters. In districts without protest, I employ nationally representative survey responses to gauge constituents' preferences.

4.2.1 Support of Protest Demands

To begin, I use the DCA to create the *Support* variable in districts where there is a protest. I start by identifying the US House of Representatives member(s) representing protesters using the location of every collective action event reported in the DCA and GIS software.[10] This process may identify multiple legislators as representatives of collective action participants. For example, consider the November 2, 1995, rally in Times Square against Medicare and Medicaid cuts. Many of the 10,000 workers who attended the Manhattan protest likely lived in other New York City neighborhoods. Therefore, a member of Congress representing any one of the thirteen congressional districts in New York City could find the event informative for how their constituents will react to a roll-call vote on the salient issue of health insurance for people with limited income and other resources. Accordingly, I recognize all thirteen New York representatives as representing constituents protesting in Manhattan.

---

[10] The DCA sometimes lists the exact address of a protest but more frequently indicates the neighborhood or city in which a protest occurred. GIS software uses maps to determine the congressional district(s) that overlap with the collective action event's more general or specific location.

Protest Claims and Ideology
I then find the specific claim or concern of each protest in the DCA. The claim may concern specific legislation but more frequently relates to a general policy or issue. For example, several protests took place on January 20, 1992, to promote white supremacy and racism or to commemorate Martin Luther King Jr. and condemn racial violence.

I only evaluate claims relating to the Policy Agendas Project (PAP) Civil Rights, Minority Issues, and Civil Liberties major topic classification. Choosing one major topic classification ensures a comparison of collective actions with similar issue area concerns. Legislative behavior, political participation, and even resource disparities can vary with different issue areas. These variations could make it difficult to discern how legislators respond to protest in their district. I chose Civil Rights, Minority Issues, and Civil Liberties because it is the most popular major topic classification in the DCA. More than two-thirds of events in the DCA list Civil Rights, Minority Issues, and Civil Liberties as the major topic classification.

Figure 4.1 displays the topics within the Civil Rights, Minority Issues, and Civil Liberties issue area classification with a relevant roll-call vote from 1991 through 1995. This issue area classification embraces various concerns, including abortion, hate crimes, and civil rights issues relating to First Amendment freedoms, access to education, affirmative action, immigration, globalization, and discrimination based on gender, age, sex, sexuality, race, and religion. The most common collective action issues for all protesters are abortion, hate crimes, and LGBT civil rights concerns. While there is a diversity of protest claims represented by this issue area, they are united by a common theme: protection of individual freedoms and protection from discrimination.

Protesters may demand policies on either side of these Civil Rights, Minority Issues, and Civil Liberties issues. For 1991 through 1995, the majority of protest demands were for more liberal policies. Figure 4.2 shows that about 58 percent of protest demands with a roll-call vote in Congress relating to the protest grievance were for liberal policies, about 31 percent were for conservative policies, and about 11 percent had no clear ideology.

Eligible Roll-Call Votes
After locating the protest claim, I retrieved the legislator's roll-call vote on the first bill relating to the protesters' demand. As discussed in Chapter 2,

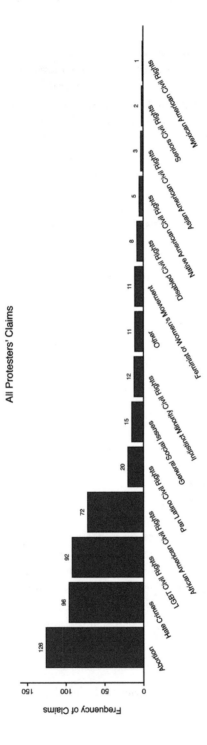

FIGURE 4.1 Civil Rights, Minority Issues, and Civil Liberties issue area claims

Note: The general issue areas with the PAP Civil Rights, Minority Issues, and Civil Liberties issue area classification and receiving roll-call vote.

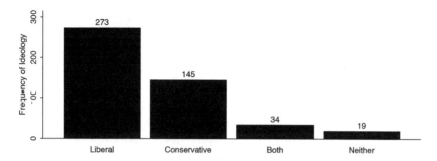

FIGURE 4.2 Ideology of protesters' claims

Note: Ideology of general issue areas with the PAP Civil Rights, Minority Issues, and Civil Liberties issue area classification and with a roll-call vote in the same Congress relevant to the protest issue.

roll-call votes are not the only way that legislators can support protest demands. Legislators can also issue public statements, meet with protesters, or sponsor legislation to address protest demands, but roll-call votes are an ideal measure of legislators' support of protest demands because they are not optional legislative behaviors. For every roll-call vote presented before the US House of Representatives, legislators have three options: vote in support of the bill, vote in opposition to the bill, or abstain from voting. Whether and how the legislator votes is a matter of public record. Constituents can observe their legislator's behavior on a protest-related roll-call vote and determine whether their legislator is responsive to protest demands. Consequently, roll-call votes force legislators into making a strategic decision about whether to represent protest demands.

Legislators have less freedom to strategically vote with their constituents' interests on procedural bills and amendment roll-call votes.[11] Legislation brought before the House for a final vote, also called a final passage vote, is less susceptible to party pressures. I want to evaluate how legislators respond to protest demands. So, I only assess legislative behavior on the first bill on an issue relevant to protest demands presented before the House for a final vote. I locate the first, final passage roll-call vote relating to protest demands using www.govtrack.us, an independent

[11] Procedural roll-call votes are the most likely to be subject to party control (Cox and McCubbins 2005; Crespin 2010). Some amendments, like the Social Security Amendments of 1965, which established Medicaid and Medicare, are highly visible and not likely to be subject to party pressures. Others are inundated with party-line votes.

website publishing information on federal legislation and congressional voting behaviors.

Recall that I employ empirical analyses for the most recent events available in the DCA, 1991 through 1995. The overall analysis is based on legislative behavior from 1991 through 1996 (i.e., the 102nd, 103rd, and 104th Congresses). The empirical models enable a legislator to represent their constituents' protest demands until the end of the congressional term.[12] For example, a protest that occurs on December 13, 1995, could be represented by a roll-call vote put before the US House of Representatives on December 31, 1996. I focus on the end of the congressional term as the end point for responsiveness because the Congress can change considerably from one term to the next.[13]

Legislators may be responsive to protest demands after they have won reelection. Legislation addressing protest demands may not have been presented before Congress for a final vote until after the end of the congressional term in which the protest occurred. Perhaps it is only in a new congressional term that the legislation gets the majority party's support to be presented before the chamber for a vote. Perhaps the protest occurred later in the congressional term, and there was not enough time for a protest-related bill to reach a final roll-call vote. In any case, the decision to restrict the empirical analyses to protest-related roll-call votes in the congressional term in which the protest occurs potentially underestimates the influence of costly protest on legislative behavior. There may have been more final passage roll-call votes addressing the protesters' concerns following the first vote. But, only sixty-four roll-call votes occur after a protest but before the end of the congressional term.

A legislator supports, or is responsive to, protesters if they vote in support of the claims specified during a protest on the first, final passage roll-call vote occurring after the event and before the next congressional term. If protesters' preferences relating to the roll-call vote align with their legislator's vote, *Support* takes on a value of 1, and 0 otherwise. If the legislator does not cast a vote, then the variable is set to missing

---

[12] I describe the data and empirical strategy in more detail in subsequent pages.

[13] US House of Representatives members run for reelection every two years. Senators serve six-year terms, but a third of senators run for reelection every two years. Reelections change the composition of the legislatures and often shape the legislators serving in leadership positions. These changes have implications for the content of legislation and legislators' strategic considerations for casting a vote. Furthermore, reelection is when constituents can hold their legislators accountable for previous legislative behaviors.

for that observation. To continue the previous example, a yea vote on H.R.5678 (a bill that appropriates funds for the MLK commission) supports Martin Luther King Jr. commemorators. A nay vote aligns with the interests of White supremacists.

4.2.2 Support in Districts without Protest

Once again, I argue that legislators are more likely to support protest demands than constituents' preferences not communicated via protest because protest can better convey issue salience than conventional information sources. For example, surveys and public opinion polls rely on pollsters or academics to determine which issues should be discussed. Pollsters and academics rarely ask about issue prioritization. Likewise, whether media covers salient preferences and how those issues are framed depend on editorial decisions that prioritize stories that will pique viewers' and readers' interests. Conventional information sources unreliably communicate constituents' issue salience, but they can adequately convey constituents' issue preferences.

I rely on national survey data and the multi-level regression and post-stratification (MRP) method to estimate district-level constituency preferences in districts without a protest.[14] The data and modeling technique result in a measure indicating whether most constituents in a district have preferences that align with their legislator's vote on a bill that I identified as relating to a protest demand. In districts without a protest on a roll-call vote relevant to protest demands made elsewhere, *Support* takes on a value of 1 if a legislator's vote aligns with constituency preferences measured using ANES data and MRP. Otherwise, *Support*

---

[14] See Warshaw and Rodden (2012) and Lax and Phillips (2009) for more information on MRP. Specifically, for each of the 1992, 1994, and 1996 American National Election Study (ANES) surveys, I partially pooled responses across districts for questions appearing in all three surveys relating to Civil Rights, Minority Issues, and Civil Liberties issues. (These questions are available in the Chapter 4 Appendix.) I code a respondent as 1 – pro–Civil Rights, Minority Issues, and Civil Liberties issues – if the legislator supports at least half of the issue area–related questions, and 0 otherwise. Using the glmer package in R, I estimate the individual survey responses with a hierarchal model of the binary dependent variable (whether they are pro–Civil Rights, Minority Issues, and Civil Liberties issues) as a function of individual characteristics (race, age, income, survey), district, district characteristics (income, percentage Black, percentage Hispanic, percentage urban), region, state, and state characteristics (veteran population). I then post-stratified the estimates using breakdowns of congressional district demographics by race, age, and income. I obtained population estimates from the 1990 Decennial Summary File 3, accessible via the US Census Bureau's DataFerret tool.

takes on a value of 0. If the legislator does not cast a vote, then the variable is set to missing for that observation.

4.2.3 Empirical Findings on Legislators' Support of (Non) Protesters

Before proceeding to the results, I want to briefly summarize the coding of the dependent variable, *Support*. For each collective action event in the DCA, I searched for a bill put before Congress for a final vote with language relating to the protesters' demand. I found sixty-four protest-related bills that had a final vote after a protest but before the end of the congressional term. For each of those protest-related bills, I indicated whether a legislator supported their constituents' preferences based on whether there was a protest in the legislator's district. If there was a protest in the legislator's district, a legislator supported protest demands (i.e., *Support* = 1) if their vote aligned with the expressed preferences of protesters in their district. If there was no protest in the district, *Support* = 1 if the legislator's vote aligned with most constituents' preferences on similar issues as stated in national survey data. If their vote did not align with constituents' preferences, then *Support* = 0. If the legislator did not cast a roll-call vote, then they are excluded from the analyses for that roll-call vote. I indicate whether there was a protest in the legislator's district with the independent variable *Protest*. Together, these variables evaluate whether constituency preferences communicated during protest are more informative than preferences revealed using other methods – in this case, survey data.

Figure 4.3 displays the results from a multi-level mixed-effects logistic regression evaluating the influence of protest on legislative support.[15] The model also includes several control variables accounting for the

---

[15] The logistic regression is often employed for dichotomous dependent variables. In this case, it uses a logistic function to model the probability that a legislator will support constituents' preferences. The multi-level models include congressional district random effects to help address the possibility that a protest may appear multiple times in the analyses. The congressional district random effects account for any atypical congressional districts. The models also include Congress year fixed effects to account for characteristics that vary across but not within each Congress (Greene 2008). A Hausman test and a variable addition test (Wu 1973) each suggest that a random effects model is more appropriate than a fixed effects model specification. Likewise, a likelihood ratio test reveals that both effects model specifications are more appropriate than a pooled logistic regression model. Even so, the primary independent variables are robust to alternative model specifications, including those that do not include random effects for congressional districts or fixed effects for the Congress year.

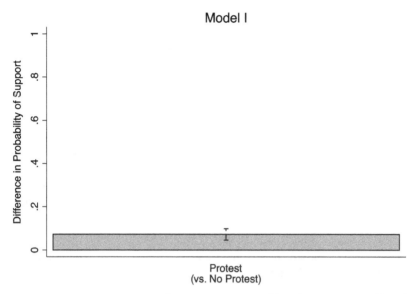

FIGURE 4.3 Constituents' preferences, protest, and legislative support (liberal only)

Model I displays the differences in the predicted probability of legislative support of preferences in districts with a protest relative to districts without a protest. The graph supports the *Protest Hypothesis* if the bar is above the x = 0 line. The difference is statistically significant if the confidence interval does not overlap with x = 0. All covariates are held at their means.

characteristics of legislators and the districts they represent.[16] As shown in Figure 4.3, the probability of the legislative support of constituency preferences is 7.2 percentage points higher (p < .05) in districts where a protest occurred than in districts without a protest when all other variables are held at their means. This result aligns with the *Protest Hypothesis*, which contends that legislators are more likely to support constituents' preferences when those preferences are articulated during protest than when protest does not occur. Compared with surveys and other information sources concerning constituents' preferences, protest communicates issue preferences and the strength of those issue preferences. Legislators who ignore or oppose protest demands risk angering a constituency that might transition to electoral participation that harms the legislators' reelection chances.

---

[16] I will describe these variables more in subsequent pages. The full tables for all figures are available in the Chapter 4 Appendix.

4.3 LEGISLATORS' SUPPORT AND PROTESTERS' RESOURCE CAPACITY

The first result supports the *Protest Hypothesis*. Legislators are more likely to support constituents' preferences when those preferences are revealed via protest than when they are revealed via national survey data. Nevertheless, the theory of costly protest and legislative behavior posits that some protests are more effective than others in communicating the salience of constituents' interests. Protesters' resource capacity is essential for revealing issue salience. The *Resource Constraint Hypothesis* asserts that groups with lower resource capacity can only protest when they have high issue salience because they face higher protest costs. Therefore, their costly protest reveals salient issue preferences. Conversely, groups with higher resource capacity can protest at will, regardless of their issue salience. Their protest less clearly communicates salient issue preferences. To assess this theoretical claim, I create several variables assessing protesters' resource capacities. Each of these variables measures resource disparities that I described in Chapter 2.

4.3.1 Protesters' Resources

One of the most valuable features of the DCA is its information concerning the resource capacity of protesters. The DCA includes several measures relating to protesters' race and ethnicity, income, and organizational resource capacities. These group characteristics help explain empirical differences in participation and representation. They are also helpful in capturing the resource disparities that legislators and their staffers recognize as relevant for the ability of groups to engage in protest.[17]

One dimension of protesters' resource disparities is in the economic, social, and political capital that groups have based on their skin color, facial attributes, perceived ancestry, and historical experiences in the United States. Black, Latino, and Asian American group members are more likely than their White counterparts to be marginalized politically, socially, and economically. This marginalization has implications for the costs that racial and ethnic minorities face when engaging in collective

---

[17] Recall Figure 3.4. It demonstrates that a convenience sample of legislators and legislators' staffers perceives protest as more difficult for some groups than others. Specifically, they find that protest is more difficult for poor people than rich people, Black people than White people, and individuals compared with groups.

action. Moreover, groups seeking radical or revolutionary change to the status quo are less likely to receive public support for their goals.[18] Mainstream media often misrepresent Black, Latino, and Asian American protest, particularly when events diverge from conventional, White narratives.[19] In addition, public opinion is generally less favorable toward policies benefiting Black and Latino people than those benefiting White people. Support for welfare reform decreases substantially when the policy is associated with Black people.[20] Support for punitive policies, like the death penalty, increases when Black people are exemplified as criminals.[21] Support for pro-immigration policy decreases when associated with Latino groups.[22] The mere presence of Black people, Latinos, or Asian Americans at a protest event could decrease the general public's support of Black, Latino, and Asian American participants' concerns.[23]

Groups seeking radical or revolutionary change to the status quo are also more likely to face repression than groups seeking incremental changes or groups hoping to maintain the status quo. In particular, protesters who belong to racial and ethnic minority groups are more likely than White protesters to be arrested at a protest event.[24] Elites also attempt to associate protest by racial and ethnic minorities with criminal behavior to delegitimize protest efforts and avoid capitulating to protesters' demands.[25] This can occur when city officials refuse to issue permits to allow collective action and also through elite rhetoric that refers to protesters as rioters, lawbreakers, or illegitimate actors.

Protest costs for racial and ethnic groups are also influenced by a group's ability to aggregate resources to challenge state repression or inaction by legislators. They are also influenced by a group's capacity to mobilize public support to motivate elite action. For example, racial and ethnic minorities tend to have lower levels of trust in government and political efficacy than White Americans due to a lack of descriptive

---

[18] See Tilly (1975); McAdam (1982).

[19] See Davenport (2010) on media's failed attempts to characterize protest that challenges the status quo.

[20] See Gilens (1999).

[21] See Gilliam and Iyengar (2000); Mendelberg (2001).

[22] See Brader, Valentino, and Suahy (2008).

[23] For example, foreign imagery at a protest is enough to increase adverse reactions to protest and decrease support for immigration (Wright and Citrin 2011).

[24] See Stockdill (2003); Davenport, Soule, and Armstrong (2011).

[25] See Weaver (2007).

representation and political incorporation.[26] Additionally, people with ancestors from Asia, like Korean Americans, are perceived to be superior to African Americans due to stereotypes of their greater intellect or work ethic but are simultaneously ostracized for being too foreign and unable to integrate into White culture and society.[27] These adverse outcomes and stereotypes increase the costliness of protest for Black, Latino, and Asian American participants.

The DCA includes six "Initiating Group" variables, which record up to two characteristics of up to three groups.[28] This variable is used to measure the resource capacity of protesters due to the protesters' race, ethnicity, or both. The *Black Protesters* variable compares protests with Black people with those involving White protesters.[29] *Latino Protesters* compares protests with Latino people[30] with those involving White protesters. Finally, the *Asian American Protesters* variable evaluates protesters belonging to Asian ethnic groups[31] relative to White protesters. For each of these variables, I code the variables as 1 if protest participants are identified as Black, Latino, or Asian American, respectively. I code the variables as 0 if the protesters are identified as belonging to undifferentiated White, Jewish, or European racial or ethnic groups.

Income is also associated with a group's ability to engage in collective action. Groups with more income find it easier to afford transportation, child care, or other financial collective action costs. They are also more likely to have internal and external political efficacy and access to networks that encourage political participation. I measure economic resource capacity using the variable *Low-Income Protesters,*

---

[26] For examples, consult Bobo and Gilliam (1990); Soss (1999); Gay (2002); Philpot, Shaw, and McGowen (2009); Hajnal and Lee (2011).

[27] See Kim (2000).

[28] The coding manual (available at web.stanford.edu/group/collectiveaction/cgi-bin/dru pal/) states that coders identified and recorded from the *New York Times* "the most salient social characteristics of the people initiating the collective action event."

[29] First, I code *Black Protesters* = 0 if any protesters are identified in the DCA as belonging to undifferentiated White, Jewish, or European racial or ethnic groups. Then, I code *Black Protesters* = 1 if the DCA indicates any protesters are Black or African American. This coding order ensures that none of the Black protests include significant numbers of White protesters. I code the Latino and Asian American protester variables using the same process.

[30] Latino protesters belong to Mexican, Chicano, Central American, South American, Puerto Rican, Cuban, or Undifferentiated Hispanic groups.

[31] These include Asian, SE Asian, Vietnamese, Chinese, Japanese, Korean, Indonesian, Malaysian, Other Asian, Pacific Islanders, Filipino, Hawaiian, Samoan, Tongan, Melanesian, Fijian, Micronesian, Chamorro, and Guam.

which denotes whether the DCA describes any protesters at an event as being low income or homeless. If poor or homeless is listed in any Initiating Group variable, *Low-Income Protesters* takes on a value of 1. Otherwise, it takes on a value of 0.

Resource disparities are also revealed in the organizational capacity of a group. I measure organizational capacity with a binary variable indicating whether a formal interest group is present at the event. *No Formal Interest Group* is the low-resource group.[32] The presence of a formal interest group suggests an agent that can coordinate events and mobilize participation even when issue salience is low.

Groups can exist within multiple categories. They can be members of both Black and Latino communities. They can also have lower resource capacities due to their race or ethnicity but higher resource capacity based on their income or organizational capacity. Furthermore, some groups are more likely than others to have multiple disadvantaged identities. For example, Black and Latino community members are more likely to have lower incomes than White or Asian American community members. The group's country of origin also matters. While Asian Americans are among the most educated and highest-earning Americans, they are also the most economically divided group.[33] How much income and education someone of Asian descent has is related to their country of origin. Even though resource disparities may be overlapping, the previous discussion demonstrates that resource disparities are also distinct. Therefore, I evaluate each of these resource capacities separately while acknowledging that these variables assess overlapping yet distinct measures of a group's resource capacity.

4.3.2 Issue Area Claims by Protesters' Resource Capacity

Figure 4.4 displays the topics within the Civil Rights, Minority Issues, and Civil Liberties issue area classification with a relevant roll-call vote from 1991 through 1995. It is similar to Figure 4.1, but it separates claims based on the resource capacity of the protesting groups. In Figure 4.1, the most common collective action issues for all protesters from 1991 through 1995 were abortion, hate crimes, and LGBT civil rights concerns. Figure 4.4 shows that these three issues are only the

---

[32] This measure is from the DCA variable indicating the presence of a social movement organization.

[33] See Kochhar and Cilluffo (2018).

most frequent collective action issues for high-resource groups. For low-resource groups, civil rights for their respective groups and hate crimes are the most prevalent collective action issues.

I distinguish hate crimes by whether collective action participants are perpetrating or supportive of the hate crime, whether they are opposed to the hate crime, or whether the participants' position on the hate crime is unclear. The hate crimes categories for White protesters predominately includes anti-LGBT protests, protests against anti-Semitism, anti-Black hate crimes and a similar number of pro- and anti-White suprematist protests. For Black collective action participants, the hate crimes category involves support for anti-Semitism and involvement in ethnic conflicts occurring primarily in urban centers. Collective actions by higher-income participants were almost equally split between supporting and opposing hate crimes. Finally, when analyzing a group's organizational capacity, collective actions were slightly more likely to oppose hate crimes than support them.

Figures 4.1 and 4.4 provide a decent picture of the grievances that mobilize groups to collective action. Still, using newspapers to track the claims of high-resource groups does present some challenges. High-resource groups are more likely to engage in institutional tactics, like letter-writing campaigns or petitions, than extra-institutional tactics.[34] And, as Figure 4.1 shows, institutional tactics appear much less frequently in newspaper data than extra-institutional tactics. Nevertheless, high-resource groups are represented in the data. Depending on the specific resource capacity, high-resource groups protest more frequently than low-resource groups.

Overall, Figure 4.4 demonstrates that collective action participants protest about different Civil Rights, Civil Liberties, and Minority Issues grievances, but the issues motivating their protests are similar. Much of the protests involved civil rights concerns, group conflict, and even direct attacks on other groups, regardless of resource capacity. However, what people are protesting about is inherently tied to their resource capacities. For example, abortion is a much more popular collective action topic among high-resource groups than low-resource groups. This does not mean that low-resource groups are not concerned about abortion but that other issues, like protections against hate crimes and employment opportunities, are more pressing.

---

[34] DiGrazia (2014) finds that the likelihood of institutional (relative to extra-institutional) tactics increases with socioeconomic status.

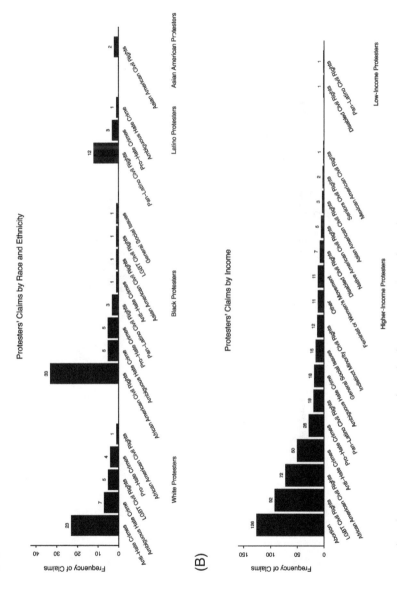

FIGURE 4.4 Civil Rights, Minority Issues, and Civil Liberties issue area claims by protesting group

Note: The general issue areas receiving a roll-call vote subsetted by the resource capacity of the group. The high-resource group, on the left, is the reference category in the forthcoming empirical models. The low-resource groups are on the right.

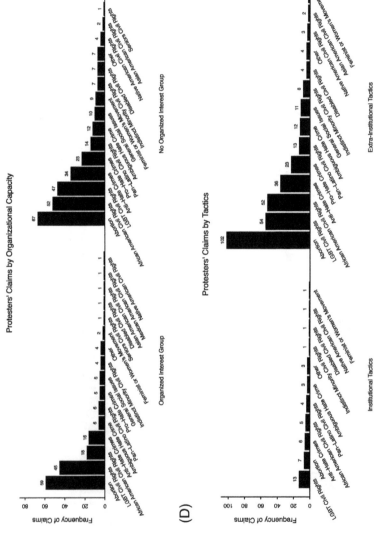

FIGURE 4.4 (*Continued*)

4.3.3 Empirical Findings on Legislators' Support of (Costly) Protest

The differences in predicted probabilities of legislative support for protest demands displayed in Figure 4.5 confirm expectations from the theoretical model in Chapter 2 and survey results in Chapter 3 that some protests are better able to inform legislative behavior than others. Specifically, legislators are 46 percentage points more likely to support protest demands if protesters are Black than if protesters are White. Legislators are also 40 percentage points more likely to support protesters if protesters are Latino than if White. Additionally, legislators are 32 percentage points more likely to support protest demands made by low-income protesters than those made by higher-income protesters. Each of these differences is statistically significant at the .05 level.

Figure 4.5 also demonstrates that legislators are more likely to support Asian American protesters' demands than White protesters' demands. They are also more likely to support protest demands by grassroots protesters than those mobilized by formal interest groups. While these differences in predicted probability are in the expected direction, they fail to meet conventional standards of statistical significance. For Asian American protesters, the lack of statistical significance is due to data constraints. Figure 4.4 shows that only two unique collective action events with Asian American protesters received a roll-call vote in this period.

The weakest differences in legislative support given the resource capacity of protesters occur when evaluating protesters' organizational

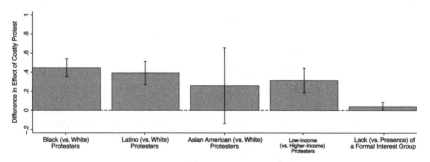

FIGURE 4.5 Constituents' preferences, protesters' resources, and legislative support (liberal only)

Each bar displays the difference in the predicted probability of legislative support of low-resource groups relative to high-resource groups. Each bar supports the *Resource Constraint Hypothesis* if the bar is above the x = 0 line. The difference is statistically significant if the confidence interval does not overlap with x = 0. All covariates are held at their means.

capacity. Legislative support is just 3.9 percentage points more likely following grassroots protest relative to formally organized protest. This difference in the predicted probability of legislative support is not statistically significant at the .05 level. Although organizational capacity influences groups' ability to engage in protests, it may not be a clear indication of a group's resource levels and, subsequently, issue salience. I maintain that the issues that protesters discuss are tied to their resource capacities. However, Figure 4.4 shows that protesters have similar protest claims regardless of their organizational resource capacity. The similarities in protest demands are another indication that organizational capacity may not be the strongest signal of costly protest or salient constituency preferences.

As a whole, the results in Figures 4.3 and 4.5 suggest that protesters' resource capacity is meaningful for legislative behavior. The average legislator is generally more likely to support the preference of low-resource protesters than those of high-resource protesters. Legislators are also more likely to support the preferences of protesters than the preferences of constituents who do not engage in collective action. Indeed, in none of the analyses does legislative support favor high-resource protesters or constituencies without a protest.

4.4 PUBLIC SALIENCE, PARTISANSHIP, AND LEGISLATOR'S PREFERENCES

Legislators do not cast roll-call votes in a vacuum. The theory of costly protest and legislative behavior acknowledges that legislators make voting decisions while also considering the issue salience and preferences of non-protesting constituents, partisan pressures, and their personal preferences. Respondents also mentioned these considerations in the survey of legislators and staffers discussed in the previous chapter. In each of the empirical models that I present in this chapter, I include several control variables that measure the influence of constituents' issue salience, public opinion, partisanship, and legislator's preferences on the likelihood that legislators support constituents' preferences.[35]

I argue that legislators' roll-call voting behavior is influenced by protest in their district, especially when constituents engage in costly protest. Still, public opinion could also be responsible for legislators' support

---

[35] Unless otherwise noted, variables are generated using David Lublin's replication dataset for his book, *The Paradox of Replication* (Lublin 1997).

of constituents' preferences.[36] Protest might only influence legislative behavior when it produces a shift in public opinion. Therefore, I include *Education* to account for changes in legislative behavior due to changes in public opinion. Constituents with higher levels of formal education are more economically conservative than those with lower educational attainment, except for the most educated who are more liberal than those with only a college degree.

Additionally, as education levels increase, support for socially liberal policies typically increases.[37] Most of the protest demands with the Civil Rights, Minority Issues, and Civil Liberties PAP major topic code concern abortion, hate crimes, and civil rights issues.[38] While abortion claims are split ideologically, the majority of claims are for liberal social policies.[39] So, congressional districts with more highly educated constituents are expected to have policy preferences that align with legislators supporting protest demands.

Table 4.1 shows, however, that the legislative support of protesters' preferences is less likely as the education level in congressional districts increases. The coefficient only reaches statistical significance at the .05 level in Models II and IV, which evaluate legislative voting behavior for legislators with Black and White or Asian American and White protesting constituents. In most models, public opinion, as measured by the education level of the constituents, has a statistically insignificant influence on the legislative support of protesters' preferences. So, it does not appear that public opinion is solely responsible for the legislative representation of protest demands.[40]

In Chapter 2, I posited that public opinion is more likely to influence legislative behavior when the public has salient issue preferences regarding protest demands. Consequently, I create a variable, *Public Salience*, measuring the percentage of people in a congressional district who

---

[36] For examples, see Burstein (1998); Lee (2002); Soule and Olzak (2004); Agnone (2007); Zepeda-Millán and Wallace (2013); Wallace et al. (2014); Mazumder (2018); Gillion (2020); Wasow (2020).

[37] See McCall and Manza (2011).

[38] See Figure 4.1.

[39] The abortion claims are split ideologically, with about 52 percent anti-abortion, 43 percent pro-abortion, and 4 percent ambiguous. Most hate crime protest claims are against hate crimes. Most civil rights protest claims are supportive of civil rights and civil liberties.

[40] The empirical models do not assess whether public opinion shifted because of protest. They do evaluate how public opinion based on the district's education level influences legislator's support of constituency preferences on protest-related bills.

TABLE 4.1 *Influence of legislator and district characteristics on legislative support (liberal only)*

	Model I Protest	Model II Black	Model III Latino	Model IV Asian American	Model V Low Income	Model VI Informal Interest Group
Education	0.172	-2.377**	-2.794*	-17.07**	-0.259	-0.252
	(0.109)	(0.945)	(1.453)	(7.285)	(0.325)	(0.325)
Public Salience	-0.00430	-0.743	-0.671	3.253	-0.640*	-0.704**
	(0.105)	(0.805)	(1.514)	(3.589)	(0.335)	(0.337)
Democratic Representative	0.530***	0.337	-0.160	-1.668	0.422***	0.437***
	(0.0315)	(0.406)	(0.647)	(1.609)	(0.149)	(0.150)
Length of Service	-0.0949	1.047	-0.458	5.476	0.130	0.0678
	(0.0897)	(1.125)	(1.908)	(4.854)	(0.412)	(0.415)
Margin of Victory	0.350***	0.171	-0.484	-7.897	0.297	0.360
	(0.111)	(1.462)	(2.253)	(5.772)	(0.478)	(0.478)
Black Representative	-0.0944	-1.548***	-2.632***	-5.541**	-0.464**	-0.477**
	(0.0595)	(0.576)	(0.963)	(2.635)	(0.202)	(0.203)
Latino Representative	0.129	-1.119	-2.620**	-5.099*	-0.297	-0.318
	(0.0828)	(0.701)	(1.105)	(3.009)	(0.252)	(0.253)
Female Representative	0.158***	0.0268	0.595	0.607	0.202	0.196
	(0.0498)	(0.466)	(0.800)	(1.801)	(0.174)	(0.174)
Observations	29882	472	294	176	2301	2285
Groups	453	94	70	64	213	212

The primary independent variables are excluded from this table but indicated under each model number. The primary independent variables are represented in Figures 4.3 and 4.5. The full table (Table 8.1) is available in the Appendix. For each model, the dependent variable, legislative support, is binary taking, on a value of 0 or 1. All covariates are coded 0 to 1. Coefficients are Log Odds. Standard errors in parentheses. $* p < 0.10$, $** p < 0.05$, $*** p < 0.01$

believe that issues within the Civil Rights, Minority Issues, and Civil Liberties issue area are among the most important problems facing the nation. I create the *Public Salience* measure in a process similar to how I crafted the measure of constituents' issue preferences in districts without protest. I rely on national survey data and multi-level regression and post-stratification (MRP) to create an estimate of the percentage of the district that believes that Civil Rights, Minority Issues, and Civil Liberties are among the top three most important problems facing the nation for each of the 102nd, 103rd, and 104th Congresses.[41]

As public salience within a congressional district increases, the legislative support of protest demands may decrease. Table 4.1 suggests support for this expectation only in Model VI comparing the organizational capacity of protesting groups. However, generally, public salience, like education, has a statistically insignificant influence on the legislative support of protesters' preferences.

A legislator's political party is also a well-known indicator of how a legislator will vote. Democratic legislators tend to vote more liberally than Republicans on roll-call votes.[42] To account for this variation, I include *Democratic Representative* in the empirical models to account for the influence of legislators' political partisanship on their roll-call voting behavior. This variable compares the legislative support of constituents' preferences by Democrats with other US House of Representatives members. Table 4.1 suggests that Democrats are more likely than Republicans and Independents to support protest demands, albeit only in three out of the six models.

Additionally, a legislator's *Length of Service* is likely to explain legislative voting behavior. The greater the length of service, the less susceptible

---

[41] See Warshaw and Rodden (2012) and Lax and Phillips (2009) for more information on MRP. For each of the 1992, 1994, and 1996 American National Election Study Post-Election Surveys, I partially pooled survey responses across districts for the survey question indicating whether respondents believed that Civil Rights, Minority Issues, and Civil Liberties were among the top three most important problems facing the nation. Using the glmer package in R, I estimate the individual survey responses with a hierarchal model of the binary dependent variable (whether civil rights issues is one of the most important problems facing the nation) as a function of individual characteristics (race, age, income, survey), district, district characteristics (income, percentage Black, percentage Hispanic, percentage urban), region, state, and state characteristics (veteran population). The estimates are post-stratified using breakdowns of congressional district demographics by race, age, and income. I obtained population estimates from the 1990 Decennial Summary File 3 and accessible via the US Census Bureau's DataFerret tool.

[42] See Poole and Rosenthal (1997); Hutchings (1998); Carrubba, Gabel, and Hug (2008).

a legislator is to district pressures. Similarly, the smaller the *Margin of Victory* in the previous election, the more sensitive members are to constituency pressures.[43] Table 4.1 suggests that a legislator's electoral security is only meaningful for legislative behavior in Model I. More generally, neither the length of service nor the margin of victory appears to have a statistically significant influence on the legislative support of protesters' preferences.

While legislators are concerned with reelection, they also have their own policy goals that they desire to pursue.[44] Black, Latino, and female legislators tend to vote more liberally than White and male representatives.[45] These individual characteristics influence the voting behavior of legislators through preferences and their ability to legislate.[46] So, I include *Black Representative*, *Latino Representative*, and *Female Representative* variables. In general, Table 4.1 suggests that Black legislators are less likely to support protesters' preferences than their counterparts. However, there are few differences in the support of constituents' preferences between Latino and non-Latino legislators or between female and male legislators.

The models in Table 4.1 include but do not display the primary independent variables shown in Figures 4.3 and 4.5. The control variables in Table 4.1 suggest that legislators are likely responding to constituents' preferences even as they consider other factors that influence their voting decisions. In Chapter 5, I explore how these factors influence the likelihood of legislative support of low-resource groups compared with their higher-resourced counterparts.

4.5 OTHER PROTEST INDICATORS OF ISSUE SALIENCE

So far, I have provided empirical support for the argument that protesters' resource capacities inform how legislators vote on protest-related legislation. Even so, legislators could be less concerned about protesters' resource levels than they are about issue salience revealed by

---

[43] The Margin of Victory variable is attained using the CQ Press Voting and Elections Collection (CQ Press 2015). See Fiorina (1977), Mayhew (1974), and Fenno (1973) on how a legislator's performance in their last election changes how concerned they are about constituents' preferences.

[44] See Fenno (1973); Fiorina (1974); Kingdon (1977); Hall (1996).

[45] See Lublin (1997); Whitby (1997); Tate (2004).

[46] See Hawkesworth (2003).

other protest characteristics. That is, if most of the protests by grass-roots protesters consist of thousands of participants; however, protests by organized interest groups involve dozens. Then, the fact that legislators are more responsive to grassroots protesters than formally organized protesters could be a function of the size of the event rather than the resource capacity of participants. Indeed, legislators' and legislative staffers' responses in Chapter 3 indicate that the size, disruptiveness, and public attention given to a protest are essential for how legislators perceive and respond to protesters' issue preferences. I address this concern by including in the subsequent models an interaction between the resource of protesters and another indicator of protesters' issue salience.

4.5.1 Protest Size and Resource Capacity

Figure 4.6 displays the difference in the probability of legislative support of protesters for low- versus high-resource groups for differently sized protests.[47] For each racial and ethnic group, legislative behavior is more likely to support the preferences of the low-resource group over White protesters for all values that can be empirically evaluated.[48] In only one case – for collective action with only a handful of Latino or White protesters – does the difference in legislative support not reach conventional levels of statistical significance.

A trend emerges for Figures 4.6B and 4.6E. When the protest is extremely small or large, there is generally no statistically significant difference in the legislative support of low- relative to high-resource protesters. Perhaps when an event is extremely large, it is difficult for a legislator to infer that no one cares about the issue being protested. However, legislators may not detect issue salience when very few people show up for a protest. Following moderately sized protests, legislators appear to be more likely to support low-resource protesters than their higher-resource counterparts. These models suggest that protest size may inform legislators about how many constituents in their district likely hold an issue preference. Even so, the resource capacity of protesters remains informative for legislators seeking to discover their constituents' issue salience.

---

[47] There are missing observations and models for some predicted probabilities in Figures 4.6 through 4.8 because of the rarity of some events in the DCA.

[48] There is not enough data to properly evaluate the difference in legislative support given to Asian American compared with White protesters due to the small number of instances of collective action by Asian American protesters.

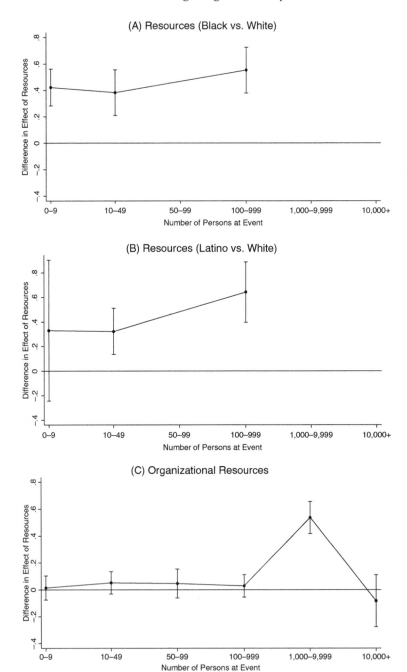

FIGURE 4.6 Resources, salience (size), and legislative support

The figures reveal the differences in the predicted probability of legislative support of low-
relative to high-resource groups at different protest sizes. All covariates are held at their
means.

4.5.2   Protest's Media Coverage and Resource Capacity

Legislators may be more likely to support low-resource groups after protest because those events receive more coverage in the *New York Times*. I consider the *New York Times* as a proxy for the presence of protests on legislators' radar. The newspaper's coverage of events could also incite salience or give a more significant platform to events covered in the newspaper.[49] Figure 4.7 demonstrates that regardless of the number of times the *New York Times* covers a protest, legislators are more likely to support low-resource groups following protest than they are to support high-resource groups. In other words, legislators are generally more responsive to the preferences of low-resource protesters than protesters with greater resource capacity, even when taking into account the *New York Times* coverage of collective action events.

4.5.3   Protest's Disruptiveness and Resource Capacity

Finally, Chapter 3 discussed how legislators are sometimes concerned about supporting disruptive collective action events. Moreover, the disruptive politics literature identifies protest featuring property damage, police presence, arrest(s), weapons, injuries, or deaths as indicators of issue salience.[50] The literature is ambiguous about whether disruptive collective action increases or decreases support for protesters' interests. Nevertheless, I argue that costly protest informs legislative behavior regardless of whether the collective action is disruptive. Figure 4.8 suggests the same. Legislators are generally more likely to support low-resource groups than high-resource groups following collective action regardless of whether the event is disruptive. Once again, costly protest remains a valuable source of information for legislative behavior.

4.6   INFLUENCE OF PROTEST DEMANDS ON OTHER ROLL-CALL VOTES

Theoretically, legislative roll-call voting behavior should align with the preferences of constituents engaging in costlier participation only on roll-call votes related to the interests of protesters. That is, legislators' roll-call voting behavior should align less often with constituents engaging in

---

[49] See Wouters and Walgrave (2017).
[50] See Lipsky (1968); Piven and Cloward (1977); Browning, Marshall, and Tabb (1984).

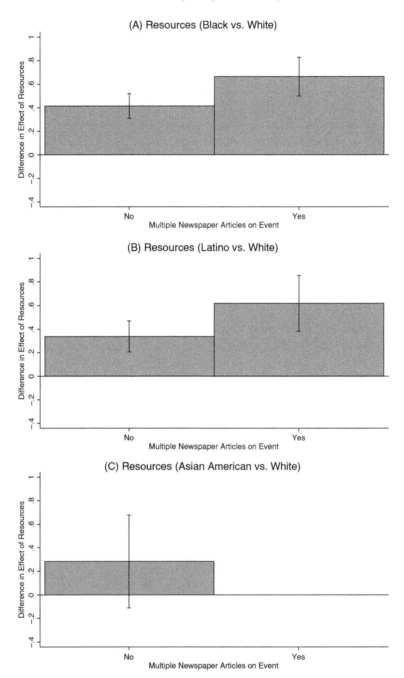

FIGURE 4.7 Resources, salience (media coverage), and legislative support

The figures reveal the differences in the predicted probability of legislative support of low-
relative to high-resource groups for protests covered in one (the left bar) or multiple (the
right bar) *New York Times* articles. All covariates are held at their means.

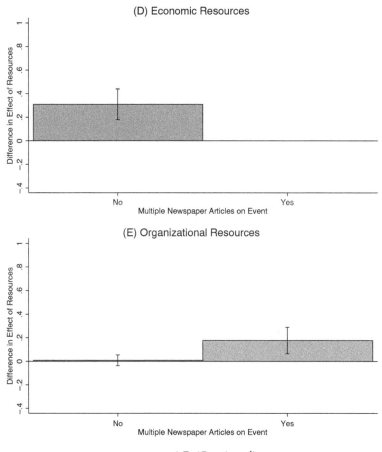

FIGURE 4.7 *(Continued)*

costlier participation on bills that are unrelated to issues raised during protest. Figure 4.9 evaluates these expectations by examining two additional sets of roll-call votes.

Figure 4.9A examines legislative support of constituency preferences on minority roll-call votes. The minority roll-call votes include all legislation with the Civil Rights, Minority Issues, and Civil Liberties major topic classification. There are few final roll-call votes with these classifications, particularly in the 102nd Congress. So, the minority roll-call votes also include social welfare and inequality issues.[51] The minority roll-call votes are generally related to constituents interested in Civil

---

[51] Following Gillion (2013), I add social welfare and inequality issues since they tend to concern issues salient for racial and ethnic minority communities.

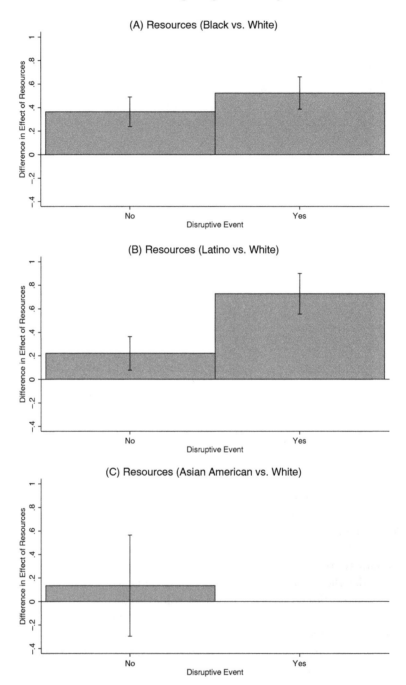

FIGURE 4.8 Resources, salience (disruptiveness), and legislative support

The figures reveal the differences in the predicted probability of legislative support of low-
relative to high-resource groups for protests with no (the left bar) or at least one (the right
bar) disruptive protest characteristic. All covariates are held at their means.

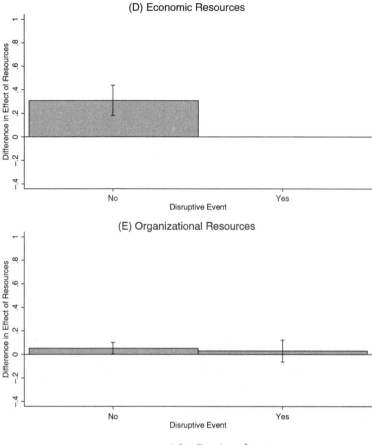

FIGURE 4.8 (*Continued*)

Rights, Minority Issues, and Civil Liberties issues. Unlike the selected roll-call votes in previous empirical tests, this subset of votes may not be indicative of legislators' responses to protesters for two reasons.

First, the timing is imprecise. Some of the minority roll-call votes may have occurred before a protest. Second, the minority roll-call votes subset includes legislation on which there was no protest on an issue, even if the votes may be relevant to constituents' preferences on Civil Rights, Minority Issues, and Civil Liberties issues. In both cases, any correlation between a legislator's roll-call votes and protesters' preferences is unlikely due to the information communicated during protest.

Figure 4.9B examines legislative support of constituency preferences on all roll-call votes in the 102nd, 103rd, and 104th Congresses. Legislation relevant to concerns articulated during protests is only a tiny

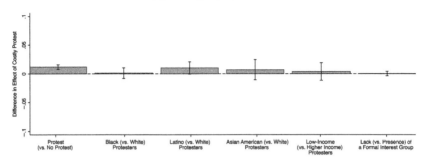

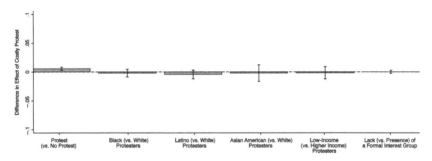

FIGURE 4.9 General legislative support (via w-NOMINATE scores) and
constituency preferences (liberal only)

The figures are derived from mixed-effects logistic regression models. Model I displays the
differences in the predicted probability of legislative support of preferences in districts
with a protest relative to districts without a protest on protest-related roll-call votes.
Models II–VI display the differences in the predicted probability of legislative support of
low-resource groups relative to high-resource groups. All covariates are held at their
means.

proportion of legislation during these congressional terms. Thus, I expect
a small, if any, empirical relationship between legislative behavior and
costly protesters' concerns. The general legislation in Figure 4.9B also
suffers from the imprecise timing that affects the minority roll-call votes
subset.

The results in Figure 4.9 confirm these expectations. The first bar
in Figures 4.9A and 4.9B show that on both minority roll-call votes
and all roll-call votes, legislators remain more likely to support issues
expressed during protest relative to concerns not expressed during protest. However, the difference in favor of protesters decreases as the subset

of roll-call votes becomes less relevant for protesters' concerns. Legislative behavior is only .5 percentage points more likely to support protesters than non-protesters on all roll-call votes in the 102nd, 103rd, and 104th Congresses. For minority roll-call votes, legislative behavior in favor of protesters' interests relative to constituents in districts without a protest is slightly larger (about 1.2 percentage points). Both of these differences in favor of protesters are statistically significant. Yet, they are substantively smaller than the difference in legislative behavior in favor of protesters on exclusively protested-related roll-call votes immediately following protests (7.2 percentage points, shown in Figure 4.3).

Figure 4.9 further demonstrates that legislators' roll-call voting is unlikely to align with the preferences of constituents engaging in costlier participation on roll-call votes unrelated to protesters' concerns. Observe that in Figures 4.9A and 4.9B, the difference in legislative support in favor of either high- or low-resource protesting groups never reaches statistical significance at the .05 level. Moreover, the size of the differences in legislative support is essentially zero. In sum, Figures 4.3 and 4.9 confirm that legislative roll-call voting behavior aligns with the preferences of constituents engaging in costlier participation only on protest-related roll-call votes that occur in time for legislators to respond to the issue preferences and salience communicated during protest.

4.7 SUMMARY OF FINDINGS AND NEXT STEPS

The benefits of protest by low-resource groups are not lost on observers. Recognizing the advantages of low-resource groups' protest, well-financed organizations sometimes subsidize participation to give the appearance of grassroots efforts.[52] As an example, Americans for Prosperity, a political organization funded by wealthy conservative businessmen Charles and David Koch, has been reported as masquerading as a grassroots organization marching against Medicaid expansion and the Environmental Protection Agency in an effort to entice legislative support for their interests.[53] Whether this particular organization successfully misrepresented the resource and salience levels of protesters is unknown. This example does demonstrate that participants' resource levels could be strategically beneficial for groups wishing to communicate salient constituency concerns.

[52] See Walker (2009).
[53] For example, see Fish (2014).

In this chapter, I empirically assess whether legislators are typically more likely to support the preferences of constituents engaging
in protests than those who do not engage in protest. I find that legislators are more likely to support the preferences of protesters than
non-protesters. Still, protests are most effective in altering legislative
behavior when performed by the most marginalized populations. The
theory presented in Chapter 2 suggests that legislators will be more
likely to support the interests of low-resource protesters than they are
to support high-resource protesters because the former are more likely
to have participation-enabling salient concerns. The empirical analyses
corroborate the theoretical results.

The likelihood of legislative support increases with the costliness of
protest. Black, Latino, and Asian American protesters' preferences are
more likely to gain legislative support than White protesters' preferences. Furthermore, the preferences of low-income protesters are more
likely to receive legislative support than the preferences of higher-income
protesters. There is also some evidence that grassroots protesters gain
legislative support more often than formally organized protesters. However, there is no statistically significant difference in legislative support
based on protesters' organizational resources. In no case does legislative
behavior favor higher-resource groups.

The primary empirical analyses are strengthened by a series of placebo
tests and empirical analyses assessing how other indicators of protesters'
issue salience influence legislators' responsiveness to protesters' resource
capacity. The placebo tests validate that the findings are unlikely to be
spurious. Legislative support of protesters' preferences decreases as roll-
call votes become less relevant to protesters' concerns. Moreover, there
are no statistically significant differences in the legislative support of protest demands based on protesters' resource capacity on bills that may
precede protest activities.

Finally, the empirical analyses demonstrate that legislative behavior is
responsive to issue salience revealed by the resource levels of protesters,
even when evaluating other salience-revealing characteristics of collective
action. Collective action literature and the legislators' survey responses
in Chapter 3 both suggest that the size, media attention, and disruptiveness of a collective action are important for how legislators perceive and
respond to it. Nevertheless, the results in this chapter demonstrate that
the influence of protesters' resource capacity on legislative behavior is
distinct from the influence of other salience-revealing characteristics.

The difference in favor of low-resource groups is not always statistically significant when accounting for the size, media coverage, or disruptiveness of the protest. Still, the empirical results generally support the theoretical expectations. After protest, the average legislator is more likely to support the preferences of low-resource groups than high-resource groups, even while considering other salience-revealing characteristics of collective action.

This chapter purposefully explores the average legislator's support of costly participation to establish empirical support for the theory of costly protest. The empirical results demonstrate that costly protest is informative for legislative behavior, even while considering other factors that influence how legislators cast their roll-call votes. However, the empirical models do not adequately assess whether certain legislators or certain types of districts are more likely to see legislative behavior that advantages low-resource groups over high-resource groups.

For example, the control variables in Table 4.1 suggest that Democrats are more likely than Republicans to support constituents' preferences on protest-related bills. Additionally, Black and Latino legislators are less likely than their counterparts to support constituents' preferences on identical bills. When included as control variables, however, these results do not indicate which protesting groups legislators are more likely to support. In the next chapter, I look in greater detail at different types of legislative districts to discover whether some legislators and electoral contexts are more likely than others to comport with the theory of costly protest and legislative behavior.

5

The Limits of Costly Protest

Collective action erupted in Los Angeles and all over the United States after the jury failed to convict the four police officers filmed beating unarmed motorist Rodney King. The congressional response was mixed but attentive. Democratic Congresswoman Maxine Waters responded to the event by calling attention to the economic and social conditions that had been plaguing urban centers like the one she represented in Los Angeles. In contrast, Republican Congressman Elton Gallegly used the collective action to introduce legislation addressing illegal immigration. Representing the mostly White Simi Valley district, Congressman Gallegly argued, "A significant percentage of those who were rioting and looting and participating in what we could accurately refer to as anarchy was illegal aliens. ... It would be very hard to argue that their mission was to defend Rodney King's honor."[1]

The US Congress responded by passing the Dire Emergency Supplemental Appropriations Act (H.R.5132) for disaster assistance to meet urgent needs in Los Angeles and other communities.[2] Congresswoman Waters voted to support the bill, which would provide some economic relief to the property damages that occurred in the district she represented.[3] In a deviation from his typical voting behavior, Republican Congressman Jerry Lewis cast a vote in support of the bill. His vote was likely motivated by the protests that spread 60 miles east of Los

---

[1] Quoted in Sneiderman (1992).
[2] The House first passed H.R.5132 on May 12, 1992. Congress enacted as law an amended version on June 22, 1992.
[3] www.govtrack.us/congress/votes/102-1992/h125.

Angeles to his district representing San Bernardino, California. In line with the preferences of his more conservative congressional district, Congressman Gallegly and the majority of his Republican colleagues voted in opposition to the bill.

In Chapter 2, I describe the theory of costly protest and legislative behavior. The theory contends that legislators' decisions to support the salient interests expressed during the Los Angeles uprisings were motivated by reelection incentives. They were likely concerned that voters would hold them accountable electorally for whether or not they supported protest demands.

Legislators' voting decisions are typically influenced by their reelection incentives. Reelection concerns motivate legislators to support their constituents' salient issue preferences since groups with salient interests are willing to impose future repercussions for legislative behavior in opposition to the groups' preferences.[4] Reelection concerns also cause legislators to consider the directives of their political parties. Political parties provide legislators with a brand name and platform that increase the legislator's likelihood of winning elections. To reap the reelection benefits supplied by their political party, legislators submit to the authority of their party leaders.[5]

How legislators are held accountable electorally also depends on the characteristics of the legislator. Constituents with salient interests are sometimes more critical of legislators and political parties that traditionally fail to represent their interests.[6] They may be more forgiving of legislators who share a salient descriptive identity.[7] The opinions of legislators and staffers that I depict in Chapter 3 demonstrate that at least some legislators acknowledge that reelection concerns influence how they respond to protesters.

In Chapter 4, I controlled for legislator's constituency pressures, partisanship, and personal preferences in search of empirical evidence for the average legislator's support of protest and costly protest. In this chapter, I evaluate legislators' electoral context to evaluate whether certain legislators or congressional districts do not align with the theory of costly protest and legislative behavior. I focus exclusively on Black and

---

[4] See Fiorina (1977); Arnold (1990).
[5] See Cox and McCubbins (1993). Also see Cox and McCubbins (2005).
[6] See Canes-Wrone, Minozzi, and Reveley (2011).
[7] See Gay (2002); Tate (2004).

Latino protesters, relative to White protesters, due to the unique resource disparities that plague these communities.[8]

5.1 GEOGRAPHIC DISTRIBUTION OF DCA PROTESTS

To evaluate how legislators' electoral context influences their voting behavior, I rely again on the Dynamics of Collective Action (DCA) dataset.[9] Figure 5.1 displays the frequency of protests for Civil Rights, Minority Issues, and Civil Liberties issues in each congressional district for the 102nd, 103rd, and 104th Congresses. Most protests occurred in large urban centers, namely New York City and Los Angeles, California, but protests were not exclusive to urban centers.

In the 102nd Congress, the most frequent protest locations also included areas in and around Atlanta, Georgia; Wichita, Kansas; and Philadelphia, Pennsylvania. The 103rd saw frequent protests in and around Jackson, Mississippi, and Cincinnati, Ohio. Outside of New York and Los Angeles, frequent protests in the 104th Congress took place in and around Boston, Massachusetts.

Figure 5.1 demonstrates that protests represented in the DCA took place across the United States. Some occurred in urban districts with a heavy presence of racial and ethnic groups. Others appeared in more suburban and rural areas. There is variation in whether Democrats or Republicans represented protesters. There is also variation in the race, ethnicity, and gender of legislators representing protesters.

The geographical variation of collective action events will assist in evaluating how different electoral contexts might challenge legislators' support of costly protesters' demands. The variation enables analyses that assess whether certain legislators or congressional districts do not advantage the protest demands of low-resource groups over their higher-resource counterparts.

5.2 CONGRESSIONAL DISTRICT HETEROGENEITY

One explanation that I offer for the difference in Congresswoman Waters's and Congressman Gallegly's support of the 1992 Los Angeles uprisings' participants is the composition of their congressional districts.

---

[8] Review Chapters 1, 2, and 4, where I include extensive discussions on resource disparities between Black and White protesters and Latino and White protesters.

[9] For more information on the DCA, refer to Chapter 4.

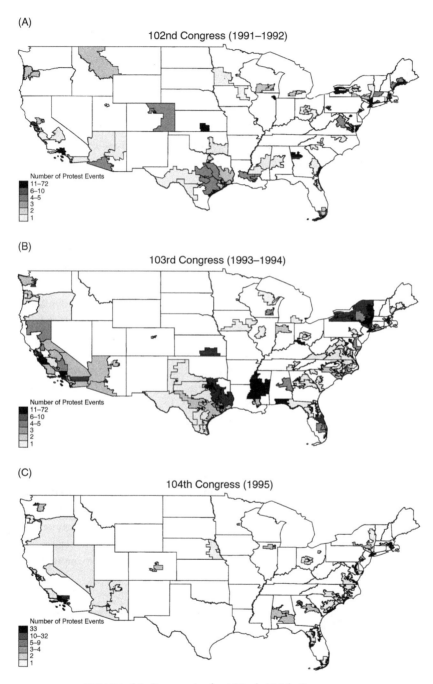

(A)

102nd Congress (1991–1992)

(B)

103rd Congress (1993–1994)

(C)

104th Congress (1995)

Number of Protest Events
11–72
6–10
4–5
3
2
1

Number of Protest Events
11–72
6–10
4–5
3
2
1

Number of Protest Events
33
10–32
5–9
3–4
2
1

FIGURE 5.1 Protests in the 102nd–104th Congresses

Note: These maps display the frequency of protests for Civil Rights, Minority Issues, and Civil Liberties in each congressional district for the 102nd, 103rd, and 104th Congresses. The DCA data closed in 1995, so only protest data from 1995 appears for the 104th Congress map.

Congresswoman Waters represented a large urban district with high percentages of Black, Latino, and Asian American residents. In contrast, Congressman Gallegly represented a mostly White congressional district.

Public opinion among non-protesters in their districts would likely vary considerably with their districts' racial and ethnic composition. Black and Latino constituents might favor legislators who support protesters' demands for liberal policies within the Civil Rights, Minority Issues, and Civil Liberties major topic classification. Congressional districts with more White constituents might support more conservative policies.

In general, legislators representing districts with greater racial or ethnic diversity might be more concerned about their reelection prospects. In districts with conflicting constituency opinions, any vote has the potential to alienate those who might have otherwise supported the legislator's reelection.[10] However, electoral insecurity is what makes legislators most responsive to the preferences of Black and Latino protesters relative to their White counterparts. With electoral insecurity, legislators are apprehensive about the potential electoral participation of a voting block with salient concerns.

Legislators may have less constraining reelection concerns when representing constituents with similar preferences, for example, when districts are racially and ideologically homogenous. They can easily identify and vote with the median voter in the district.[11] They also have more leeway to sometimes vote with the preferences of constituents who might not align with the median voter.[12]

These aberrations to vote in support of protesters with salient preferences might be motivated by goals external to legislators' reelection incentives. Legislators may desire to increase their prestige, make good public policy, or have more influence in their political party, or legislators may only feel secure about their reelection when they consistently represent the salient interests of their constituents. They may do so regardless of whether or not they have a sufficient percentage of constituents who will contribute to their reelection.

Overly ambitious legislators behave as if there is no level of constituency support that will reassure them of reelection. These legislators may

---

[10] See Fenno (1978).

[11] See Gerber and Lewis (2004). At least this is the case for final passage votes, which are less susceptible to party pressures than procedural votes (Crespin 2010).

[12] See Fiorina (1974).

be relentlessly insecure about their reelection prospects regardless of their knowledge of their district, length of service, margin of victory in the previous election, or the composition of their district. They could also desire to increase their likelihood of reelection out of pride or arrogance. In any case, legislators may still be responsive to costly protest even if they face fewer electoral threats due to the uniformity of their constituents' preferences.

To evaluate how legislators respond to costly protest based on their district's racial and ethnic heterogeneity, I evaluate empirical models based on the data I describe in Chapter 4. The dependent variable, *Support*, is a dichotomous measure of whether the legislator votes in support of a protest-related liberal Civil Rights, Minority Issues, or Civil Liberties issue. The vote must take place on the first final passage roll-call vote after the protest and before the next Congress convenes. I measure resources using two variables: *Black Protesters*, which compares collective action by Black protesters with that of White protesters, and *Latino Protesters*, which compares collective action by Latino protesters to that of White protesters. I interact each of these resource capacities with variables assessing the racial and ethnic heterogeneity of the district. Specifically, one set of models interacts each of the resource capacity variables with *Percentage Black Voting-Age Population*. Another set of models interacts each of the resource capacity variables with *Percent Latino Voting-Age Population*.

Figure 5.2 demonstrates how the difference in a legislator's support of protesters' preferences changes with the percentage of Black voters in the legislator's district.[13] In both Figures 5.2A and 5.2B, legislators appear more likely to support low-resource protesters than high-resource protesters. However, this difference in legislative support in favor of Black protesters is not statistically significant in districts with the highest percentages of Black voters. In districts with more Black voters, legislators may be adequately informed about Black voters' preferences because they represent a larger voting block. Alternatively, legislators representing majority Black districts could be as unresponsive to Black protest as to White protest because Black voters are unlikely to hold the legislators accountable for their voting behavior.[14]

---

[13] The tables producing these predicted probabilities and the predicted probabilities in subsequent figures are available in the Chapter 5 Appendix.

[14] See Swain (1993).

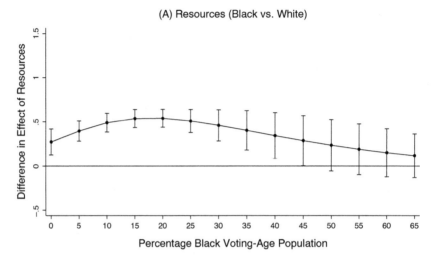

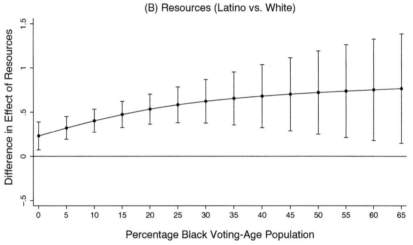

FIGURE 5.2 Protesters' resources and legislative support by percentage Black
voting-age population

Note: Differences in the predicted probability of legislative support of Black relative to
White protesters (A) and Latino relative to White protesters (B). All covariates are held at
their means. If the difference in predicted probabilities is positive (i.e., the confidence
interval for each bar is above the zero line), then the empirical estimate corroborates the
Resource Constraint Hypothesis.

The differences in the effect of Black voting-age population on the
predicted probability of legislative support, given the race of protesters,
suggest another possibility.[15] Legislators are more likely to support

[15] See Figure 8.1 in the Chapter 5 Appendix for this figure.

both White protesters and Black protesters as the Black voting-age population increases. However, the size of the coefficient is bigger for White protesters. It appears that legislators are changing their behavior in response to White protesters more often than Black voters as the Black voting-age population increases.

Perhaps legislators are more responsive to White voters because White protesters in majority Black districts have more intense preferences. Their interests may be represented less often than desired. Black legislators usually represent majority Black districts. All voters are less trusting of legislators who do not share their ascriptive characteristics.[16] Whatever the case may be, legislators are generally more responsive to Black protest and Latino protest than to White protest, regardless of the size of the Black voting age population.

Figure 5.3 displays similar patterns for legislative behavior given a district's Latino voting-age population as those revealed for the Black voting-age population. In general, after collective action, legislators appear more supportive of low-resource than high-resource protesting groups. As Figure 5.3B suggests, however, legislators are no more likely to support Latino protesters than White protesters in districts with the greatest percentage of Latino voters. Again, this may be because legislators are already responsive to the Latino community's salient interest, even in the absence of protest, since they represent such a large voting block. More generally, legislators remain more responsive to Black protest and Latino protest than to White protest. The greater responsiveness to low-resource group's protest is irrespective of the size of the Latino voting age population.

5.3 PARTISANSHIP AND IDEOLOGY

Another explanation that I offer to explain Congresswoman Waters's and Congressman Gallegly's differential support of the 1992 Los Angeles uprisings participants is their partisanship. Congresswoman Waters was a member of the Democratic Party and tended to cast more liberal roll-call votes than her Republican counterpart. Republican legislators are generally less responsive than Democrats to new information concerning the saliency of constituents' concerns because they have stronger policy motivations and more ideological party supporters.[17] Given the more conservative racial policy preferences among Republicans, these

---

[16] See Gay (2002).
[17] See Henderson and Brooks (2016); Broockman and Skovron (2018).

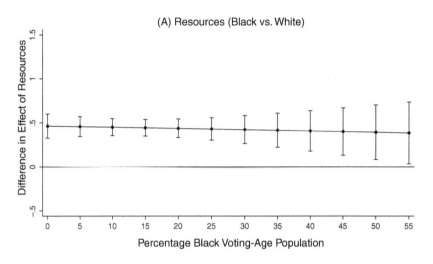

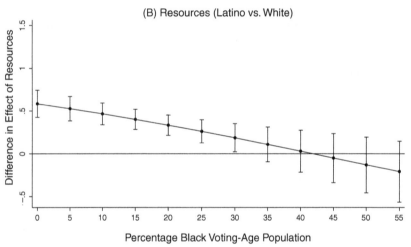

FIGURE 5.3 Protesters' resources and legislative support by percentage Latino
voting-age population

Note: Differences in the predicted probability of legislative support of Black relative to
White protesters (A) and Latino relative to White protesters (B). All covariates are held at
their means. If the difference in predicted probabilities is positive (i.e., the confidence
interval for each bar is above the zero line), then the empirical estimate corroborates the
Resource Constraint Hypothesis.

legislators may have little incentive to support the more ideologically
liberal-leaning protest demands raised during collective action on Civil
Rights, Minority Issues, and Civil Liberties issues by participants of any
race. Republicans' reelection incentives might suggest otherwise.

Republicans and conservatives rarely represent liberal Civil Rights, Minority Issues, and Civil Liberties issue preferences. So, they are less likely than Democrats and liberals to be given the benefit of the doubt for not representing costly protesters' preferences.[18] Furthermore, constituents perceive greater levels of responsiveness when descriptively represented by a legislator of their same race, regardless of whether that legislator is also a co-partisan.[19] This means that Black constituents are more likely than White constituents to disapprove of Republican legislators who are predominately White. Also, higher levels of disapproval among Black compared to White constituents suggests that when Republicans do decide to represent protesters' preferences, they may be more likely to represent Black constituents. Black constituents are more resolved to electorally punish the White legislator for ignoring their salient preferences.

To evaluate how a legislator's ideology influences their support of protest demands given protesters' resource capacity, I create a *Minority NOMINATE Score* – a measure of how liberal a legislator's roll-call voting behavior is relative to other legislators on minority roll-call votes. These roll-call votes include all legislation with the Civil Rights, Minority Issues, and Civil Liberties major topic classification. There are few final roll-call votes with the Civil Rights, Minority Issues, and Civil Liberties major topic classification, particularly in the 102nd Congress. So, the minority roll-call votes also include social welfare and inequality issues.[20]

Figure 5.4A suggests that the most conservative legislators are not more supportive of Black protesters' preferences than of White protesters' preferences following protests. However, legislators with moderate and liberal voting records are more supportive of Black protesters than of White protesters. Again, the predicted probabilities showing the difference in the effect of a legislator's voting behavior on minority roll-call votes on the legislative support of protesters' concerns are informative (see Figure 8.3 in the Appendix). It suggests that conservative legislators are not generally supportive of Black or White protesters' preferences, but as legislators become more liberal they are supportive of Black protesters' demands but unsupportive of White protesters'

---

[18] See Canes-Wrone, Minozzi, and Reveley (2011).

[19] See Gay (2002); Tate (2004); Bowen and Clark (2014).

[20] Following Gillion (2013), I add social welfare and inequality issues since they tend to concern issues salient for racial and ethnic minority communities.

demands. Only costly protest motivates legislators' support of protest demands.

Figure 5.4B suggests that conservative legislators do not appear to be more responsive to Black protest than to White protest, but they are more responsive to Latino protest than to White protest. Indeed, regardless of a legislator's roll-call voting behavior on minority roll-call votes, legislators are consistently more likely to support Latino protesters than White protesters. Together, Figures 5.4A and 5.4B suggest that legislators are generally more supportive of low-resource protesters' preferences than high-resource protesters' preferences. However, there are contexts in which conservative legislators may not be more supportive of costlier protest by Black participants.

Next, I compare legislators' responsiveness to costly protest based on the legislator's party affiliation (Democratic relative to Republican). Figure 5.5 suggests that legislators are generally more likely to support costlier protest. However, this difference in favor of low-resource protesters fails to reach statistical significance at the .05 level for Republican legislators' support of Black relative to White protesters. Nevertheless, it is once again generally the case that legislators are more supportive of low-resource protesters' preferences than high-resource protesters' preferences, regardless of their partisanship.

5.4 LEGISLATORS' RACE, ETHNICITY, AND GENDER

Beyond a legislator's party, their race and ethnicity can also influence how they perceive and subsequently support the preferences of their protesting constituencies. Black legislators, who are predominately in the Democratic Party, vote more liberally than White legislators on roll-call votes to advance Black interests.[21] Accordingly, Black legislators may not appear responsive to protest demands because they already support those issues. Unlike Black legislators, Latino legislators are likely to identify with both the Democratic and Republican Parties. Latino legislators vary more in their political ideologies based on their heritage, countries of origin, and the number of generations in the United States, among many other factors.

The influence of a legislator's race and ethnicity on their legislative support of protesters' preferences could vary with their party affiliation. Consequently, Figure 5.6 displays the differences in the effect of protesters' resource capacity on the predicted probability of the

---

[21] See Whitby (1997).

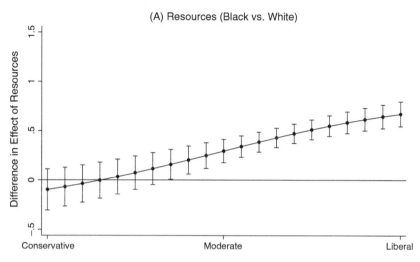

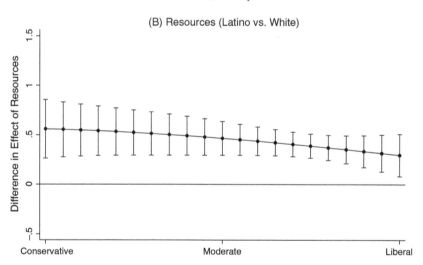

FIGURE 5.4 Protesters resources and legislative support by *Minority NOMINATE Score*

Note: Differences in the predicted probability of legislative support of Black relative to White protesters (A) and Latino relative to White protesters (B). All covariates are held at their means. If the difference in predicted probabilities is positive (i.e., the confidence interval for each bar is above the zero line), then the empirical estimate corroborates the *Resource Constraint Hypothesis.*

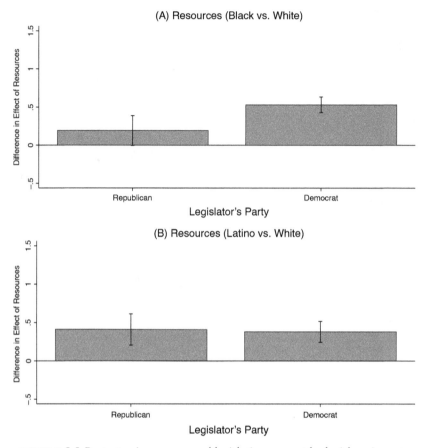

FIGURE 5.5 Protestors' resources and legislative support by legislator's party

Note: Differences in the predicted probability of legislative support of Black relative to
White protesters (A) and Latino relative to White protesters (B). All covariates are held at
their means. If the difference in predicted probabilities is positive (i.e., the confidence
interval for each bar is above the zero line), then the empirical estimate corroborates the
Resource Constraint Hypothesis.

legislative support of protesters' preferences by legislator's race, ethnicity, and party affiliation. For the first time, there is a difference
in legislative support in favor of White protesters. Mexican American
Democrats are more likely to support White collective action than Latino
collective action.[22] The difference in the likelihood of legislative support

---

[22] Only Latino legislators of Mexican descent have Black and White protests in the analyses. Since Latino groups vary considerably, I include the more specific ethnic group
classification.

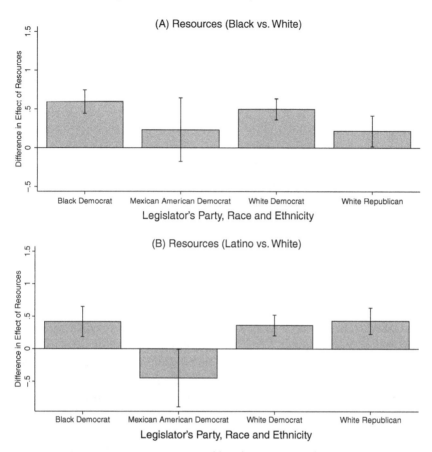

FIGURE 5.6 Protesters' resources and legislative support by legislator's race,
ethnicity, and party

Note: Differences in the predicted probability of legislative support of Black relative to
White protesters (A) and Latino relative to White protesters (B). All covariates are held at
their means. If the difference in predicted probabilities is positive (i.e., the confidence
interval for each bar is above the zero line), then the empirical estimate corroborates the
Resource Constraint Hypothesis.

for Black relative to White protesters is not statistically significant among
Mexican American Democrats. Still, for most legislators, regardless of
race and ethnicity and in both parties, legislators are more likely to
support protesters' preferences as the resource capacity of protesters
decreases.

Finally, I include variables assessing how a legislator's gender and
party affiliation influence a legislator's support of the issue raised during protests by Black and Latino protesters relative to White protesters.

Female legislators are more likely than male legislators to have liberal voting records. Indeed, women legislators have more liberal welfare policy preferences than their male colleagues, especially Republican and conservative legislators.[23] These expressed preferences may be due in part to constituency demands. For health care, education, children, and issues concerning women, the electorate perceives women as more competent and more liberal than men. Still, on matters relating to crime, foreign policy, and the economy, the electorate perceives men to be more conservative and more competent.[24]

Figure 5.7 shows similar patterns emerging for a legislator's gender and party affiliation as in previous results. Regardless of their gender, all legislators are at least marginally more likely to support low-resource protesters than high-resource protesters.

5.5 ELECTORAL SECURITY

Last, legislators may be responsive to costly protest because they barely won the previous election. Legislators with small margins of victory in the last election are likely nervous about any group that could threaten their reelection prospects. In fact, small electoral margins of victory in the previous election, even among incumbents, generally enhance legislative responsiveness to constituency pressures.[25] Therefore, I assess legislators' electoral uncertainty based on their *Margin of Victory* in the previous election.[26]

I also assess electoral uncertainty based on a legislator's *Years of Service* in Congress. As legislators increase their tenure in Congress, they are more likely to have a good understanding of the district they represent. They may also be more capable of discerning salient constituent concerns regardless of whether or not their constituents are engaging in collective action. Indeed, more senior legislators are generally less susceptible to constituency pressures than newly elected members of Congress.[27]

The point estimates in Figure 5.8 depict the difference in the marginal effect of Black protesters relative to White protesters (in Figure 5.8A) and Latino protesters relative to White protesters (in Figure 5.8B) on the likelihood of a legislator supporting protesters' interests as a legislator's

[23] See Poggione (2004).
[24] See Thomas (2014).
[25] See Ansolabehere, Brady, and Fiorina (1992).
[26] I get this measure from the CQ Press Voting and Elections Collection (CQ Press 2015).
[27] See Henderson and Brooks (2016).

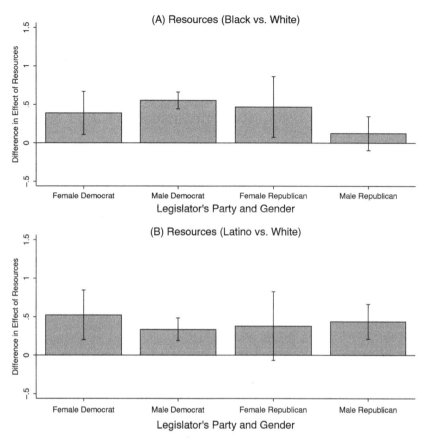

FIGURE 5.7 Protesters' resources and legislative support by legislator's gender and party

Note: Differences in the predicted probability of legislative support of Black relative to White protesters (A) and Latino relative to White protesters (B). All covariates are held at their means. If the difference in predicted probabilities is positive (i.e., the confidence interval for each bar is above the zero line), then the empirical estimate corroborates the *Resource Constraint Hypothesis*.

margin of victory in the previous election changes. The estimates suggest that regardless of how large a legislator's win was in the previous election, a legislator is more likely to support constituents engaging in costlier protest. In this case, legislators are more likely to support Black protesters than White protesters as shown in Figure 5.8A. They are also more likely to support Latino than White protesters (Figure 5.8B).

Figure 5.8 also suggests that as a legislator's margin of victory increases, the difference in the probability of supporting Black protesters

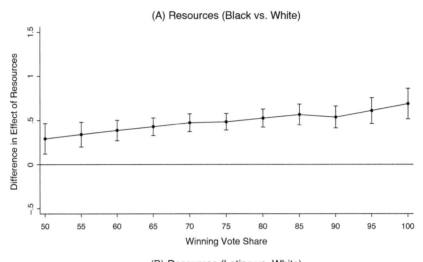

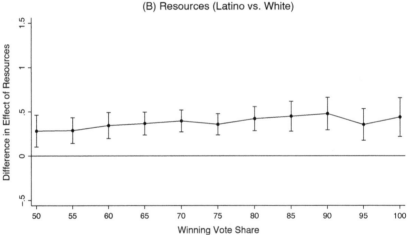

FIGURE 5.8 Protesters' resources and legislative support by legislator's margin of victory

Note: Differences in the predicted probability of legislative support of Black relative to White protesters (A) and Latino relative to White protesters (B). All covariates are held at their means. If the difference in predicted probabilities is positive (i.e., the confidence interval for each bar is above the zero line), then the empirical estimate corroborates the *Resource Constraint Hypothesis.*

compared with White protesters increases. However, the difference does not increase for Latino protesters compared with White protesters. To understand this relationship, I evaluate the marginal effects model estimating how a change in a legislator's margin of victory influences their support of White protesters and Black protesters, respectively.[28]

The marginal effects suggest that increases in a legislator's margin of victory decrease a legislator's support of White protesters, but increases in the margin of victory have no statistically significant influence on a legislator's support of Black protesters. In other words, the reason it appears that the difference in the legislative support of costly protest demands increases with legislator's margin of victory is that legislators become less supportive of White protest demands (and remain similarly supportive of Black protest demands) as their margin of victory increases.

Figure 5.9 reveals how a legislator's length of service in the House of Representatives influences the legislative support of costlier protest. The longer a legislator serves in office, the more confident they might be in their ability to discern the salient interests of their constituents. Therefore, the longer a legislator serves in office, the less likely they might be to respond to costlier protest.

Figure 5.9A suggests that regardless of how long a legislator serves in Congress, they are always more likely to support low-resource protesters than high-resource protesters. Figure 5.9B reveals a similar trend, except perhaps for the longest-serving members of Congress. The legislative roll-call voting behavior of the most senior legislators is more likely to support Latino protesters than White protesters, but this relationship is not statistically significant. The lack of statistical significance could be a measurement issue. There is a smaller number of legislators serving in Congress for more than twenty-two years, or it could be that senior legislators are confident they do not need to heed the protest demands of constituents with salient interests to avoid Election Day losses.

5.6 ELECTORAL ACCOUNTABILITY AND THE SUPPORT OF COSTLY PROTEST DEMANDS

There is much debate about whether constituents actually influence legislative behavior and when that influence is most likely to occur. Some scholars argue that legislators who narrowly win office and are uncertain about their reelection prospects are more likely than their counterparts

---

[28] This graph appears in the Appendix (Figure 8.5A).

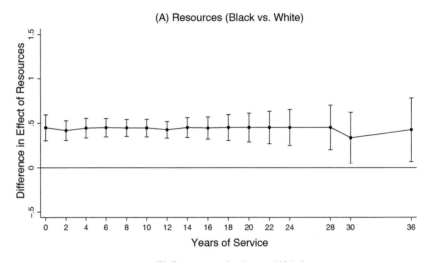

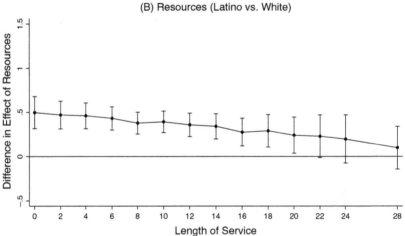

FIGURE 5.9 Protesters' resources and legislative support by legislator's years in Congress

Note: Differences in the predicted probability of legislative support of Black relative to White protesters (A) and Latino relative to White protesters (B). All covariates are held at their means. If the difference in predicted probabilities is positive (i.e., the confidence interval for each bar is above the zero line), then the empirical estimate corroborates the *Resource Constraint Hypothesis.*

to heed constituency influence.[29] Others doubt whether electoral context is ever relevant for the representation of constituency preferences.

[29] For examples, see Fiorina (1973, 1974); Gerber and Lewis (2004); Griffin (2006); Henderson and Brooks (2016).

Constituents may influence policy outcomes only when the election results in a new elected official.[30] Conversely, legislators may be responsive to constituency opinion even when there appears to be little accountability for legislative behavior during an election.[31] Consequently, how a legislator's electoral context influences their responsiveness to salient constituency preferences is up for debate.

I do not intend to resolve the debate about the influence of electoral accountability on legislative behavior in this chapter. Instead, I investigate whether different electoral contexts challenge the theory of costly protest and legislative behavior. The short answer: legislators remain more likely to support low-resource protesters over high-resource protesters, regardless of the characteristics of their districts, partisan pressures, or personal preferences.

In only one circumstance are legislators more likely to support high-resource protesters over low-resource protesters. Mexican American Democrats are more likely to support White protesters than Latino protesters. There are a few cases where the differences in the legislative support of protest demands based on protesters' resource capacity do not reach statistical significance. For example, there is no statistically significant difference in support of Black and White protest demands among conservative and Republican legislators.

In the previous chapter, I found that Black and Latino legislators were less likely than their counterparts to support collective action demands. This chapter demonstrates that when they do support protest demands, they favor those made by Black and Latino groups more often than those by White protesters. The legislators who share salient descriptive identities with low-resource protesters appear more responsive to those protest demands.

I find little evidence that legislators who are objectively more insecure about their reelection prospects are more responsive to costly protest than legislators who are less concerned about winning reelection. Legislators with smaller margins of victory in the previous election or with fewer years in Congress are not more responsive to costly protest than legislators who objectively have more electoral security. The lack of evidence for differences in legislative behavior based on objective reelection concerns does not mean that reelection incentives are not responsible for the legislative support of costlier protest demands. There may be no

---

[30] See Lee, Moretti, and Butler (2004); Poole (2007).
[31] See Bartels (1991); Gay (2007).

level of electoral security where a legislator feels that they can ignore the preferences of their constituents.[32]

This research has important implications for scholarship on the representation of Black and Latino constituency interests. Black participants must overcome greater barriers to engage in participation equal to that of their White counterparts. Hence, their participation suggests to legislators that they have greater salience than White protesters for the issue inciting the protest. Greater levels of salience suggest that high-salience participants are more willing than lower-salience participants to reward or punish their legislator for their voting behavior. Consequently, reelection-minded legislators have greater levels of responsiveness to Black and Latino protesters than to their White counterparts.

---

[32] See Arnold (1990); Ansolabehere, Brady, and Fiorina (1992).

6

Costly Protest in a Digitized World

On March 28, 2012, Congressman Bobby Rush provocatively donned a hooded sweatshirt before the US House of Representatives. Explaining his actions, Rush told CNBC, "The floor of the House ... should not ever be disconnected nor distant from the cries of the American people for justice. That's one of the reasons I wore the hoodie to the floor."[1] The hoodie was a symbol for protests held throughout the nation as groups expressed outrage over the delayed arrest and later failed conviction of George Zimmerman, a neighborhood watchman. Zimmerman killed teenager Trayvon Martin after fearing that he might be "suspicious."

The death of Trayvon sparked the protests, but the events embodied a dissatisfaction over current and historical injustices for African Americans. Rush elaborated, "I'm outraged because this pattern [of Black men being racially profiled] has existed in this nation for a long time. ... I wore a hoodie because I wanted to identify with [the demonstrators] and tell them to keep demonstrating, because be it not for them we wouldn't even be discussing Trayvon Martin."

Congressman Rush was not the only one donning hoodies in response to the injustice toward Trayvon Martin. Collective action condemning the circumstances surrounding Trayvon Martin's death was widespread. The events were coordinated through traditional and digital media outlets. Photos of doctors, professional athletes, celebrities, and other sympathizers wearing hoodies circulated on social media websites like Facebook and Twitter. Locations and times of rallies, vigils, and demonstrations were shared using email, text messages, and websites.

[1] See Navarro (2012). Retrieved on March 23, 2014, from www.cnbc.com/id/46886308.

141

Additionally, various online petitions calling for justice for Trayvon, demanding an end to stand your ground laws or supporting George Zimmerman received thousands of signatures.

The collective action was remarkable. It was also eerily similar to collective action events of the past. The collective outrage following the murder of Trayvon Martin is akin to the discussions noted in previous chapters surrounding the nationwide collective action following the acquittal of police officers charged with brutally beating Rodney King. In both situations, legislators took notice and expressed their insights on the salient concerns sparking the protests. Congressman Rush's discussion of the persisting injustices plaguing the Black community is analogous to speeches by Congresswoman Maxine Waters. Both Rush and Waters emphasized the collective outrage felt within the Black community about social, political, and economic inequities in the early 1990s.

One of the many differences between the collective action surrounding Rodney King's beating and that surrounding Trayvon Martin's death was the influence of digital technologies. The Rodney King collective action relied heavily on coverage by television, print media, and traditional social networks to spread news of the incident and coordinate protest. Collective action surrounding Trayvon Martin's murder was facilitated by digital technologies, including websites, smartphones, and social media pages.

The ability of digital technologies to decrease the information, communication, and coordination costs associated with engaging in collective action is an important consideration for the central argument of this book. Suppose digital technologies decrease participation costs to the point where costs no longer prohibit participation. In that case, resource disparities may not help legislators uncover the salient interests of their constituents. Consequently, this chapter explores how digital technologies have evolved since the 1990s and considers the potential implications of that evolution for legislative behavior following protest.

6.1 EVOLUTION OF DIGITAL TECHNOLOGIES

Digital technologies were in their infancy in the early 1990s (see Figure 6.1). The first public website was introduced in 1990. The World Wide Web was launched in August 1991. By 1995, just 42 percent of US adults had heard of the Internet; only 14 percent of US households

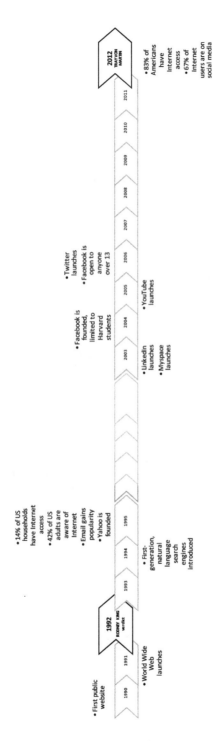

FIGURE 6.1 Notable moments in the evolution of digital technologies

had Internet access.[2] Even then, accessing the Internet was slow using a then–cutting edge dial-up connection.

Once online, there was little to do. Websites were only present for the most resourced, forward-looking organizations able to hire technologically advanced website developers. First-generation, natural language search engines introduced in 1994 made it easier to find websites, but user functionality was still limited. Email was beginning to gain popularity among the fortunate minority with Internet access, but it was used infrequently. Only 53 percent of Internet users sent or received an email at least once a week. The average Internet user sent only three messages a day and received only five.[3] Imagine only receiving five emails a day!

This was the beginning of the digital age.[4] This was the time of the Rodney King and Crown Heights protests and other collective actions for issues salient from 1990 through 1995. Few collective actions in that period benefited from the nascent digital technologies of the times. However, digital technologies evolved quickly.

Since 2000, the Pew Research Center has conducted several surveys of Internet access and usage. According to these surveys, about 50 percent of Americans used the Internet in 2000 (Figure 6.2B). Still, less than 40 percent had any form of Internet access at home (Figure (6.2A). Dial-up connections dominated home Internet connectivity.

The next decade marked a decrease in home dial-up connections and a steady increase in broadband connectivity. Libraries, public Wi-Fi, cell phones, and technology in the workplace supported a smaller but steady increase in individuals' Internet usage. These Pew Internet connectivity figures appear comparable to data collected by other sources. Findings from the US Census Bureau's Current Population Survey demonstrate that in 2009 almost 63.5 percent of American households had a home broadband connection.[5] The white, vertical line in Figure 6.2A shows a similar number (62 percent) of US households with a home broadband connection in 2009.

The turn of the twentieth century began the embrace of social networking websites and increased user functionality (refer again to Figure 6.1). The popular Myspace platform launched in 2003 alongside

---

[2] Last accessed May 8, 2017, from www.pewinternet.org/2014/02/27/part-1-how-the -internet-has-woven-itself-into-american-life/#fn-10743-4.

[3] Last accessed May 8, 2017, from www.people-press.org/1995/10/16/americans-going-online-explosive-growth-uncertain-destinations/.

[4] I associate the digital age with the rise and pervasiveness of digital technologies.

[5] See NTIA (2010).

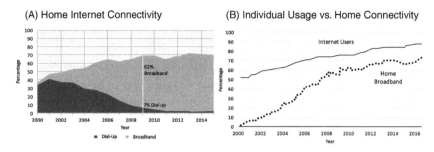

FIGURE 6.2 Internet usage over time (Pew Research Center)

Source: Pew Research Center data from surveys conducted 2000–2016. (A) "Three Technology Revolutions." Retrieved from www.pewinternet.org/three-technology-revolutions/ on May 28, 2017. (B) "Internet/Broadband Fact Sheet." Retrieved from www.pewinternet.org/fact-sheet/internet-broadband/ on May 28, 2017. For Internet users, data for each year were based on a pooled analysis by Pew of all surveys conducted during that year. I created an average trend line in Excel for the home broadband users based on data for each survey conducted in 2000–2016.

the then–less popular LinkedIn. YouTube launched in 2005. The following year marked the beginning of Twitter and Facebook accessibility to anyone older than age 13 with a valid email address.[6]

By 2012, about 83 percent of Americans had Internet access,[7] and 67 percent of Internet users were present on social networking websites, like Twitter, Facebook, and YouTube.[8] It was on these platforms that #blacklivesmatter found its beginnings – in the social media posts of people expressing their anger, grief, and disbelief. Indeed, the widespread Trayvon Martin protests were possible due largely to the capacity of digital technologies to decrease participation costs.

6.2 ORIGINAL DATASET OF DIGITALLY ENABLED PROTESTS

The data in previous chapters rely heavily on the Dynamics of Collective Action (DCA) database – a compilation of collective action events reported in the *New York Times* from 1991 through 1995.

---

[6] Facebook was initially exclusive only to Harvard students.

[7] Last accessed May 8, 2017 from www.pewinternet.org/2014/02/27/part-1-how-the-inter net-has-woven-itself-into-american-life/#fn-10743-4.

[8] Last accessed May 8, 2017 from www.pewinternet.org/2013/02/14/social-networking-site-users/.

While comprehensive, the DCA is insufficient in uncovering how digital technologies might influence how legislators respond to contemporary protests in their districts. To address this question, I created a unique dataset of digitally enabled protests with the help of several research assistants. The dataset includes every collective action event reported in 2012 in newspapers across the United States. Specifically, I collected protests reports in the newspaper with the largest circulation in the twenty largest US metropolitan areas. Information on the data collection process is available in the Chapter 6 Appendix.

6.2.1   DCA vs. 2012 Data

The DCA is limited to events reported in the *New York Times*, which is more likely to cover major cities like New York, Los Angeles, and Washington, DC. The unique dataset of 2012 includes events covered in any of twenty newspapers of the most populated metropolitan areas in the United States. The map in Figure 6.3 suggests that the 2012 data result in more geographical coverage than that in the DCA. Collective action events are reported in major cities, including Los Angeles, Philadelphia, Charlotte, Milwaukee, and Washington, DC. Despite the increase in geographic coverage, a descriptive look at collective action across time suggests that contemporary collective action may not be much different from that occurring in the early 1990s.

Figure 6.4 counts the number of collective action events for each year in the DCA and compares those numbers with the number of events

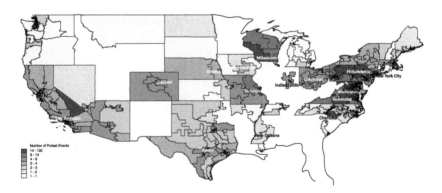

FIGURE 6.3 Geographical coverage of 2012 data

Note: This map does not include events that occurred nationwide or exclusively online
with no indication of a physical location.

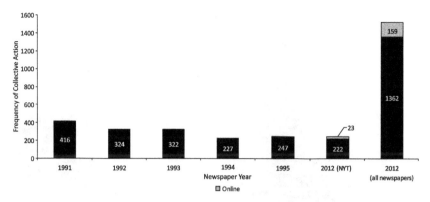

FIGURE 6.4 Frequency of collective action across time

Note: Years 1991 through 1995 are from the DCA, which only includes the *New York Times*. The 2012 is from original data collection.

covered in 2012 by the *New York Times* and then all newspapers. The *New York Times* covered 245 collective action events in 2012. It averaged just more than 300 collective action events for each year from 1991 through 1995. Many forces can explain the ebb and flow of collective action, including constituents' level of contentment and feelings of efficacy. This cursory look at the frequency of collective action suggests there were about as many collective action events in 2012 as there were in the initial analyses. So, if there are differences in contemporary legislative behavior in response to collective action, those differences are not likely due to the frequency of events.

Despite the comparability of the *New York Times* coverage over time, the newspaper does appear to miss many collective action events. Only 16 percent of collective action events in the 2012 data were reported by the *New York Times*. Figure 6.5 shows that the *New York Times* covers similar collective action as other newspapers. It gives slightly more coverage to rallies and less coverage to petitions and letter-writing campaigns than other newspapers, but the differences are small.

There may be disparities in news coverage with respect to the race or ethnicity of the participants. Figure 6.6 shows that compared with other newspapers, the *New York Times* coverage of collective action events underrepresents collective action by Black participants. It does give more significant coverage to collective action featuring Latino protesters. Thus, the frequency and nature of collective action do not differ much when comparing the *New York Times* with other newspapers; there

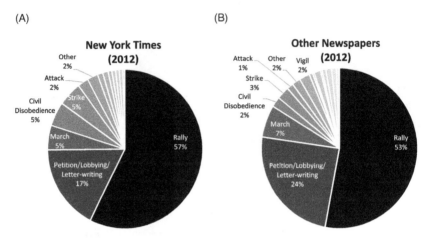

FIGURE 6.5 Comparing newspaper coverage by type of events

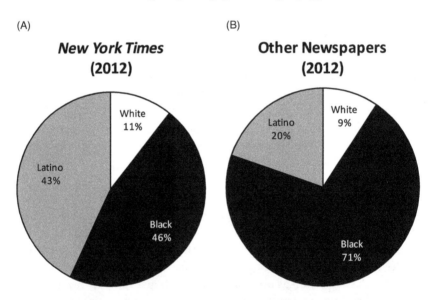

FIGURE 6.6 Comparing newspaper coverage by race of participants

are differences in which participants are likely to receive coverage in newspapers, perhaps due to the newspapers' geographical scope.

These differences have implications for the empirical tests of legislative behavior following protest using the DCA data, which rely exclusively on *New York Times* coverage of collective action. The newspaper data serve as a proxy for information that legislators have concerning collective action in their districts, but legislators depend on more than just newspaper coverage for that information. The fact that the *New York Times* misrepresents collective action at least partly based on who is participating means that the empirical results in this work may underestimate the influence of collective action on legislative behavior.

In addition to providing more geographical coverage to the protest data, the 2012 data also include an array of online and offline collective action events. Figure 6.7 demonstrates that about 62 percent of the collective action events reported in the nation's largest newspapers in 2012 occurred online. The majority of online events in the 2012 data are petitions, symbolic displays (like changing one's profile picture in solidarity of a protest demand), or boycotts conducted online. Underrepresented in this data are various online petitions promoted on www.change.org and other petitioning websites. Also underrepresented are the numerous hashtag collective action campaigns, including #Kony2012, #BringBackOurGirls, and #JusticeforTrayvon.

Over the past two decades, the Internet has evolved from being a novel technology accessible to few Americans to a staple of the ordinary citizen. Social networking websites, personal blogs, public and private web pages, and smartphone apps facilitate collective action. They also provide opportunities for individuals to organize and participate in collective action more easily. These technological tools can

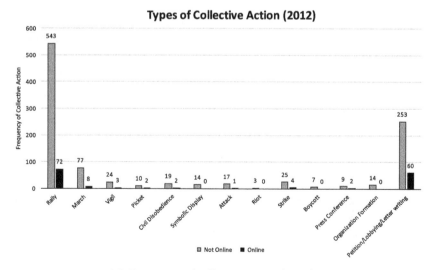

FIGURE 6.7 Frequency of collective action by online presence

reduce participation costs and forever change the way people engage in collective action.

The new dataset on collective action events reported in 2012 enables an evaluation of legislative behavior following digitally enabled collective action. It allows for a comparison of collective action events that occur online and those that occur in physical locations with the assistance of digital technologies. Furthermore, it provides greater geographical coverage than analyses conducted in previous chapters. While comprehensive, these new data still have limits.

Traditional media sources, like newspapers, are skilled in reporting on events that occur in physical locations. Reporters monitor applications to police departments for permits to protest. They also have sources that can inform them when an event is taking place. Monitoring the universe of collective action events that occur in online locations is more complicated. New websites pop up every day. Viral hashtag campaigns and online petitions are a dime a dozen and hard to predict. Efforts are being made to account for the copious accounts of collective action events occurring throughout the world. Still, newspapers may not be the best source for this information. This does not mean that the 2012 data are useless.

Legislators also find it challenging to collect information on collective action occurring in the online universe. They rely on traditional media sources to communicate pertinent information concerning salient constituency concerns. Thus, the 2012 data collection effort attempts to mirror the information available to legislators when deciding whether to support protest demands on roll-call votes. It includes more newspapers to capture the biggest, nationwide events and local events occurring primarily in legislators' congressional districts. These data effectively capture protest activity in the digital age.

6.3 DIGITAL TECHNOLOGIES AND PROTEST ACTIVITY

Digital technologies influence collective action in two ways. First, they change the context in which collective action occurs. Technological advances enable the development of ideas and concerns in a virtual world of digital interactions. The digital interactions complement the physical spaces (e.g., dinner tables, churches, civic organizations, labor unions), where individuals build community, frame ideas, and improve their capacity to influence politics.

In digital forums, the communication of grievances and ideas is almost instantaneous. Provocative blog posts stimulate commentary. Opinions circulate widely, sometimes even internationally, through user-generated posts and shares, and active debates are fueled by live-streamed, firsthand accounts.

Information is also more readily accessible. Individuals no longer have to wait for traditional media to cover an event. They also do not have to depend on elites to frame debates or offer perspectives that may not resonate with them.

Curious minds are limited only by their imaginations and dedication to finding information. They can comb social media to access multiple viewpoints on the merits of a government policy. They can consult online databases for how their elected representatives voted on that legislation. They can also visit an interest group's website to find out how to become more involved on any given issue.

There is some evidence that exposure to political information online is associated with increased political activity,[9] even independent of an individual's interest in politics.[10] In an analysis of the American National Election Study (ANES), Tolbert and McNeal (2003) discover that people who view election information online are more likely to vote, even when controlling for traditional media use, political interest, political efficacy, respondents' demographic characteristics, and several other factors. The association between accessing political information online and participation is reflected in different types of political behaviors. People who access political information online score higher on an index of electoral participation activities, including attending rallies; talking about politics; participating in a campaign; and giving money to candidates, parties, or interest groups.[11]

---

[9] See Kenski and Stroud (2006).

[10] See Xenos and Moy (2007) and Borge and Cardenal (2011).

[11] See Tolbert and McNeal (2003). But also, the association between accessing political information online and political participation is not absolute. Using the 1996 and 1998 National Election Study surveys and an original dataset of nationwide telephone surveys, Bimber (2001) finds little association between accessing campaign information online and political participation. Also questioning this relationship, Jennings and Zeitner (2003) find no influence of Internet use on political activity nor engagement when controlling for individual characteristics associated with political activity and past civic orientation measures. Despite the lower costs of accessing political information that digital technologies provide, there may be no increase in traditional forms of political participation, even though there is an increase in individualized participation more generally.

The second way that digital technologies influence collective action is by altering how people engage in collective action. Earl and Kimport (2011) separate digitally enabled collective actions into three categories: offline protest with online components (e-mobilizations), online protest with little to no offline elements (e-movements), and a hybrid category of protest with online and offline features (e-tactics).

E-mobilizations mirror protests of the past. Marches down city streets, acts of civil disobedience in front of government buildings, and swarms of people contacting their elected officials are but a few digitally enabled protest tactics with rich, historical foundations. Digital technologies facilitate how people find out about events, coordinate on a specific time or place, and convince their friends to participate in collective action. Many of the Trayvon Martin protests can be categorized as e-mobilizations. Calls to action and information about when and where to show up for protests were shared in online and offline forums. They were disseminated quickly and broadly by word of mouth; with print flyers; and through social media platforms, emails, and interest group websites.

While e-mobilizations occur predominately offline in physical spaces, e-movements prevail almost exclusively in virtual spaces. With e-movements, individuals engage digital technologies to share information, coordinate, and actually protest. In the same year of the Trayvon Martin protests were the collective actions by the English Wikipedia community against the proposed Stop Online Piracy Act (SOPA) and PROTECT IP Act (PIPA).[12]

The English Wikipedia community was concerned about freedom of speech, Internet security, and the flawed and potentially excessive application of the legislation. So, they organized a twenty-four-hour global blackout of their website for January 18, 2012. Google, Twitter, Reddit, Tumblr, Craigslist, and more than 115,000 other websites joined the day of online protest. The collective action spurred tens of thousands of mass emails, petitions, Tweets, and phone calls condemning the legislation. The protests forced Senate Majority Leader Harry Reid to indefinitely postpone the roll-call vote on the legislation.

---

[12] The US House of Representatives introduced the legislation to impede illegal content and actions on websites outside of United States jurisdiction. Media companies supported the legislation for their ability to combat copyright infringement and counterfeiting. Technology and Internet companies were in strong opposition to the bills.

Lastly, e-tactics are characterized as a hybrid of e-mobilizations and e-movements. They tend to have both online and offline components. Many e-tactics were traditionally conducted offline but have now moved to online forums. The most common e-tactic is petitioning.

Petitioning has a long tradition of communicating collective interests to policymakers and engaging constituents in the political process.[13] In the digital age, someone creates the petition and makes it available online for others to sign. Sometimes the signatures are delivered electronically. Other times the petitions are downloaded and then returned by mail or in-person to an accountable party.[14]

Not all petitions are related to politics, but policymakers do recognize the value of the tool for responsiveness. To increase participation and government transparency, the Obama administration implemented the online platform "We the People," which initially pledged to respond to any petition reaching 5,000 signatures within thirty days. The website's popularity prompted an increase in the threshold to 25,000 signatures two weeks after the website launched in 2011 and then to 100,000 in January 2013.

Earl and Kimport (2011) advise that whether digital technologies alter the underlying processes of collective action (e.g., the types of organization, participants, and participation) depend on how effectively digitally enabled protests leverage the affordances of reduced costs and the diminishing necessity for co-presence and group behavior. Similarly, Bennett and Segerberg (2013) argue that digital technologies may alter the underlying processes of collective action in some areas but not others. Digital technologies enable a logic of "connective action" in which rigid organizational structures and collective identities are rejected for loose networks of like-minded individuals united by a desire to share ideas and actions.

Nevertheless, the logic of collective action, characterized by high levels of organizational resources and the formation of collective identities, remains unchanged. This burgeoning literature on collective action in the digital age provides novel insights into how individuals engage in collective action. However, it does not focus much on how changes in collective action might shape legislative outcomes. I rely on these insights to evaluate legislative behavior following digitally enabled protest.

---

[13] See Carpenter and Moore (2014), Carpenter and Schneer (2015), and Carpenter (2016).

[14] Popular online petitioning websites include MoveOn.org, founded in 1998, and Change.org, founded in 2007.

6.4 ONLINE VS. OFFLINE COLLECTIVE ACTION

Digital technologies enhance collective action by reducing participation costs, but reduced participation costs also make it difficult for legislators to determine whether protesters have salient protest demands. Digital technologies lower transaction and reputation costs to the point where participants need not care about a political issue to participate online.

Consider, for instance, the Ice Bucket Challenge, in which participants filmed themselves dumping a bucket of ice over their heads to raise awareness and funds for amyotrophic lateral sclerosis (ALS). Participants would then post the video on social media while naming other people to either complete the challenge or donate to the cause. Despite the campaign's initial success in raising more than $115 million for ALS research, "it is questionable whether the campaign did anything to substantially improve people's understanding of serious neurodegenerative diseases such as ALS, or foster any type of sustained long-term support for its cause."[15] Google searches and donations for ALS peaked in the initial months of the campaign but soon waned; efforts to revive the campaign to viral levels have been unsuccessful.

The inability of the ALS fundraising campaign to replicate its initial success is unsurprising. As Margetts and colleagues (2016) find, most online collective action events fail, and they fail quickly. Successful online collective actions benefit from the early participation of well-networked extroverts and individuals with a strong belief in their ability to control their fate.[16] In online collective action, "it is not the existence of the leader who brings the success, but the existence of a sufficient number of starters with low thresholds [for participation], and the readily available and disseminated social information about other participants that draws in the followers with higher [participation] thresholds."[17]

Peer production, when individuals are motivated to participate in collective action because of social media culture, also plays a role in motivating individuals to participate in online protests.[18] Peer production occurs when many individuals join in collective action to avoid social condemnation or to receive personal gratification. Simply seeing friends being rewarded for their participation with likes, shares, comments, and view counts in the Ice Bucket Challenge was enough to make the event

[15] van der Linden (2017), p. 2.
[16] See Chapter 7 of Margetts et al. (2016).
[17] Margetts et al. (2016), p. 193.
[18] See Benkler (2006).

go viral. It was peer production and not the issue of ALS that motivated people to participate. Once the novelty of the collective action expired, the ability to encourage additional participation faded.

It is not simply that online collective action fails to effectively communicate salient interests because the participation can come from people with little concern for the issue. Online collective action could also be unintentional.[19] Someone might post a comment that they intended for a small groups of friend but it ends up circulating to larger audiences. An individual might include a hashtag in a message without understanding or recognizing the hashtag's meaning for an existing collective action. A person might even be included on a publicly available group membership list simply because they entered their email address to access information on a website. The fact that individuals may unintentionally participate in online collective action makes it difficult for legislators and other outside publics to distinguish between salient and fleeting issue preferences.

The communication of salient concerns is more difficult with online collective action not only because of extroverts, peer production, and unintentional collective actions. It is also due to the generally reduced participation costs. Participation in online protest can materialize relatively quickly with the press of a button. Online participation also means that individuals do not incur the opportunity or material costs from relocating to participate in an event. Emotional costs due to repression, stigmatization, threats, and bullying are possible online, but even these can be avoided with the anonymity that some online collective actions provide.

The virtual costlessness of online collective action makes it difficult to discern how much participants actually care about the issue instigating participation. An electronic signature on an online petition could mean the participant cares deeply about the issue, or it could mean that a person inadvertently signed, or they could have signed the petition to receive recognition for supporting a popular cause. Writing a lengthy response in a comment section or posting information about an issue may be a better indicator of salience. However, these are still low-cost activities relative to collective actions that occur in physical spaces.

This is not to say that offline protests do not benefit from the affordances of digital technologies. If someone were to receive a flyer on their door or Facebook wall about a demonstration in their city center, they could seek more information about the event online. They could

---

[19] See Bimber, Flanagin, and Stohl (2005).

search a public transportation website for the most appropriate route and schedule. They could text their friends to find out if they are attending. They could even arrange childcare services through an online website. The tasks of deciding whether and how to participate in collective action are all more manageable due to digital technologies that benefit both online and offline collective action. The task of actually engaging in offline collective action presents opportunity, material, and physical costs that are not required for online collective action activities.

Digital technologies may make participation easier for individuals to engage in collective action, mainly when participation occurs in online spaces relative to offline ones. They also make it more difficult for legislators to infer the salience of the issue preferences motivating participation. Therefore, I expect to see the following in the roll-call voting behavior of legislators:

> Offline vs. Online Collective Action Hypothesis: A legislator is more likely to support the preferences of collective action participants engaging in offline activities relative to those engaging in online activities.

As in previous chapters, I empirically evaluate the legislative support of protest demands based on the resource capacity of protesters. For this hypothesis, the low-resource group is represented by offline collective action participants.[20] The empirical analyses confirm the Offline vs. Online Collective Action Hypothesis.

Figure 6.8 displays the difference in the predicted probability of legislative support following offline collective action relative to online collective action.[21] The predicted probability is calculated from estimates of the influence of collective action venue on the likelihood of legislative support given other legislative considerations, like the demographic characteristics of the legislator's congressional district or the legislator's party, race, or voting record. Figure 6.8 shows that legislative support is 10 percent more likely following offline collective action than following online collective action. The difference in the probability of support reaches conventional levels of statistical significance ($p < .05$).

As shown in previous chapters, legislators are more likely to support protest demands involving costlier participation. Protest demands made

---

[20] Details of the empirical models in this chapter are available in the Chapter 6 Appendix.

[21] The empirical models producing Figures 6.8 and 6.11 are available in Table 8.15 in the Appendix.

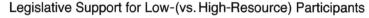

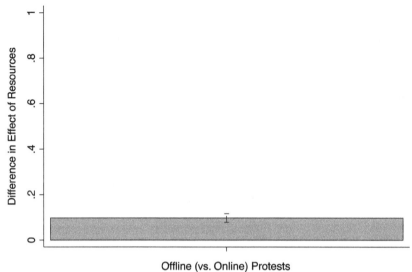

FIGURE 6.8 Digitally enabled protest, resources and legislative support

Note: Difference in the predicted probability of legislative support of low-resource group relative to the high-resource group. All covariates are held at their means. If the difference in predicted probabilities is positive (i.e., the confidence interval for each bar is above the zero line), then the empirical estimate corroborates the *Offline vs. Online Collective Action Hypothesis*.

in physical spaces, like marching or attending a rally, require more time and effort than virtual collective action events, like signing online petitions or participating in viral social media campaigns. They also present more risks, like arrests in events that become disruptive. When groups protest despite participation costs, it demonstrates that the issue motivating the collective action is salient for participants. When issue salience is high, constituents are more likely to punish their legislator for not representing their salient interests.

6.5 OFFLINE AND ONLINE DIGITALLY ENABLED PROTEST

Digital technologies enhance both online and offline collective action, but they are not accessible to everyone. Internet connectivity rates differ considerably by socioeconomic status. Figures 6.9A and 6.9B demonstrate that even with increases in Internet access, a large proportion of those with lower socioeconomic status still lack access to the digital technologies that could make collective action easier. In 2012, only 70 percent of the lowest-income earners were Internet users, while 97 percent of the highest-income earners used the Internet (Figure 6.9A). Relatedly, only 52 percent of Americans without a high school degree and 75 percent of Americans with a high school degree had access to the Internet in 2012 (Figure 6.9B).

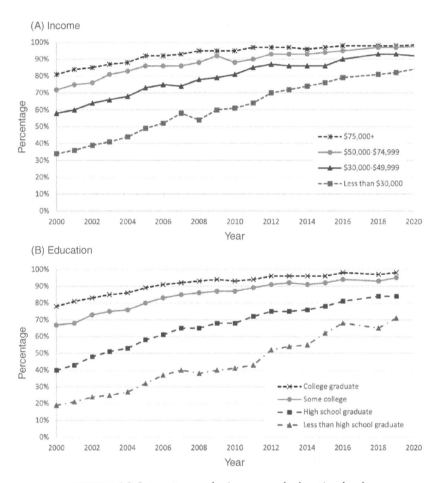

FIGURE 6.9 Internet usage by income and education levels

Source: Pew Research Center data from Surveys conducted 2000–2020. Data for each year based on a pooled analysis of all surveys conducted during that year. Retrieved from www.pewinternet.org/fact-sheet/internet-broadband/ on May 21, 2021.

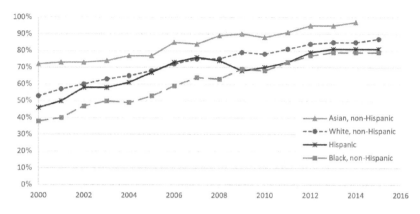

FIGURE 6.10 Internet users by race and ethnicity over time

Note: Figure reproduced from Rainie (2016). Retrieved from
www.pewinternet.org/2016/07/14/digital-divides-2016/ on May 8, 2017.

Disparities in access to digital technologies also exist based on race and ethnicity (Figure 6.10). Asian Americans (95 percent in 2012) are most likely to have access to the Internet, while Black (77 percent) and Latino individuals (79 percent) lag behind their White (84 percent) and Asian American counterparts. Differences in Internet usage are explained, in part, by differences in home Internet access. As the 2009 US Census reports, 63 percent of American households had Internet access, but the numbers were lower among Black (45 percent) and Latino (40 percent) households.[22]

In an analysis of the 2008 Pew Internet and American Life Survey, Schlozman, Verba, and Brady (2010) find that even among Internet users, White respondents and people with higher socioeconomic status are more likely to be contacted by political mobilizers and more likely to participate than racial and ethnic minorities and lower socioeconomic status respondents, respectively.[23] The reasons for these similar patterns of participation may be attributable to differences in political mobilization.

Krueger (2006) argues that even though the costs of sending one email or having one follower on a social media platform are virtually the same as the costs of sending thousands of emails or having thousands of followers, the populations that are contacted through these digital technologies are far from uniform. Internet etiquette highly discourages

---

[22] See NTIA (2010).

[23] See also, Best and Krueger (2005) and Krueger (2002).

unsolicited political contact. Individuals must first consent to being contacted by an organization, political party, or group.[24] Although coercion is sometimes used,[25] signing up to be contacted usually occurs after individuals become aware of the institution through their own personal networks or a specified search. This requires a level of political interest and technological skill that favors young, White, highly educated, and high-income citizens.

6.5.1 How E-Mobilizations Communicate Issue Salience

Digital technologies can decrease the costs of e-mobilizations by making it easier for potential participants to become informed, communicate, disseminate information, and coordinate collective actions. Yet, large sectors of the US population are unable to benefit from these affordances. Low-income constituents and racial and ethnic minorities may benefit the most from digital technologies. They face more significant economic, opportunity, physical, and emotional costs for participation in collective action than their higher-resource counterparts, and they are less likely to have access to digital technologies that can decrease their barriers to participation. Nevertheless, costly participation is a more legitimate signal of salient concerns. So, after protest, legislators should be more likely to represent the concerns of racial and ethnic minorities and low-income constituents than White and affluent constituents.

Legislators should also favor informal interest groups over formal interest groups. Offline collective action that materializes without the benefit of a formal interest group with expertise in mobilizing participation is more costly – and, therefore, more likely to represent salient concerns – than collective action that relies on the expertise of a formal interest group. While digital technologies do make it easier for individuals to access and disseminate information, formal interest groups further reduce costs by diversifying and facilitating participation.[26]

> Offline Protests Hypothesis: A legislator is more likely to support e-mobilizations by constituents with low-resource capacity than e-mobilizations by constituents with high-resource capacity.

---

[24] See Krueger (2006).

[25] Some groups require that you give them your contact information to become a member or receive a perk, like access to a publication or blog.

[26] See Bimber, Flanagin, and Stohl (2012).

6.5.2 How Online Protests Communicate Issue Salience

Within online collective action, participants have the potential to benefit the most from the lower participation costs and the diminishing necessity for co-presence that digital technologies provide.[27] Online is also where people can benefit the most from forming loose, public networks of like-minded people.[28] Online, the costs of participation are low enough that collective action is abundant,[29] sometimes unintentional,[30] and motivated by incentives that make salience difficult to discern.[31] However, the ability of groups to benefit from the affordances of digital technologies online is not uniform across resource categories. Accordingly, I offer separate expectations for each group resource type concerning legislative behavior following online collective action.

As discussed in the previous section, traditionally disadvantaged, low-resource groups are less likely to have access to the Internet. Online, these groups are also less likely to be asked to participate politically,[32] and they are less likely to have the technical skills that lead to membership in networks that engage in online collective action.[33] When low-resource groups do protest online, the salience of the rare participation, even if marginal relative to offline collective action, is more likely to be perceived as credible.[34]

> Online Income and Race Hypothesis: A legislator is more likely to support online collective action by low-income participants and racial and ethnic minorities than online collective action by higher income and White participants, respectively.

In previous chapters, I argued that formal interest groups are less likely to gain legislative support because their organization and mobilization capabilities make it difficult for legislators to infer whether selective incentives or salient issue preferences dominate the motivations of protesters to engage in collective action. Due to digital technologies,

---

[27] See Earl and Kimport (2011).
[28] See Bennett and Segerberg (2013).
[29] See Lupia and Sin (2003).
[30] See Bimber, Flanagin, and Stohl (2005).
[31] See Benkler (2006) and Margetts et al. (2016).
[32] See Schlozman, Verba, and Brady (2010).
[33] See Krueger (2006).
[34] See Lupia and Sin (2003).

the provision of selective incentives by formal interest groups is becoming obsolete in online spaces. Individuals are self-motivated to participate online. They self-select into networks of like-minded people[35] and are rewarded for their participation with likes, shares, view counts, and comments that recognize individuals for their contributions.[36] Moreover, many activities that were once private are more readily public, which makes it easier for outside publics to become aware of individuals' concerns.[37] Instead of providing incentives for individuals to engage in online collective action, formal interest groups have become important for their role in communicating constituents' preferences.

With lowered coordination and communication costs, a diversity of perspectives and concerns floods virtual spaces. This is ideal in a pluralistic or democratic sense. Still, the variety of voices makes it difficult for collective voices to coalesce into a central frame. Indeed, outside publics, including traditional media, politicians, and potential allies, crave leaders they can engage with to better understand the reasons for and solutions to salient concerns.

Nevertheless, the concerns about complex protest demands may be overstated. Sometimes diverse and occasionally competing opinions do coalesce into easily digestible narratives.[38] The calls for Justice for Trayvon and #blacklivesmatter evolved into Black Lives Matter (BLM) and the Movement for Black Lives. Furthermore, discontent over rising inequality led to Occupy Wall Street (OWS), and the "We are the 99%" slogan. However, these examples may be extraordinary.

In online collective action, the primary role of formal organizations is to create opportunities for individuals to narrate their own experiences. Formal interest groups facilitate and communicate the self-motivated, personalized "sharing of already internalized or personalized ideas, plans, images, actions, and resources with networks of others."[39] Among many activities, organizations sponsor websites to house user-generated petitions, invite users to share their experiences in short videos or blogs, and initiate discussion boards in which members articulate and debate topics of interest to them.

[35] See Bennett and Segerberg (2013).
[36] See Benkler (2006).
[37] See Bimber, Flanagin, and Stohl (2005).
[38] Bennett and Segerberg (2013) advise that informally organized collective actions may not be any less cohesive than those developed by formal interest groups.
[39] Bennett and Segerberg (2013), p. 36.

Formal interest groups do more than provide leadership or structure to collective actions. Organizations "provide a durable brand, an object for the potential development of sustained trust and identification by members and participants" in ways that informal networks and other organization-less collective action cannot.[40] A diversity of opinions and leadership types means that informal collective actions are more viable in the digital era than they may have been in the past. Additionally, frames can emerge from within a group instead of being applied to group concerns, but it also means that spurious collective actions may be less capable of producing lasting change.

When self-motivation is the primary mode of participation, it is difficult to keep participants focused and engaged on a particular interest. If a new issue emerges that provides more recognition or exposes a cleavage of the loosely formed coalition, and there is no leader or structure to encourage cohesion, then it is unlikely that the participation will be sustained. Furthermore, relatively low barriers to participation increase instances of collective action to the point where the perceived legitimacy of any one protest is difficult to discern.[41] Formal interest groups can provide the necessary legitimacy for collective actions to be taken seriously.

Informal interest groups are important because they enable individuals to dictate their interests and participate whenever an issue is salient. In the digital age, formal interest groups can more easily tap into those interests on platforms they sponsor. They can observe trending topics in search engines or social media platforms. They can monitor discussions in comment sections or create relatively costless participation opportunities that provide feedback. Once this information is acquired, formal interest groups can provide a collective frame and a brand that outside publics can comprehend. With the increased diversity of perspectives provided by digital technologies, the role of facilitating and communicating salient concerns is more imperative than ever before.

Online Organizational Capacity Hypotheses: A legislator is more likely to support online collective action featuring a formal interest group than online collective action featuring an informal interest group.

---

[40] Bimber, Flanagin, and Stohl (2012), p. 28.
[41] See Lupia and Sin (2003).

As a whole, the theoretical expectation for digitally enabled protest is consistent with those in previous chapters. Legislators should support low-resource protesters more often than high-resource protesters. There is one exception. Because of the multitude of online collective action, formal interest groups are crucial for facilitating and communicating salient protest demands. The empirical results confirm these expectations for collective action taking place within online and offline spaces.

6.5.3   Empirical Support for Offline and Online Collective Action

Figure 6.11 is a graphical representation of the difference in the predicted probability of legislative support for low- relative to high-resource capacity groups.[42] Figures 6.11A and 6.11B display the results for the influence of Black and Latino protesters, both compared with White protesters. Figure 6.11C presents the results for the influence of a formal interest group on legislative behavior.

For most models, low-resource groups should be more likely than the higher-resource counterparts to receive legislative support after collective action. The greater likelihood of legislative support for low-resource groups occurs regardless of whether the event is in person or online. The height of the bars for each of the models should be above zero. An exception exists in Figure 6.11C in online collective action where legislative support should be more likely for formal interest groups than for informal interest groups.

Once again, the empirical results generally correspond to the theoretical expectations. The difference in the predicted probability of legislative support is positive in favor of the low-resource group in Figures 6.11A and 6.11B for Black vs. White and Latino vs. White collective action participants, respectively. Legislators are just over 20 percent more likely

---

[42] Low-income and Asian American Participants are not included due to the infrequency of their collective action coverage. There are also no online collective action events that mention Latino groups. So, those models only assess the difference in legislative support of Latino relative to White collective action events that occur offline. This could relate to the relatively lower propensity of Latinos to have Internet access (Figure 6.2B). The absence of online collective action by Latino participants could also relate to the decreased ability of observers to detect when Latinos are participating in online collective action events. Latino is an ethnic group classification that relates to a person's country of origin rather than physical characteristics, like skin color or facial features. Consequently, observers may be more likely to indicate that participants are Black, White, or Asian instead of Latino. This misidentification then creates a measurement error in the number of online Latino collective action events.

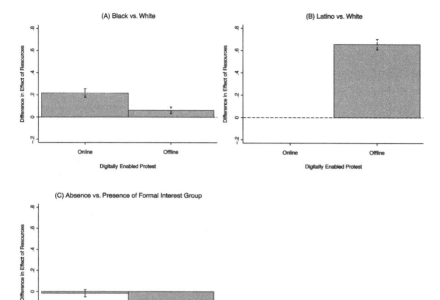

FIGURE 6.11 Resources and legislative support by digitally enabled protest

Note: Differences in the predicted probability of legislative support of low-resource group relative to high-resource group by type of digitally enabled protest. All covariates are held at their means. If the difference in predicted probabilities is positive (i.e., the confidence interval for each bar is above the zero line), then the empirical estimates corroborate the theoretical expectations. An exception exists for online collective action in Figure 6.11C. Legislative support should be more likely to following collective action with an interest group than collective action without an interest group (i.e., a negative coefficient) due to the smaller likelihood that resource disparities can effectively communicate salient concerns during virtually costless collective action.

to support collective action by Black participants than by White participants in online spaces. They are about 6 percent more likely to support Black collective action than White collective action occurring offline. Even more, legislators are more than 60 percent more likely to support the interests of Latino protesters than those of White protesters. Moreover, the difference in legislative support is in the expected direction but not statistically significant for grassroots collective action than for collective action featuring a formal interest group in Figure 6.11C.

Unexpectedly, the coefficient is negative and statistically significant in Figure 6.11C for offline collective action, suggesting that while digital technologies have decreased collective action costs, they may be making it more difficult for informally organized protests to communicate salient concerns. In a digitally enabled environment, it is more difficult for average citizens to communicate the legitimacy of their salient concerns without a formal interest group that can provide a cohesive frame and longevity to a salient problem, particularly for events occurring in physical spaces.

Despite this unexpected finding, the primary argument for the greater likelihood of legislative support for costlier collective action is generally supported even in a universe where digital technologies are pervasive. The reduced protest costs have not invalidated the role of traditional resource disparities in communicating salient issue preferences. Legislators remain more likely to support Black protesters than White protesters following online and offline collective action efforts. They also remain more likely to support Latino protesters than White protesters. However, there is no evidence to assess whether this relationship prevails following online collective action.

6.6 DISCUSSION

On July 16, 2012, Dan Cathy, the chief operating officer and son of Chick-fil-A founder, S. Truett Cathy, wrote in the *Baptist Press* to reassert his family's religious views on same-sex marriage. He stated, "We are very much supportive of the family – the biblical definition of the family unit. We are a family-owned business, a family-led business, and we are married to our first wives. We give God thanks for that."[43] Dan Cathy's statement was not abnormal. The family has been transparent in their opposition to same-sex marriage and homosexuality and their support for other conservative religious values. This time, however, calls for collective action, including a boycott of Chick-fil-A, circulated widely on social media.

One New Yorker, Carly McGehee, used his online presence to organize a "Kiss In." The collective action event involved activists taking pictures of themselves kissing someone of the same sex at Chick-fil-A restaurants. The Gay & Lesbian Alliance Against Defamation (GLAAD) backed the event while encouraging participants to "keep the kisses on the conservative side."[44] In counter-protest, Arkansas Governor Mike Huckabee

---

[43] Brumfield (2012).
[44] Brumfield (2012).

called for a "Chick-fil-A Appreciation Day" on his Facebook page. Politicians, activists, supporters, and opponents joined in the debate. They were called to action by ordinary citizens, activists, and politicians on social networking platforms.

As this example highlights, digital technologies enable information to be produced and disseminated by novices, experts, and those in between. Social networking platforms, inexpensive website domains, and adaptable templates empower almost anyone with Internet access to organize collective action. Many of the coordinating capabilities traditionally exclusive to formal interest groups and activists with a background in organizing and mobilizing collective action are available to a wider variety of individuals due to the lower participation costs that digital technologies provide.

Still, this chapter demonstrates that digitally enabled collective action comports with the theory of costly protest and legislative behavior described in previous chapters. I argue that while digital technologies decrease the information, communication, and coordination costs associated with collective action, they do so more for online collective action than for offline collective action. Moreover, the reduced costs have yet to mitigate the disparities in political participation leading to an advantage in political representation for traditional politically marginalized protesting groups.

Even in a world of smartphones, websites, and social media platforms, protest remains more costly for low-resource groups, which are less likely to have Internet access and are disconnected from the networks that could encourage political participation. There remains a clear disparity in the ability of groups to engage in collective action. Consequently, legislators remain more likely to represent the interests of low-resource groups than those of high-resource groups after protest.

The role of formal interest groups, however, has changed due to the presence of digital technologies. In the past, formal interest groups were necessary for aggregating group resources and encouraging people to participate in collective action. They provided information about why, where, and how to protest, and they subsidized participation costs with transportation and connections with media or policymakers.

In comparison, digital technologies provide platforms for ordinary citizens to discuss issues and coordinate strategies for solutions.[45] They also

---

[45] See Earl and Kimport (2011).

motivate everyday people to participate in collective action with likes, shares, and page visit counts.[46] Nevertheless, digital technologies make it more difficult to distinguish between collective action materializing due to salient concerns and those attracting large participation because of reduced participation costs.[47] The virtual costlessness and abundance of digitally enabled collective action have transformed the role of interest groups from organizing and mobilizing collective action to facilitating and communicating the salient issue preferences that materialize in collective action instigated by ordinary citizens.

I find support for these arguments using an original dataset of collective action events reported in 2012. I empirically compare online collective action (mostly petitions; boycotts; and symbolic displays, like wearing a hoodie) to events conducted in-person, including marches, rallies, and strikes. I find that legislators are more likely to support protest demands made in person than those made in the virtual spaces. Additionally, I find that legislative roll-call voting behavior favors Black and Latino protesters over White protesters within online and offline collective action events.

Interestingly, the expectations for protesters' organizational capacity appear to play out more for offline collective action than for online collective action. Following offline collective action, formal interest groups are more likely to receive support than informal interest groups in online collective action. After online protests, the likelihood of legislative support in favor of formal interest groups is not statistically significant.

Digital technologies are not the only difference between the early 1990s and contemporary collective action. To be sure, economic inequality has continued to grow. The US Congress is now more ethnically and racially diverse. The electoral participation of racial and ethnic minorities is beginning to comport with that of White voters. The election of the nation's first Black president and subsequent election of Donald Trump have called into question racial progress in the United States. Many previously disengaged groups are beginning to participate more politically. Despite these changes, the theory of costly protest and legislative behavior remains largely intact. Legislators are still responsive to costly protests in their districts.

These analyses provide a mere snapshot of legislative responses to collective action in a constantly evolving world of digital technologies. At

---

[46] See Benkler (2006).
[47] See Lupia and Sin (2003).

some point, digital technologies may alleviate barriers to participation for all groups so that resource disparities cease to be informative for legislative behavior. It does not look like that will be the case any time soon.

Digital technologies remain distant from many low-income and minority constituents, and political elites remain disconnected from politically marginalized communities. Resource disparities persist. Moreover, collective action efforts to address the concerns of low-resource groups continue to outperform similar efforts by high-resource groups. These findings challenge the conventional wisdom that legislative behavior more often represents high-resource groups. I hope that they also provide some optimism for individuals seeking to use protest as a resource for better representation.

7

The Democratic Value of Costly Protest

Tensions were flaring on March 5, 1770. Yet another brawl had erupted between American colonists and the British soldiers who had recently arrived in town to enforce the British Parliament's tax laws. The evening began with a confrontation between several angry colonists and a British soldier guarding the king's money. The evening ended with soldiers shooting and fatally wounding several colonists, including Crispus Attucks, a man of Native American and African descent.

In defense of the British soldiers' actions at the Boston Massacre, John Adams deflected responsibility from respectable, White Bostonians toward lower-class and non-White people.[1] Adams described the agitators as "a motley rabble of saucy boys, negroes and mulattoes, Irish teagues and outlandish jack tars."[2] He called special attention to the presence of Crispus Attucks. Adams asserted that the crowd was "under the command of a stout mulatto fellow, whose very looks was enough to terrify any person, what had not the soldiers then to fear?"[3] In a common trope that persists to this day, Adams defended the British soldiers by insisting that the mere image of a man with darker skin and African features was enough to warrant his death by armed law enforcement agents.

John Adams was no friend of the British government. He was a founding member of the Sons of Liberty, a group of American colonists who formed in opposition to the Stamp Act and other tax laws imposed on the colonies by the British Parliament. In admiration of the Boston Tea

---

[1] See Carp (2010), p. 143.
[2] Wemms and Hodgson (1824), p. 112.
[3] Wemms and Hodgson (1824), p. 116.

Party, Adams wrote in his diary: "This is the most magnificent Movement of all. There is a Dignity, a Majesty, a Sublimity, in this last Effort of the Patriots, that I greatly admire.... This Destruction of the Tea is so bold, so daring, so firm, intrepid and inflexible, and it must have so important Consequences, and so lasting, that I cant but consider it as an Epocha in History."[4] Adams's admiration for the Boston Tea Party is unmistakeable. He despised the British Parliament for taxing the colonists without the colonists' representation in the governing body. He praised the Boston Tea Party as a defining moment that would eventually lead to the American Revolution.

Like John Adams, many members of the Sons of Liberty were wealthy, highly regarded Bostonians. They often scapegoated lower-class and non-White groups in their protests against Great Britain. Adams cast blame for the Boston Massacre on Irish, Black, and lower-class participants. Years later, Boston Tea Party protesters crudely disguised themselves as Mohawk people to play "on the community's paranoia about non-white and lower-class rioters ... as a way of provoking fear in their enemies."[5] The disguises made it difficult for the British to hold any particular individuals accountable for the lost tea. They also helped maintain support among American colonists nervous about conflict with Great Britain. Furthermore, the disguises heightened stereotypes of lower-class and non-White groups as violent and dangerous. These stereotypes helped absolve the British soldiers of their actions at the Boston Massacre.

Adams justified the soldiers' violence and aggression toward the protesters by emphasizing the participation of Crispus Attucks, a man of Native American and African descent whose mere appearance induced fear. His defense resulted in the British soldiers being found not guilty, despite the growing contempt in the colonies toward Great Britain. Only two of the soldiers received any punishment for their actions. They were convicted of manslaughter and branded on their thumbs with the letter M.

7.1 UNEQUAL PARTICIPATION AND REPRESENTATION

Black people have been protesting against the devaluation of their lives since before arriving in the American colonies. They have been feared, condemned, and blamed for problems they did not create. When Black

---

[4] Retrieved from founders.archives.gov/documents/Adams/01-02-02-0003-0008.
[5] Carp (2010), p. 145.

people protest, they are called criminals and their protest demands are disregarded as illegitimate. In comparison, when White people protest, the general public sees them as patriotic defenders of freedom and justice even during violent collective action and even when they protest to infringe on the rights of others.

I argue throughout this book that the different lived experiences and realities that groups face heighten protest costs for some groups more than others. For example, because of slavery, Black people were robbed of the economic benefits of their labor for centuries. Black people were prevented from building familial and social networks. They were stripped of their histories and cultures.

Since slavery, institutions have been created to keep Black people from accessing wealth and building economic, political, and social power. Policing practices and criminal laws harass Black citizens and keep them from exercising the right to vote, housing, employment, and other basic human and civil rights.[6] Policing practices and criminal laws also make it difficult for families and communities with experiences with the criminal justice system to build wealth, political power, and social networks.[7] Moreover, the electoral college, poll taxes, gerrymandering, voter ID laws, and other political institutions have crippled Black people's ability to acquire political power. Stereotypes about Black people's mental acumen, physical prowess, civility, and ability to self-govern continue to influence public opinion and public policies concerning education, employment, housing, and social welfare. These historical and contemporary realities mean that Black people have fewer economic, political, and social resources available for protest than their White counterparts.

Other racial and ethnic groups vary in their resource capacities but typically have less political, social, and economic power than White people but more resources than Black people.[8] People with less income and wealth are less able than higher-income people to afford material collective action costs, including transportation, bail if arrested during an event, or lost wages due to protest participation. Low-resource groups also tend to be disconnected from the political and social networks that facilitate participation.

Because low-resource groups face profound obstacles to expressing their concerns in collective action, they can only aggregate their scarce

[6] See Alexander (2012).
[7] See Burch (2013).
[8] See Kim (2000); Masuoka and Junn (2013).

resources for protest when they have intense issue preferences. But when groups with low-resource capacity do protest, their collective action suggests a constituency that is willing to pool together scarce resources to hold their legislators accountable for their legislative behavior on salient protest demands.

In contrast, high-resource groups can protest at will. Their ready access to collective action resources makes it possible for them to protest even if the issue they are protesting about is not their most important policy goal. The unrestrained protest by high-resource groups makes it more difficult for reelection-minded legislators to know whether the representation of the protest demand will determine how high-resource protesters will participate in the next election. Protest by high-resource groups is a less clear signal of protesters' salient issue preferences. Consequently, the central argument of this book is that legislators are more likely to support the protest demands of low-resource groups than those of high-resource groups.

I develop this argument with a formal theory of costly protest and legislative behavior. The theory characterizes the relationship between a legislator and their constituents based on literature in sociology and political science on social movements, protests, political participation, and representation. Formal theories are beneficial for their ability to expose logically inconsistent arguments and uncover counterintuitive behaviors. For example, a common and persistent finding in political science is that White and affluent constituents are more likely than their lower-resource counterparts to have their interests politically represented.[9] Generally, legislators are more likely to favor wealthier constituents over the less affluent.[10] They are also more responsive to White constituents than Black or Latino constituents.[11] However, I demonstrate with the formal theory that it is logical for legislators to shift their voting behavior away from high-resource groups toward low-resource protesting groups. Protest delivers information about constituents' issue salience that is otherwise unavailable to legislators. This new information motivates legislators who are almost always concerned about their reelection prospects to represent the protest demands of politically marginalized groups more often than the protest demands of high-resource groups.

---

[9] See Schattschneider (1960).
[10] See Bartels (2008); Ellis (2012); Gilens (2012); Carnes (2013); Miler (2018).
[11] See Griffin and Newman (2007); Butler and Broockman (2011).

For the theory of costly protest and legislative behavior to be accurate, legislators must be aware of collective action – they cannot be responsive to participation that is not on their radar. Legislators must also believe that collective action is valuable to them. Otherwise, legislators would simply ignore any collective action they perceive. Third, for legislators to respond more often to some collective action more than others, their legislative behavior must be influenced by (any) collective action. Next, the theory requires that legislators respond strategically to collective action. Indeed, legislators do not blindly support collective action. They support protest demands to reach a desired outcome - reelection. Finally, for the theory to be accurate, legislators must observe and respond to group differences in protest costs.

In Chapter 3, I presented the survey responses from a convenience sample of legislators and legislative staffers to demonstrate that legislators perceive themselves acting in ways that align with the mechanisms motivating the theory. The sample is small, and the survey respondents are mostly Democrats, but they represent policymakers from local, state, and national legislative offices. More importantly, the survey responses corroborate each of the theoretical mechanisms described in the previous paragraph.

In Chapters 4 through 6, I conducted a series of empirical analyses to test the theoretical argument. Chapter 4 demonstrated that legislators are more likely to support constituents' preferences communicated during protest than those communicated via other channels, like survey data. I also evaluated multiple resource disparities and presented overwhelming evidence for the argument that legislators are more likely to support low-resource groups than high-resource groups after protest. Next, I considered the argument alongside other theories of protests' influence on legislative behavior, like the size of the protest, the disruptiveness of the protest, and the amount of media attention a protest received. These empirical analyses suggest that protesters' resource capacities persist as an explanation for legislators' roll-call voting behavior.

Chapter 5 considered how a legislator's electoral context influenced their support of protest demands. In general, regardless of a legislator's partisanship, voting record, race, ethnicity, gender, and electoral security, legislators remain more likely to support low-resource groups than high-resource groups. The results suggest that a legislator's electoral context sometimes alters the extent but rarely the direction of legislators' roll-call voting behavior in favor of low-resource protesters.

Still, some doubt may remain that the conclusions reached in Chapters 4 and 5 are generalizable. The DCA only includes events reported in the *New York Times*. There is more coverage of events transpiring in a major city or having a national focus relative to smaller protests. Consequently, while these data include hundreds of protest and provide a good test of the theory, the empirical analysis is limited to relatively visible collective action. Nevertheless, the theory suggests that the visibility of the event should not alter legislative behavior after protest. Legislators respond to protest because they are responding to a group that is communicating a willingness and ability to hold legislators accountable for their legislative behavior. Furthermore, the empirical analyses accounting for variability in media attention suggest that legislators are more responsive to costlier protest demands when protests receive a large amount of media coverage than when news coverage is minimal.

Another concern may be that the data in Chapters 4 and 5 are limited to the early 1990s. This period avoids the infamous social movement activity of the 1960s through the 1980s in which many politically marginalized groups participated in social movements. Collective action was more frequent, media were more attentive to protest, and public issue salience for civil rights– and civil liberties–related issues was relatively high. Hence, assessing protests occurring from 1991 through 1995 enables a more straightforward, albeit conservative, empirical test of legislative behavior given protesters' resource capacity. When social movements are active, legislative behavior is more susceptible to public opinion due to the heightened attention to protest activity.

Nevertheless, perhaps the 102nd, 103rd, and 104th Congresses were different from those that preceded it or those that followed. For instance, in Chapter 6, I explored the evolution and influence of digital technologies on collective action. I also empirically evaluated the influence of protest costs on legislative behavior. The results demonstrate that technological advances substantially alter the context in which collective action occurs. While digital technologies facilitate many contemporary collective action events, protest costs remain more consequential for the participation of some groups than of others. Attending a protest march remains more costly for low-resource groups than for high-resource groups. Smartphone applications and websites make it easier to discover which transportation mode will be the most efficient for reaching an event, but the costs of taking public transportation or putting fuel in one's car are still more significant for lower-income participants. Internet accessibility is more common among White, younger, more financially stable, and educated Americans than their lower-resource counterparts.[12] Political operatives continue to be less likely to appeal to low-resource groups.[13] Moreover, low-resource groups remain outside of the personal, professional, and social networks of politicians who, despite the increasing diversity and participation of the electorate, are still predominately White, male, and affluent.[14] So, while the early 1990s may be different from recent periods, things have not changed enough to alter many of the circumstances that make low-resource groups more likely than high-resource groups to receive legislative support for concerns raised during protest. Disparities in resource capacity and representation persist.

7.2 INCENTIVES AND MOTIVATIONS FOR LEGISLATORS' SUPPORT OF COSTLY PROTEST

I contend that legislators are motivated to support low-resource protesting groups more often than high-resource protesters out of a concern for their reelection. Legislators are cautious of ignoring or angering a constituency that could shift from protest to electoral participation that could cost legislators their reelection. Reelection concerns could reflect objective realities. Legislators who are newer in Congress or who barely won their previous election and other legislators uncertain about their reelection prospects might be more likely to support costly protest than legislators who are more confident about reelection.[15] On the other hand, legislators might be responsive to constituents' demands even if there is no objective accountability for their legislative behavior.[16] Perhaps legislators are overly ambitious and want to gain the highest possible vote margins, or maybe they are always concerned that a previously silent constituency could challenge their reelection.[17]

I do not find much evidence that legislators are motivated to be responsive to costly protest due to objective reelection concerns. Legislators with conservative roll-call voting records do not appear more responsive to Black protest than White protest, although they are more responsive

---

[12] See NTIA (2010).
[13] See Best and Krueger (2005); Schlozman, Verba, and Brady (2010).
[14] See Carnes (2012).
[15] For examples, see Fiorina (1973, 1974); Gerber and Lewis (2004); Griffin (2006); Henderson and Brooks (2016).
[16] See Bartels (1991); Gay (2007).
[17] See Arnold (1990).

to Latino protest than to White protest. Democrats are more consistent in legislatively supporting the protest demands of low-resource groups more often than high-resource groups, but Republican legislators are also responsive to costlier protest. Moreover, legislators who narrowly won their previous election are no more likely than legislators with larger vote margins to support costlier protest demands.

There is no definitive evidence that legislators with objective reelection threats are more likely to support costly protest than legislators with more secure reelection chances. Nevertheless, the reelection concern could still motivate legislators' more frequent support of costlier protest. Legislators are often concerned about their reelection, even if the threat is only subjective. Besides, other explanations for the legislative support of costly protest are inconsistent with the theory and empirical results regarding costly protest and legislative behavior.

To begin, political opportunity or political process theories contend that the context in which a protest develops determines when a protest emerges and how much influence it will have.[18] According to these theories, external shocks to the economy, war, political realignments, and other circumstances create shifts in protest costs that make it easier for protest to emerge. They also shape whether protest will influence public policy. For example, in more liberal congressional districts, public opinion may be more aligned with liberal protest demands, which reduces public support for tactics geared toward suppressing protests and for legislators who ignore protest demands.

Little evidence supports the contention that political opportunities motivate legislators to vote in support of low-resource protesters' preferences more often than high-resource protesters' demands. The results in Chapter 5 demonstrate that legislators across ideological and partisan lines are generally more likely to support low-resource protesters than high-resource protesters. In most cases, legislators are more likely to support costlier protest despite the demographic makeup of the congressional district. In only one case is a legislator more likely to support low-resource groups less often than high-resource groups.

Another potential explanation for legislative behavior following protest is that the issues articulated by low-resource protesters are simply more likely to be represented than issues expressed by high-resource protesting groups. This explanation is at odds with conventional

---

[18] See Tilly (1978); McAdam (1982); Meyer (2004).

understandings of public opinion and political representation. Low-resource groups, by definition, tend to be politically, socially, and economically marginalized. They have issues preferences that are less likely to be politically represented,[19] and they tend to protest for issues that public opinion is against, even among liberals.[20] It is difficult to imagine that low-resource groups would only protest for issues that nonparticipants would support and that their selection of protest issues would be more efficient than that of high-resource groups. Consequently, protesters' issue selection fails to explain why the data show legislators, including Republicans and conservatives, supporting low-resource protesters' preferences more than high-resource protesters' preferences. Legislators have little incentive to represent low-resource groups beyond the reelection incentives described in the theory of costly protest and legislative behavior.

When I asked legislators and staffers why they support protest demands, they freely recounted their reelection incentives. One respondent was explicit in saying that reelection motivated the behavior of his boss. Another respondent mentioned that he preferred responding to events that occurred around elections or at city council meetings. Many respondents talked about the need to respond to protesters who lived in their districts. Their geographic constituents would have the most opportunities to leverage electoral participation that could influence the legislator's reelection prospects.

7.2.1 Voting and Nonvoting Constituents

While the reelection incentive motivates legislators to support low-resource protesters more often than high-resource protesters, it does not require that protesters be voters. Voting is the most direct way for constituents to hold their legislators accountable for their actions while in office, but it is not the only way. Successful electoral campaigns depend on campaign contributions, volunteers, and good press. Whether they choose not to or do not have the legal right to cast a ballot, people who do not vote can influence a legislator's reelection through many channels. They can withhold their financial contributions or volunteering. They

---

[19] See Schattschneider (1960); Griffin and Newman (2007); Bartels (2008); Butler and Broockman (2011); Ellis (2012); Gilens (2012).

[20] For example, see Sniderman and Carmines (1997) on how ideology shapes White Americans' public opinion regarding Black people.

can choose to shift their support to another candidate. Moreover, constituents can sway other voters during formal and informal conversations or social media posts in support of or opposition to a candidate.

Legislators may not be as wary of the electoral participation of nonvoters as they are of voters. Groups that do not vote are unlikely to participate in other electoral activities.[21] However, they are concerned that felons, children, noncitizens, and other nonvoting citizens could shift their electoral participation in ways that could threaten their reelection effort. Groups that demonstrate their willingness to incur collective action costs because of a salient issue are also likely to participate electorally.[22] This concern motivates legislators to be responsive to protesters, even those who do not vote.

7.3 LESSONS LEARNED FROM FERGUSON AND ANTI-POLICE BRUTALITY PROTESTS

On August 9, 2014, Ferguson police officer Darren Wilson fatally shot Michael Brown, an 18-year-old Black male, after stopping the teen on suspicion of theft. Accounts of the altercation, which lasted less than two minutes, vary. Some witnesses and sources declared that Wilson shot Brown as he was trying to retreat, while others proclaimed that Brown was shot while moving toward Wilson.[23] In the end, both a St. Louis County grand jury and the US Department of Justice concluded that there was insufficient evidence to warrant an indictment of Darren Wilson.

In the days following Brown's death, candlelight vigils, marches, looting, vandalization, and police armed with riot gear and military-grade weapons began to flood the streets of Ferguson, Missouri. Wellspring United Methodist Church stood as a refuge amid chaos. The church offered prayer vigils and a safe haven for protesters fleeing police deploying tear gas and rubber bullets.[24] The church also provided childcare when violent clashes between police and angry protesters prompted the Ferguson-Florissan School district to cancel classes.[25] The Wellspring

---

[21] See Rosenstone and Hansen (1993).

[22] See Rosenstone and Hansen (1993).

[23] See the Department of Justice Report regarding the Criminal Investigation into the Shooting Death of Michael Brown by Ferguson, Missouri Police Officer Darren Wilson available at: www.justice.gov/sites/default/files/opa/press-releases/attachments/2015/03/04/doj_report_on_shooting_of_michael_brown_1.pdf.

[24] See Hahn (2014) and Yokley (2015a).

[25] See Hahn (2014).

Church was the site of healing, recovery, and perseverance. It was also the site where Representative William Lacy Clay Jr. joined nine of his Congressional Black Caucus colleagues at a Sunday morning church service on January 18, 2014, to express his support for the protesters.

Congressman Clay was a Democrat and had represented Missouri's First Congressional District, which included Ferguson, for ten terms in Congress. Standing before the congregation, Congressman Clay lamented, "Just like 52 years ago, today we are faced with the obvious failure of local officials who are either unable, or unwilling, to provide equal justice under the law.... So once again, our community looks toward the federal government to make the promises enshrined in the Constitution finally ring true."[26] Congressman Clay responded to his constituents' protest demands by sponsoring legislation to address policing practices. The legislation did not go far. Republicans had control of both the US House and Senate. Despite Congressman Clay's push for policing legislation, he received criticism for not doing enough to address his constituents' protest demands.

Missouri State Senator Maria Chappelle-Nadal showed her support for protesters by marching on the street with them. She criticized the Democratic establishment, which included Congressman Clay, for allowing poverty and racism to continue in the St. Louis suburb.[27] State Senator Chappelle-Nadal backed up her criticisms with an unsuccessful bid for Congressman Clay's congressional seat in 2016. The criticism of Clay did not stop there. After ten consecutive terms in Congress, Congressman Clay lost his congressional seat in 2020 to another Ferguson activist Cori Bush.[28] Bush's win ended the fifty-two-year representation of the congressional district by Clay and his father, William "Bill" Lacy Clay.

There are several lessons to be learned from the Ferguson protests and ensuing responsiveness from representatives. First, Black protesters in Ferguson were met with enormous protest costs. They protested in an electoral context that was not open to representing the protesters' interests. At the time of Michael Brown's death, the St. Louis suburb was about 67 percent Black; yet, the mayor and chief of police were White, and only one of six city council members was Black. Their collective

---

[26] Yokley (2015*a*).

[27] See Yokley (2015*b*).

[28] Bush lost to Clay in the 2018 primary election, but in the 2020 general election, she was elected to represent Missouri's First Congressional District.

action was met with police in riot gear deploying rubber bullets and tear gas. When they protested Michael Brown's death, media, elected officials, and other observers discredited their version of events and called their protest demands illegitimate. They were willing to incur the protest costs because their concerns were salient.

Regardless of the circumstances that led to Michael Brown's death, the failed indictment of Officer Darren Wilson was another in an endless list of Black people killed by police officers with impunity. The Department of Justice report into Michael Brown's death cited no evidence to refute armed police officer Wilson's claim that he feared for his life against unarmed Michael Brown.[29] A separate Department of Justice investigation revealed that the Ferguson Police Department routinely violated the constitutional rights of Ferguson citizens in a pattern of police bias and excessive use of force.[30]

Many types of elected officials in offices across the United States recognized the salient protest demands as potential electoral threats after viewing the costly protest in Ferguson and other US cities. At the federal level, Congressman Clay and other members of the Congressional Black Caucus responded by introducing policing legislation. President Obama made available $75 million for body cameras for law enforcement officers to address aggressive and dishonest police tactics. He also created a commission to diagnose and make recommendations for broad police reform. State legislatures proposed and passed policing legislation to address protesters' concerns.[31] At the local level, the Ferguson police chief was replaced by Delrish Moss, the first permanent African American chief in Ferguson. The long-serving prosecuting attorney, Bob McCulloch, who presented the case for Wilson's indictment, also lost his reelection in 2018.[32]

---

[29] See p. 7 of the Department of Justice Report regarding the Criminal Investigation into the Shooting Death of Michael Brown by Ferguson, Missouri Police Officer Darren Wilson available at www.justice.gov/sites/default/files/opa/press-releases/attachments/2015/03/04/doj_report_on_shooting_of_michael_brown_1.pdf.

[30] See the United States Department of Justice Civil Rights Division's Investigation of the Ferguson Police Department (March 4, 2015) available at www.justice.gov/sites/default/files/opa/press-releases/attachments/2015/03/04/ferguson_police_department_report.pdf.

[31] Whether the legislation called for more police accountability or autonomy corresponded with whether news coverage framed the police or protesters' demands as legitimate (Arora, Phoenix, and Delshad 2019).

[32] McCulloch served as St. Louis County's prosecuting attorney for twenty-eight years.

Another lesson from the Ferguson activism and elected officials' responses is that the time horizon for protest influence is unpredictable. The first Ferguson protests took place in August 2014 following Michael Brown's death. The criticism against Congressman Clay and other elected officials was immediate and insistent. Congressman Clay survived his first electoral challenge from State Senator Chappelle-Nadal in 2016. He also survived an electoral challenge from nurse and activist Cory Bush in 2018. By 2020, Bush's organizing efforts to represent Ferguson protesters' interests in Congress succeeded. She received prominent endorsements from progressive organizations, including Justice Democrats, Sunrise Movement, and Democratic Socialists of America.[33] She also received endorsements from Senators Bernie Sanders and Ed Markey and Congresswomen Ayanna Pressley and Rashida Tlaib. Bush's efforts took time, but after years of organizing, she and the activist community that supported her campaign eventually held Congressman Clay accountable for his representation of his constituents' costly protest demands.

In the empirical analyses in Chapters 4 through 6, I measure the legislative support of protest demands with roll-call votes occurring after a protest and within the same congressional term. In some cases, a protest emerged so late in the congressional session that there was only a matter of days or weeks for a legislator to support protest demands. The limited time frame for responsiveness means that legislators might have had more opportunities to represent protest demands in the future. Therefore, results using this time horizon likely underestimate the greater legislative support of low-resource protesters relative to high-resource protesters. To be sure, issue salience is not stagnant. It often peaks alongside external shocks and wanes once people have found ways to cope with their new realities. The longer the time between a shock and the legislative responsiveness to protest demands, the less likely the group will have issue salience that is high enough to be translated into electoral participation.

The best indication that a highly salient protest demand could threaten a legislator's electoral prospects over a longer time horizon is the costliness of the initial protests. Costly protest communicates salient issues that can remobilize for future electoral participation. Indeed, Cory Bush's ability to gain the electoral support of progressive organizers

---

[33] Retrieved November 29, 2020, from coribush.org/endorsements.

and mobilize a constituency that infrequently participated in previous elections was due to organizing efforts that capitalized on the latent issue salience of Black Ferguson protesters. The costly protest occurring after Michael Brown's death demonstrated a constituency with salient concerns about policing and racial inequality. The grievances did not go away when the initial protests dwindled. So, when elite mobilizers and organizers asked Ferguson residents to channel their grievances into electoral participation to hold elected officials accountable, their efforts eventually delivered on the electoral threat that their costly protest promised.

Could Congressman Clay have done more? To directly address Ferguson protesters' demands, Clay introduced policing legislation, but the bill did not progress far in the legislative process due to the Republican-dominated US Congress. Clay was not able to legislatively support Ferguson protest demands with a roll-call vote.[34]

I focus on roll-call votes throughout this book because a legislator's roll-call voting is public record. Roll-call votes are a visible form of legislative behavior that empowers constituents to become aware of how legislators vote on protest-related legislation and, in turn, hold their legislators accountable for their representation of protest demands. Roll-call votes create opportunities for legislators to claim credit for responding to protesters' claims, and they force legislators into a response to protest demands. Legislators must support, oppose, or abstain from voting on every roll-call vote put before the legislative body, but roll-call voting behavior is not the only way that legislators can represent protest demands.

State Senator Chappelle-Nadal participated in Ferguson protests, and she mobilized electorally to hold Congressman Clay accountable for his representation.[35] The survey respondents discussed in Chapter 3 talked about taking meetings with activists and directly communicating with communities about what they were doing to address protest demands. Perhaps Congressman Clay could have participated in some of the protests to demonstrate his support for protesters or done more to

---

[34] The House of Representatives voted on the Death in Custody Reporting Act (H.R.1447) on December 12, 2013, which was before the Ferguson protests. Democratic and Republican members of Congress have introduced several law enforcement bills in response to protest for police reforms. Still none have been put up for a final roll-call vote. See the Congress and Police Reform: Current Law and Recent Proposals (*Congress and Police Reform: Current Law and Recent Proposals* 2020). Also, see Bade (2015).

[35] See Yokley (2015*b*).

communicate his legislative support of protest demands. He may have miscalculated his electoral prospects or believed that the way he represented his constituents in the past would be sufficient in addressing reemerging protest demands against policing practices. Perhaps there was nothing Congressman Clay could have done to demonstrate his commitment to addressing protesters' concerns. In their challenges to Congressman Clay's congressional seat, both State Senator Chappelle-Nadal and Cory Bush criticized him for not doing enough during his long tenure to address systemic racism and inequality.[36]

In general, the strategic representation of protest demands means that legislators respond to protest only as much as they believe necessary to appease protesters. The more costly the protest, the more pressure the legislator will experience to produce more substantive policy changes. The costliness of the protest reveals whether the protesters might hold legislators responsible for voting in favor of a roll-call vote that does not (substantively) address the protesters' concerns. After costly, salience-revealing protest, even strategic legislators will act to produce more substantive policy change.

Amid unprecedented, far-reaching protests against police brutality and systemic racism in the summer of 2020 after the death of George Floyd at the hands of Minneapolis police officer Derek Chauvin, elected officials across the political spectrum scrambled to introduce legislation to address protest demands.[37] The Democratically controlled House of Representatives passed H.R.7120 (the George Floyd Justice in Policing Act of 2020); however, Republicans put no bills before the Republican-controlled Senate for a final roll-call vote.[38] Perhaps the Republican leadership did not feel an electoral threat from the costly protests occurring in their districts.[39] Perhaps they thought that the attempt to craft

---

[36] See Yokley (2015*b*) and thehill.com/hilltv/rising/507087-black-lives-matter-activist-cori-bush-on-running-for-congress-we-have-to-have.

[37] See Putnam, Chenoweth, and Pressman (2020) and *Congress and Police Reform: Current Law and Recent Proposals* (2020).

[38] Republican Senator Tim Scott introduced S.2985 (JUSTICE Act) to improve and reform policing practices, accountability, and transparency, but it failed cloture and did not receive a final-passage roll-call vote. Republicans introduced and passed a related bill, S.2163 (Commission on the Social Status of Black Men and Boys Act), established a commission to study and make recommendations to address social problems affecting Black men and boys and for other purposes. The bill became law on August 14, 2020.

[39] Democrats criticized S.2985 for not going far enough to address policing. Republicans did not have enough support for the tougher policing provisions in H.R.7120, including limitations on qualified immunity, "a court-created legal shield that protects police

legislation to address protest demands was sufficient representation to appease their protesting constituents.

Sometimes legislators get their responses wrong. They may understand the electoral threat posed by costly protest, but they may not know how to respond. In a failed attempt to symbolically support protest demands, House Democrats donned Ghanaian kente cloth while kneeling on the floor of the US Capitol.[40] The House Democrats were attempting to stand in solidarity with protesters and provide symbolic representation since they could not substantively represent protest demands with legislation. Yet, the response from their constituents demonstrated that their symbolic efforts were not enough to appease protesters.[41]

The responses to the Ferguson protests and other collective action surrounding police brutality suggest that costly protests pose electoral threats that prompt elected officials across the political and ideological spectrum and at different levels of government to support salient protest demands. Successful electoral challenges may not be immediate. Some elected officials remain in office for multiple terms. With sustained mobilization and organizing efforts, however, constituents with salient issue preferences can punish legislators who do not adequately represent their interests.

Still, roll-call votes are not the only way that legislators can represent protest demands. Legislators can attend protests, symbolically introduce legislation, and communicate directly with their constituents about what they are doing to address salient concerns. Nevertheless, roll-call votes are essential for the ability of constituents to hold their legislators accountable. If they were not, legislators would not have been working as hard to address protesters' salient demands concerning policing with legislation.

In general, legislators are cautious of costly protest and eager to find ways to represent salient protest demands. Sometimes they get things wrong. They may miscalculate protesters' issue salience, misunderstand protest demands, or misstep in how they choose to represent protesters' salient preferences. In the end, legislators' ability to survive electoral threats depends on whether and how they support costly protesters' salient issue preferences.

---

officers from civil lawsuit if their use of force is determined to be 'reasonable'" (Turner 2020).

[40] See Paquette (2020); Sarmiento (2020).

[41] See Paquette (2020); Sarmiento (2020).

7.4 TOWARD A PLURALIST HEAVEN?

The Death in Custody Reporting Act (DICRA) of 2013 became law on December 18, 2014. The legislation requires local law enforcement agencies to report any death occurring while in police custody to the federal government.[42] It was passed by voice vote in the House of Representatives and unanimous consent in the Senate, making it difficult for constituents to hold legislators accountable for their vote on the legislation. Even then, some legislators might have cast their vote with the belief that the bill would not have a lasting impact on how police and legislators deal with officer-involved deaths. A previous version of the bill, cosponsored by Asa Hutchinson (R-AR) and Bobby Scott (D-VA), was passed in 2000 in response to a scathing investigative report by journalist Mike Masterson.[43] By the time the bill expired in 2016, little progress in reporting had been made.[44] Supporters of the new bill might have expected a similar fate.

The bill's sponsor, Representative Bobby Scott (D-VA), made several efforts over the years to get the bill reauthorized. After pressure from Black Lives Matter and related collective action, Congress finally enacted the bill in December 2014. Legislators' votes were not recorded for the legislation. Still, if they were, a roll-call vote on DICRA could be coded as a success per the empirical methods employed throughout this book. The votes in favor of data on deaths in police custody support the demands of protesters seeking greater accountability for police actions. Explaining his reasoning for sponsoring the legislation, Representative Scott asserted, "You can't begin to improve the situation unless you know what the situation is. We will now have the data."[45] Nevertheless, the example also demonstrates the limitations of policy advances made through protest.

A condition of the Death in Custody Reporting Act of 2013 is that upon successful data collection, the attorney general of the United States would report to Congress how the data might reduce the number of deaths in police custody. The attorney general would also report any connection between those deaths and the actions of police and facility officials. The attorney general released the report on December 16,

---

[42] www.congress.gov/bill/113th-congress/house-bill/1447.

[43] The report asserted that many deaths in police custody are incompetently determined to be suicides.

[44] See Schwarz (2014).

[45] Schwarz (2014).

2016, detailing efforts toward collecting and improving existing data collection methods and the Department of Justice's intention to hire an external consultant to study the data.[46] These efforts have been criticized within the Black community for being "too narrow and potentially ineffective."[47] They also illustrate a common concern regarding attempts to stop protest participation with small economic or symbolic concessions.[48]

Data from reports are only the first step in a long process toward improved interactions between police and suspected criminals. In addition to reporting on deaths in police custody, there have also been mandates for police to wear body cameras. However, the way people interpret the data and images depends heavily on prior beliefs about the circumstances of the interaction. Previously filmed police interactions, including the beating of Rodney King by LAPD officers and the death of George Floyd caused by Minneapolis police officer Derek Chauvin kneeling for seven minutes on the dying man's neck, show that people viewing the same videos can reach completely different conclusions about what was occurring. If they do agree on the interaction, they disagree about what preceded it and what should follow it.

Protest is hailed as a tool of the powerless who pursue extrainstitutional tactics to seek remedies for their grievances.[49] Yet, there has been little evidence that it benefits the groups with the most to gain from the representation of protest demands. I demonstrate throughout this book that protest efforts are more successful for politically marginalized groups than their higher resource counterparts. Legislators are more likely to cast roll-call votes that support protest by low-resource groups than votes that support high-resource groups' protest, but to what end? Does the legislative support of costly protest improve inequalities in representation that continue to marginalize low-resource groups?

The answers to these questions depend on the ability of costly protest to communicate to legislators that a constituency is willing and able to hold a legislator accountable for their representation of protest demands. This is no small order. Costly protest is demanding. It requires marginalized groups with limited resources to overcome seemingly

[46] www.justice.gov/archives/page/file/918846/download.
[47] Retrieved January 20, 2015, from www.nbcnews.com/politics/barack-obama/wake-police-shootings-obama-speaks-more-bluntly-about-race-n278616.
[48] See Piven and Cloward (1977).
[49] See Lipsky (1968); Gamson (1975); McAdam and Su (2002).

insurmountable odds to communicate their needs. It also requires elected officials to interpret the costly protest as a credible threat to their reelection prospects.

Moreover, substantive policy change requires legislators to be in institutional arrangements that allow policy to be passed and implemented and for legislators to propose the correct solutions to pressing issues. However, legislators are imperfect, strategic, and unable to pass policy unilaterally. Sometimes legislators misunderstand protesters' grievances. Sometimes they have a solution but cannot implement it because it is not popular in the legislature or because of reelection threats posed by other constituencies. Other times the legislator reluctantly represents protest demands solely out of concern for their reelection. In any of those scenarios, substantive policy gains are possible, but they require sustained mobilization.

Sustained mobilization can pressure even the most ideologically distant legislators to support protest demands. Sustained mobilization not only demonstrates an unceasing threat to a legislator's reelection, but it also influences media representations and public opinion on protest demands. Protesting groups receive the most significant policy gains when they can convince outside publics to support their protest demands.[50] For example, years of organizing against police brutality and costly protests during a pandemic were responsible for shifts in public opinion, media framing, and policies concerning police brutality following the deaths of Ahmaud Arbery, Breonna Tayler, and George Floyd in the summer of 2020.

The good news is that costly protest efforts do pay off. The more frequent legislative support of costlier protest does not mean that high-resource groups never receive legislative support for their protest demands. For example, as legislation for police accountability has been developed in response to Black Lives Matter and anti-police brutality protests, police autonomy bills have also been introduced and implemented in response to Blue Lives Matter protests. Founded by a group of law enforcement officers, Blue Lives Matter protesters exemplify a high-resource protesting group with more political, social, and economic power than the mostly Black participants of the Black Lives Matter movement. Law enforcement officers are granted a considerable amount of discretion and autonomy.[51] They are often represented by police

[50] See McCarthy and Zald (1977).
[51] See Lipsky (1980).

unions that create bargaining leverage for officers with the government and the general public to maintain their authority and independence. There is also a high degree of solidarity within law enforcement communities, which facilitates collective action. However, in line with the central argument of this book, police are less likely to receive legislative support for their protest demands than lower-resource groups protesting for more police accountability. To be sure, police accountability bills introduced from 2013 to 2016 in support of anti-police protesters outnumber policy autonomy bill introductions 2 to 1, and the number of policing bills passed in support of low-resource protesters outnumbers those supporting high-resource protesters about 1.5 to 1.[52]

Throughout this book, I demonstrate that protest enables low-resource groups to gain representation for themselves. This does not mean that protest removes inequalities in participation and representation. Legislators are still more likely to represent the interests of White constituents more often than other racial and ethnic groups, and representation remains more likely to favor affluent groups over the less affluent.[53] Nevertheless, the relative advantage granted to disadvantaged groups after protest can mitigate inequalities in representation that typically favor well-resourced constituencies. Because of protest, the "strong upper-class accent" of the "heavenly chorus"[54] is not as strong as voting behavior, lobbying, and other forms of political participation might suggest.

---

[52] See Arora, Phoenix, and Delshad (2019).
[53] See Bartels (2008); Butler and Broockman (2011).
[54] Schattschneider (1960), p. 34.

8

Appendices

Formal Model Proof

I develop a formal theory based on the canonical signaling model to discern how the resource capacity of protesters influences a legislator's decision to support constituents' preferences. The theory builds upon Kollman's (1998) outside lobbying as costly signaling model. One major difference is the addition of protesters' resource capacity as a consideration for protest costs.

Actors

The signaling model consists of two actors. The group, G, sends a signal communicating whether it has high or low salience for an issue. The group's type, t_i, is defined such that $i \in \{L, H\}$ and t_H is a high-salience type and t_L is a low-salience type. The group's type, or salience level, is private information to the group and is determined exogenously by nature or some player or event not involved in this interaction. The receiver is a legislator, L. The group's type is distributed such that the group is a high-salience type (t_H) with probability, λ, and a low-salience type (t_L) with probability $1 - \lambda$. This distribution is common knowledge and determined exogenously by nature or some other player or event not involved in this interaction.

Actions

The group moves first, anticipating the legislator's rational decision-making. The group can either protest, $p = 1$, or not protest, $p = 0$. After the group moves, the legislator takes an action $a \in \{0, 1\}$. With

this action, the legislator informs the group whether they are supporting the group's policy preference. After observing protest, the legislator's
posterior beliefs are that with probability σ ($0 \leq \sigma \leq 1$), the group is a
high-salience type (t_H), and $1 - \sigma$, the group is a low-salience type (t_L).
After observing no protest, the legislator's posterior beliefs are that with
probability μ ($0 \leq \mu \leq 1$) the group is a high-salience type (t_H), and $1 - \mu$
the group is a low-salience type (t_L).

Players' Utility

The group has the following utility:

$$EU_{G_i}(a, p, t_i) = a - \frac{p}{t_i} * C_r$$

In this utility function, the group receives a positive payoff if the legislator chooses to legislatively support the group ($a = 1$). If the legislator
chooses not to support the group ($a = 0$), the group receives no utility
from legislative support. Protest is costly, so when the group protests,
it pays a cost that decreases as the group's salience increases, where
$0 < t_L < t_H$. This cost decreases as group resource levels increase, where
$C_r = (0, 1)$.

The legislator's utility function is specified as follows:

$$EU_L(a, t_i) = a(t_i - k)$$

When choosing how to respond to protest, a legislator considers the
consequences of each of their actions. Supporting a high-salience group
(t_H) results in a higher payoff than supporting a low-salience interest
group (t_L). Choosing to support a group costs a legislator, k, where
$k=(0,1)$. To ensure that the legislator wants to support a high-salience
group and not support a low-salience group, I assume that $t_L < k < t_H$.

Like Kollman (1998) and unlike Lohmann (1993), this utility function does not explicitly model policy locations. In Lohmann's model, the
private information concerns the group's issue preferences. Thus, a modeling of policy locations is essential. In this formal theory, the group's
policy preferences are common knowledge and therefore known to the
legislator. The private information relates to the group's issue salience.
Therefore, modeling policy preferences is unnecessary. Furthermore, in
line with Fenno (1978) and more explicitly Fiorina (1974), I argue that
legislators are less concerned about representing the entire district or the
majoritarian or median voters' preferences in a district. Instead, they are
primarily concerned about representing the interests of their reelection

constituency. This reelection constituency is a sub-constituency of a legislator's district. It can change over time and depending on the policy
issue. This suggests that whom the legislator decides to represent depends
on which constituents are important for reelection and not necessarily
the policy preferences of constituents relative to those of the overall district. A group becomes part of the reelection constituency if and when
it is willing to reward or punish legislators on salient issue concerns.
Granted, the reelection constituency could also include partisans and the
preferences of the group could conflict with these other groups in the
reelection constituency. Instead of modeling conflicting preferences with
policy locations, these legislative considerations are implicitly modeled in
the legislator's utility function in the term k.

Perfect Bayesian Equilibria
Semi-Pooling Equilibria. A semi-pooling equilibrium exists that informs
the model's main hypothesis. Semi-pooling equilibria occur when one
or both players mix between strategies. These equilibria are particularly
interesting because they allow for comparative statics, which suggest the
conditions under which legislative support following protest is likely.

Since costs to protest are higher for low-salience groups than they are
for high-salience groups, I explore the equilibrium where a high-salience
type group (t_H) always chooses protest $(p = 1)$, a low-salience group (t_L)
chooses protest $(p = 1)$ with probability α, and a low-salience group (t_L)
chooses not to protest $(p = 0)$ with probability $1 - \alpha$.

The legislator would prefer to support a group that provides more
electoral support without discouraging existing support. Therefore, they
never support the group after seeing no protest $(a = 0|p = 0)$, they
support the group after seeing protest $(a = 1|p = 1)$ with probability γ,
and they do not support the group after seeing protest $(a = 0|p = 1)$ with
probability $1 - \gamma$.

For the legislator's strategy to be sustained in equilibrium, they must
be indifferent between supporting and not supporting the group after
seeing protest. That is, $EU_L(a = 1|p = 1) = EU_L(a = 0|p = 1)$. This is
true if $\sigma = \frac{k-t_L}{t_H-t_L}$, which is derived from equating the legislator's expected
utilities of their actions.

$$EU_L(a = 1|p = 1) = EU_L(a = 0|p = 1)$$
$$\sigma(t_H - k) + (1 - \sigma)(t_L - k) = 0$$
$$\sigma = \frac{k - t_L}{t_H - t_L}$$

Updating the legislator's beliefs using Bayes's rule reveals the following:

$$\sigma = P(t_H | p = 1) = \frac{P(p = 1 | t_H) P(t_H)}{P(p = 1 | t_H) P(t_H) + P(p = 1 | t_L) P(t_L)}$$

$$= \frac{1 * \lambda}{1 * \lambda + \alpha (1 - \lambda)}$$

$$\frac{k - t_L}{t_H - t_L} = \frac{\lambda}{\lambda + \alpha (1 - \lambda)}$$

$$\alpha = \frac{\lambda (t_H - k)}{(1 - \lambda)(k - t_L)}$$

The legislator must also be willing to not support the group after viewing no protest. This strategy is sustained if $0 \leq \frac{k - t_L}{t_H - t_L}$.

$$EU_L(a = 0 | p = 0) \geq EU_L(a = 1 | p = 0)$$

$$0 \geq \mu (t_H - k) + (1 - \mu)(t_L - k)$$

$$\mu \leq \frac{k - t_L}{t_H - t_L}$$

$$\mu = P(t_H | p = 0) = \frac{P(p = 0 | t_H) P(t_H)}{P(p = 0 | t_H) P(t_H) + P(p = 0 | t_L) P(t_L)}$$

$$= \frac{0 * \lambda}{0 * \lambda + (1 - \alpha)(1 - \lambda)}$$

$$\mu = 0$$

For the group's strategy to be sustained in equilibrium, a high-salience group must be willing to always protest. This occurs when $\gamma \geq \frac{C_r}{t_H}$.

$$EU_{G_H}(p = 1) \geq EU_{G_H}(p = 0)$$

$$\gamma (1 - \frac{C_r}{t_H}) + (1 - \gamma)(-\frac{C_r}{t_H}) \geq 0$$

$$\gamma \geq \frac{C_r}{t_H}$$

Additionally, the low-salience group must be indifferent between protest and no protest. This occurs when $\gamma = \frac{C_r}{t_L}$.

$$EU_{G_L}(p = 1) = EU_{G_L}(p = 0)$$

$$\gamma (1 - \frac{C_r}{t_L}) + (1 - \gamma)(-\frac{C_r}{t_L}) = 0$$

$$\gamma = \frac{C_r}{t_L}$$

Following are the results of this semi-pooling equilibrium. These results are derived from differentiating the equations for α and γ. These comparative statics yield a number of testable predictions with respect to protest and legislative behavior. The first set of results reveals the proclivity for protest by low-resource groups.

Result 1: The first equation reveals that as the legislator's prior belief that the group is a high-salience type increases the probability that a low-salience group will protest will also increase. The increased likelihood of participation by low-salience groups decreases the benefit of the legislator supporting protest, which sustains the legislator's indifference between supporting and not supporting a group that protests.

Since the legislator prefers to support a high-salience group over a low-salience group, this result suggests that low-salience groups will increase their participation given the increased likelihood that the legislator believes the group is a high-salience group.

$$\frac{\partial \alpha}{\partial \lambda} = \frac{t_H - k}{(k - t_L)(1 - \lambda)^2} > 0$$

Result 2: The probability that a low-salience group will engage in collective action also increases as the cost for supporting a group increases. Intuitively, this suggests that a low-resource group recognizes that with increasing legislative costs for supporting the group's interests, a legislator will be more likely to support the group if they think the group is a high-salience type group. Since the legislator knows that any group that fails to protest is not a high-salience group, the group protests to increase its likelihood of being represented.

$$\frac{\partial \alpha}{\partial k} = \frac{\lambda(t_L - t_H)}{(1 - \lambda)(k - t_L)^2} > 0$$

Results 3 and 4: The probability that a low-salience group's protests increases as the salience of both group types increases, respectively. The greater the group's salience, the less prohibitive protest is for groups. At the same time, the legislator will benefit more from protest by groups with higher salience than by those with lower salience. Consequently, both the group and legislators benefit from protest as the group's issue salience increases.

$$\frac{\partial \alpha}{\partial t_H} = \frac{\lambda}{(1 - \lambda)(k - t_L)} > 0$$

$$\frac{\partial \alpha}{\partial t_L} = \frac{\lambda(t_H - k)}{(1 - \lambda)(k - t_L)^2} > 0$$

The next set of results relates to the probability that the legislator will support a group after seeing protest. The first of these results informs the hypothesis tested in the empirical analyses.

Result 5: The probability of legislative support increases as the costs with respect to the group's resource capacity increase. This predicts that a legislator is more likely to reward protest by a low-resource group than they are to reward protest by a high-resource group as the costs of protesting for a low-resource group are higher than the costs of protesting for a high-resource groups.

$$\frac{\partial \gamma}{\partial C_r} = \frac{1}{t_L} > 0$$

Result 6: The probability of legislative support decreases as the salience of the low-salience group increases. Even though a legislator will benefit more from protest by a low-salience group as the issue salience of that group increases, the legislator will also have to expend more resources for supporting a low-salience group with higher issue salience. To be clear, $t_L \leq k \leq t_H$. As the value of t_L increases, so must the value of k.

$$\frac{\partial \gamma}{\partial t_L} = -\frac{C_r}{t_L^2} < 0$$

Pooling Equilibria. There also exist a set of pooling equilibria. In a pooling equilibrium, both group types choose the same action. In these equilibria, the protest signal is uninformative for determining the group's salience level.

The first equilibrium states that if both high- and low-salience type groups protest, then the best response of the legislator to the group's action is to support the group after seeing protest and not support the group after seeing no protest. The following proof supports this strategy.

The legislator supports the group after seeing protest if their utility of support for the group is greater than their utility of not supporting the group.

$$EU_L(a = 1|p = 1) > EU_L(a = 0|p = 1)$$
$$\sigma(t_H - k) + (1 - \sigma)(t_L - k) > 0$$
$$\sigma > \frac{k - t_L}{t_H - t_L}$$

The legislator does not support the group after not seeing protest if their utility of not supporting the group is greater than their utility of supporting the group.

$$EU_L(a = 0|p = 0) > EU_L(a = 1|p = 0)$$

$$0 > \mu(t_H - k) + (1 - \mu)(t_L - k)$$

$$\mu < \frac{k - t_L}{t_H - t_L}$$

The legislator's beliefs are updated after seeing the group's (in)action using Bayes's rule.

$$\sigma = P(t_H|p = 1) = \frac{P(p = 1|t_H)P(t_H)}{P(p = 1|t_H)P(t_H) + P(p = 1|t_L)P(t_L)}$$

$$= \frac{1 * \lambda}{1 * \lambda + 1(1 - \lambda)}$$

$$\sigma = \lambda$$

Given the legislator's strategy, the group is willing to always protest if the expected utility of protest is greater than the expected utility of not protesting, or if the following is true:

$$EUG_H(p = 1) \geq EUG_H(p = 0)$$

$$1 - \frac{C_r}{t_H} \geq 0$$

$$t_H \geq C_r$$

and

$$EUG_L(p = 1) \geq EUG_L(p = 0)$$

$$1 - \frac{C_r}{t_L} \geq 0$$

$$t_L \geq C_r$$

The pooling equilibrium is therefore that both group types protest and the legislator supports the group after seeing protest and does not support the group after seeing no protest if $\lambda > \frac{k-t_L}{t_H-t_L}$ and $t_h > t_l \geq C_r$. Off the equilibrium path, the legislator's posterior belief is that $\mu \leq \frac{k-t_L}{t_H-t_L}$.

There are also several pooling equilibria where both types of groups choose to never protest. The legislator's strategy depends on the value of μ as follows:

- If $\mu > \frac{k-t_L}{t_H-t_L}$, then L chooses a = 1
- If $\mu < \frac{k-t_L}{t_H-t_L}$, then L chooses a = 0
- If $\mu = \frac{k-t_L}{t_H-t_L}$, then L is indifferent between a = 1 and a = 0

These relationships are supported by the legislator's expected utilities of supporting a group and not supporting the group after not seeing protest. For instance,

$$EU_L(a = 1|p = 0) > EU_L(a = 0|p = 0)$$

$$\mu(t_H - k) + (1 - \mu)(t_L - k) > 0$$

$$\mu > \frac{k - t_L}{t_H - t_L}$$

The legislator's posterior beliefs, established using Bayes's Rules, are that $\mu = \lambda$.

$$\mu = P(t_H|p = 0) = \frac{P(p = 0|t_H)P(t_H)}{P(p = 0|t_H)P(t_H) + P(p = 0|t_L)P(t_L)}$$

$$= \frac{1 * \lambda}{1 * \lambda + 1 * (1 - \lambda)}$$

$$\mu = \lambda$$

Off the equilibrium path, the legislator's strategy depends on the value of σ.

- If $\sigma > \frac{k - t_L}{t_H - t_L}$, then L chooses a $= 1$
- If $\sigma < \frac{k - t_L}{t_H - t_L}$, then L chooses a $= 0$
- If $\sigma = \frac{k - t_L}{t_H - t_L}$, then L is indifferent between a $= 1$ and a $= 0$

These strategies are sustained in equilibrium if neither group type has incentive to deviate or if $EU_G(p = 0) > EU_G(p = 1)$. The assumption that $C_r > 0$ is enough to sustain the equilibrium if the legislator chooses the same response to the group's action, regardless of the group's action. If L's strategy is to always support the group, then it must be true that

$$EU_{G_H}(p = 0) \geq EU_{G_H}(p = 1)$$

$$1 \geq 1 - \frac{C_r}{t_H}$$

$$C_r \geq 0$$

and

$$EU_{G_L}(p = 0) \geq EU_{G_L}(p = 1)$$

$$1 \geq 1 - \frac{C_r}{t_L}$$

$$C_r \geq 0.$$

If L's strategy is to never support the group, then it must be true that

$$EUG_H(p = 0) \geq EUG_H(p = 1)$$
$$0 \geq -\frac{C_r}{t_H}$$
$$C_r \geq 0$$

and

$$EUG_L(p = 0) \geq EUG_L(p = 1)$$
$$0 \geq -\frac{C_r}{t_L}$$
$$C_r \geq 0.$$

If L's strategy is to never support a protesting group and to support a group that does not protest, then the group will still never protest in equilibrium because

$$EUG_H(p = 0) \geq EUG_H(p = 1)$$
$$1 \geq -\frac{C_r}{t_H}$$
$$t_H \geq -C_r$$

and

$$EUG_L(p = 0) \geq EUG_L(p = 1)$$
$$1 \geq -\frac{C_r}{t_L}$$
$$t_L \geq -C_r.$$

If L's strategy is to support a protesting group and to never support a group that does not protest, then the group will never protest in equilibrium if $C_r \geq t_H > t_L$.

$$EUG_H(p = 0) \geq EUG_H(p = 1)$$
$$0 \geq 1 - \frac{C_r}{t_H}$$
$$C_r \geq t_H$$

and

$$EUG_L(p = 0) \geq EUG_L(p = 1)$$
$$0 \geq 1 - \frac{C_r}{t_L}$$
$$C_r \geq t_L$$

These conditions sustain the pooling equilibria that neither group type protests with the legislator's strategy depending on the values of μ and σ, where $\mu = \lambda$ and the legislator chooses to support the group if $\sigma \geq \frac{k-t_L}{t_H-t_L}$ and to not support the group if $\sigma \leq \frac{k-t_L}{t_H-t_L}$.

Separating Equilibrium. Finally, there exists a separating equilibrium. In a separating equilibrium, the high-salience group and low-salience group pursue different actions. In the separating equilibrium, the high-salience group protests, and the low-salience group does not protest; the legislator supports the group after seeing protest and never supports the group after seeing no protest. This equilibrium exists if $\mu = 0$, $\sigma = 1$, and $t_H \geq C_r \geq t_L$.

Once again, the legislator's best response to the group's strategy depends on the expected utility of supporting the group relative to the expected utility of not supporting the group. After seeing protest, if $\sigma > \frac{k-t_L}{t_H-t_L}$, then L chooses a $= 1$, but if $\sigma < \frac{k-t_L}{t_H-t_L}$, then L chooses a $= 0$. Similarly, after not seeing protest, if $\mu > \frac{k-t_L}{t_H-t_L}$, then L chooses a $= 1$, but if $\mu < \frac{k-t_L}{t_H-t_L}$, then L chooses a $= 0$.

The legislator's posterior beliefs are established using Bayes's rule.

$$\sigma = P(t_H|p=1) = \frac{P(p=1|t_H)P(t_H)}{P(p=1|t_H)P(t_H) + P(p=1|t_L)P(t_L)}$$

$$= \frac{1*\lambda}{1*\lambda + 0(1-\lambda)}$$

$$\sigma = 1$$

$$\mu = P(t_H|p=0) = \frac{P(p=0|t_H)P(t_H)}{P(p=0|t_H)P(t_H) + P(p=0|t_L)P(t_L)}$$

$$= \frac{0*\lambda}{0*\lambda + 1*(1-\lambda)}$$

$$\mu = 0$$

Updating the legislator's beliefs reveals that the legislator's best response is to choose a $= 1$ after seeing protest and a $= 0$ after not seeing protest. This strategy is sustained in equilibrium. The group has no incentive to deviate from its strategy if $t_H \geq C_r \geq t_L$, where $t_H > t_L > 0$.

$$EU_{G_H}(p=1) \geq EU_{G_H}(p=0)$$

$$1 - \frac{C_r}{t_H} \geq 0$$

$$t_H \geq C_r$$

$$EUG_L(p = 0) \geq EUG_L(p = 1)$$
$$0 \geq 1 - \frac{C_r}{t_L}$$
$$C_r \geq t_L$$

8.2 CHAPTER 3 APPENDIX

Legislators and Legislative Staffers Survey Questionnaire

Q1 – Consent

Welcome to the research study!

Thank you for agreeing to participate in this research survey, which seeks to understand the perceptions of elected officials. If you agree to participate in this study, you will be presented with information relevant to representation and asked to answer some questions about it.

Research records will be kept confidential to the extent allowed by law. The names and contact information of elected officials and their staffers will be collected for contact purposes only. They will not be associated with any of the survey responses and will not be used in any published materials. Only LaGina Gause, the principal investigator will have access to the data collected in this research survey.

Your participation in this research is voluntary. You have the right to withdraw at any point during the study, for any reason, and without any prejudice. If you want additional information or have questions or research-related problems, please e-mail LaGina Gause, the principal investigator and researcher at UCSD, at lgause@ucsd.edu.

By clicking the button below, you acknowledge that your participation in the study is voluntary, you are 18 years of age, and that you are aware that you may choose to terminate your participation in the study at any time and for any reason.

o   I consent, begin the study (1)

o   I do not consent, I do not wish to participate (2)

If consent, Q2 – What is your gender?

o   Male (1)

o   Female (2)

Q3 – Are you of Spanish, Hispanic, or Latino origin?

o   Yes (1)

o   None of these (2)

Q4 – Which of the following races do you consider yourself to be? (select all that apply)

o   White or Caucasian (1)
o   Black or African American (2)
o   American Indian or Alaska Native (3)
o   Asian (4)
o   Native Hawaiian or Pacific Islander (5)
o   Other (specify) _____ (6)

Q5 – Which political party are you registered with, if any?

o   Republican Party (1)
o   Democratic Party (2)
o   None or independent (3)
o   Other (specify) _____ (4)

If Republican, Q6 – Would you call yourself a strong Republican or a not very strong Republican?

o   Strong (1)
o   Not very strong (2)

If Democrat, Q7 – Would you call yourself a strong Democrat or a not very strong Democrat?

o   Strong (1)
o   Not very strong (2)

Q8 – Where would you place yourself on this scale on which the political views that people might hold?

o   Extremely liberal (1)
o   Liberal (2)
o   Slightly liberal (3)
o   Moderate; middle of the road (4)
o   Slightly conservative (5)
o   Conservative (6)
o   Extremely conservative (7)

Q9 – Are you an elected official?

o   Yes (1)
o   No (2)

If an elected official, Q10 – In which state do you currently serve as an elected official?

o   Alabama (1)
o   Alaska (2)
o   Arizona (3)
o   Arkansas (4)
o   California (5)
o   Colorado (6)
o   Connecticut (7)
o   Delaware (8)
o   District of Columbia (9)
o   Florida (10)
o   Georgia (11)
o   Hawaii (12)
o   Idaho (13)
o   Illinois (14)
o   Indiana (15)
o   Iowa (16)
o   Kansas (17)
o   Kentucky (18)
o   Louisiana (19)
o   Maine (20)
o   Maryland (21)
o   Massachusetts (22)
o   Michigan (23)
o   Minnesota (24)
o   Mississippi (25)
o   Missouri (26)
o   Montana (27)
o   Nebraska (28)
o   Nevada (29)
o   New Hampshire (30)
o   New Jersey (31)
o   New Mexico (32)
o   New York (33)
o   North Carolina (34)
o   North Dakota (35)
o   Ohio (36)
o   Oklahoma (37)

- Oregon (38)
- Pennsylvania (39)
- Puerto Rico (40)
- Rhode Island (41)
- South Carolina (42)
- South Dakota (43)
- Tennessee (44)
- Texas (45)
- Utah (46)
- Vermont (47)
- Virginia (48)
- Washington (49)
- West Virginia (50)
- Wisconsin (51)
- Wyoming (52)
- I do not reside in the United States (53)

If an elected official, Q11 – Which elected office do you occupy?

- U.S. Senate (1)
- U.S. House of Representatives (3)
- Governor (2)
- State Senate, or upper house (5)
- State House of Representatives, Assembly, or House of Delegates (6)
- Mayor (7)
- City Council (9)
- Other, please specify: _____ (8)

If an elected official, Q12 – Are you currently a staff member in the office of an elected official?

- Yes (1)
- No (2)

If currently a staff member in the office of an elected official, Q13 – In which state do you currently work as a staff member in the office of an elected official?

- Alabama (1)
- Alaska (2)
- Arizona (3)
- Arkansas (4)

- California (5)
- Colorado (6)
- Connecticut (7)
- Delaware (8)
- District of Columbia (9)
- Florida (10)
- Georgia (11)
- Hawaii (12)
- Idaho (13)
- Illinois (14)
- Indiana (15)
- Iowa (16)
- Kansas (17)
- Kentucky (18)
- Louisiana (19)
- Maine (20)
- Maryland (21)
- Massachusetts (22)
- Michigan (23)
- Minnesota (24)
- Mississippi (25)
- Missouri (26)
- Montana (27)
- Nebraska (28)
- Nevada (29)
- New Hampshire (30)
- New Jersey (31)
- New Mexico (32)
- New York (33)
- North Carolina (34)
- North Dakota (35)
- Ohio (36)
- Oklahoma (37)
- Oregon (38)
- Pennsylvania (39)
- Puerto Rico (40)
- Rhode Island (41)
- South Carolina (42)
- South Dakota (43)
- Tennessee (44)

o   Texas (45)
o   Utah (46)
o   Vermont (47)
o   Virginia (48)
o   Washington (49)
o   West Virginia (50)
o   Wisconsin (51)
o   Wyoming (52)
o   I do not reside in the United States (53)

If currently a staff member in the office of an elected official, Q14 – In which elected office are you a staff member?

o   U.S. Senate (1)
o   U.S. House of Representatives (3)
o   Governor (2)
o   State Senate, or upper house (5)
o   State House of Representatives, Assembly, or House of Delegates (6)
o   Mayor (7)
o   City Council (9)
o   Other, please specify: _____ (8)

If currently a staff member in the office of an elected official, Q15 – Which position do you occupy?

o   Chief of staff (1)
o   Senior staff member (2)
o   Legislative assistant (3)
o   Administrative assistant (6)
o   Intern (4)
o   Other, please specify _____ (5)

If NOT currently a staff member in the office of an elected official, Q16 – Have you ever been an elected official or did you ever work for an elected official?

o   Yes (1)
o   No (2)

If they had ever been an elected official or worked for an elected official, Q17 – When did you most recently serve as an elected official or as a staff member of an elected official?

o   Within the last year (1)
o   1–3 years ago (2)
o   4–5 years ago (3)
o   6–10 years ago (4)
o   11–15 years ago (5)
o   More than 16 years ago (6)

If they had ever been an elected official or worked for an elected official, Q18 – In which state did you work as an elected official or as a staff member in the office of an elected official?

o   Alabama (1)
o   Alaska (2)
o   Arizona (3)
o   Arkansas (4)
o   California (5)
o   Colorado (6)
o   Connecticut (7)
o   Delaware (8)
o   District of Columbia (9)
o   Florida (10)
o   Georgia (11)
o   Hawaii (12)
o   Idaho (13)
o   Illinois (14)
o   Indiana (15)
o   Iowa (16)
o   Kansas (17)
o   Kentucky (18)
o   Louisiana (19)
o   Maine (20)
o   Maryland (21)
o   Massachusetts (22)
o   Michigan (23)
o   Minnesota (24)
o   Mississippi (25)
o   Missouri (26)
o   Montana (27)
o   Nebraska (28)
o   Nevada (29)
o   New Hampshire (30)

o   New Jersey (31)
o   New Mexico (32)
o   New York (33)
o   North Carolina (34)
o   North Dakota (35)
o   Ohio (36)
o   Oklahoma (37)
o   Oregon (38)
o   Pennsylvania (39)
o   Puerto Rico (40)
o   Rhode Island (41)
o   South Carolina (42)
o   South Dakota (43)
o   Tennessee (44)
o   Texas (45)
o   Utah (46)
o   Vermont (47)
o   Virginia (48)
o   Washington (49)
o   West Virginia (50)
o   Wisconsin (51)
o   Wyoming (52)
o   I do not reside in the United States (53)

If they had ever been an elected official or worked for an elected official, **Q19** – Select the option that best defines the position you once held.

o   Elected official (1)
o   Staff member of an elected official (2)
o   Other, please specify _____ (3)

If they had ever been an elected official, **Q20** – Which elected office did you occupy?

o   U.S. Senate (1)
o   U.S. House of Representatives (3)
o   Governor (2)
o   State Senate, or upper house (5)
o   State House of Representatives, Assembly, or House of Delegates (6)
o   Mayor (7)

o   City Council (9)
o   Other, please specify: _____ (8)

If they had been a staff member of an elected official, Q21 – Which elected office did the elected official you worked for occupy?

o   U.S. Senate (1)
o   U.S. House of Representatives (3)
o   Governor (2)
o   State Senate, or upper house (5)
o   State House of Representatives, Assembly, or House of Delegates (6)
o   Mayor (7)
o   City Council (9)
o   Other, please specify: _____ (8)

If they had another position, Q22 – You indicated that you were not an elected official nor were you a staff member of an elected official. What was your position or the position of the elected official that you worked for?

_____

If not currently an elected official or staff member, Q23 – What is your current position?

_____

Q24 – I am now going to ask you a series of questions about your perceptions of constituents' efforts to participate in politics. (Q25–29 presented in random order.)

Q25 – Think about the difficulties people face when participating politically. Move the slider toward the group (*Men or Women*) that you believe encounters greater difficulty when engaging in each form of political participation listed below. Moving the slider more to the right (or left) indicates stronger agreement with the statement on the right (or left).
***Forms of participation presented randomly.**

MEN face more difficulties than WOMEN				WOMEN face more difficulties than MEN	Not applicable
1	2	3	4	5	

Voting

Contributing financially to campaigns

Contacting their legislators

Protesting

Lobbying

Running for office

Voicing their opinions

Q26 – Think about the difficulties people face when participating politically. Move the slider toward the group (*Youth or Adults*) that you believe encounters greater difficulty when engaging in each form of political participation listed below. Moving the slider more to the right (or left) indicates stronger agreement with the statement on the right (or left).
*Forms of participation presented randomly.

YOUTH face more difficulties than ADULTS				ADULTS face more difficulties than YOUTH	Not applicable
1	2	3	4	5	

Voting

Contributing financially to campaigns

Contacting their legislators

Protesting

Lobbying

Running for office

Voicing their opinions

Q27 – Think about the difficulties people face when participating politically. Move the slider toward the group (*White people or Black people*) that you believe encounters greater difficulty when engaging in each form of political participation listed below. Moving the slider more to the right (or left) indicates stronger agreement with the statement on the right (or left).

*Forms of participation presented randomly.

WHITE PEOPLE face more difficulties than BLACK PEOPLE				BLACK PEOPLE face more difficulties than WHITE PEOPLE	Not applicable
1	2	3	4	5	

Voting

Contributing financially to campaigns

Contacting their legislators

Protesting

Lobbying

Running for office

Voicing their opinions

Q28 – Think about the difficulties people face when participating politically. Move the slider toward the group (*Organizations or Individuals*) that you believe encounters greater difficulty when engaging in each form of political participation listed below. Moving the slider more to the right (or left) indicates stronger agreement with the statement on the right (or left).

*Forms of participation presented randomly.

ORGANIZATIONS face more difficulties than INDIVIDUALS				INDIVIDUALS face more difficulties than ORGANIZATIONS	Not applicable
1	2	3	4	5	

Voting

Contributing financially to campaigns

Contacting their legislators

Protesting

Lobbying

Running for office

Voicing their opinions

Q29 – Think about the difficulties people face when participating politically. Move the slider toward the group (*Poor people or Rich people*) that you believe encounters greater difficulty when engaging in each form of political participation listed below. Moving the slider more to the right (or left) indicates stronger agreement with the statement on the right (or left).

*Forms of participation presented randomly.

POOR PEOPLE face more difficulties than RICH PEOPLE				RICH PEOPLE face more difficulties than POOR PEOPLE	Not applicable
1	2	3	4	5	

Voting

Contributing financially to campaigns

Contacting their legislators

Protesting

Lobbying

Running for office

Voicing their opinions

Q30 – Below is a list of names, organizations, and concepts. For each, please indicate your impression of that person, organization, or concept as of today. If you have no opinion or never heard of them, please select that option.
*Names presented randomly.

	Very Favorable	Somewhat Favorable	Somewhat Unfavorable	Very Unfavorable	Never heard of this person, organization, or concept	Heard of this person, organization or concept, but unsure
Labor unions	○	○	○	○	○	○
Pro-life organizations	○	○	○	○	○	○
Dreamers	○	○	○	○	○	○
Environmental protection organizations	○	○	○	○	○	○
Pro-choice organizations	○	○	○	○	○	○
United We Dream	○	○	○	○	○	○
Pro-life advocates	○	○	○	○	○	○
Environmentalists	○	○	○	○	○	○
Pro-choice advocates	○	○	○	○	○	○
Teachers	○	○	○	○	○	○
Police officers	○	○	○	○	○	○

Q31 – Below is a list of names, organizations, and concepts. For each, please indicate your impression of that person, organization, or concept as of today. If you have no opinion or never heard of them, please select that option.
*Names presented randomly.

	Very Favorable	Somewhat Favorable	Somewhat Unfavorable	Very Unfavorable	Never heard of this person, organization, or concept	Heard of this person, organization or concept, but unsure
Donald Trump	○	○	○	○	○	○
Me Too movement	○	○	○	○	○	○
The National Rifle Association (NRA)	○	○	○	○	○	○
Black Lives Matter (BLM) movement	○	○	○	○	○	○
Hillary Clinton	○	○	○	○	○	○
Bernie Sanders	○	○	○	○	○	○
Republican Party	○	○	○	○	○	○
Feminists	○	○	○	○	○	○
Gun rights supporters	○	○	○	○	○	○
Black Lives Matter supporters	○	○	○	○	○	○
Democratic Party	○	○	○	○	○	○

Q32 – There are many different ways that constituents can communicate to their legislators. Move the slider to indicate how *legitimate* you believe each form of participation is. Higher values indicate that you believe the participation is a more legitimate form of participation. *Participation types presented randomly.

Not legitimate	Not very legitimate	Somewhat legitimate	Very legitimate	Extremely legitimate	Not applicable

Voting

Volunteering for campaigns

Contacting their legislators

Protesting

Lobbying

Running for office

Voicing their opinions

Q33 – Which forms of participation are *likely to receive a positive response* from you? *Forms of participation presented randomly.

Extremely unlikely	Moderately unlikely	Somewhat unlikely	Neither likely nor unlikely	Slightly likely	Moderately likely	Extremely likely

Lobbying

Financial contributions

Civil disobedience

Petition

March or rally

Calls, emails, or letters

Social media posts

If Elected Official, Q34–44

Q34 – Now we'd like to ask you a series of questions about *collective action*, which includes anything from people calling their legislators or signing petitions to boycotts, marches, and acts of civil disobedience. Other examples include letter-writing campaigns, advocacy, strikes, media appeals, marches, and riots. These don't have to target an elected official.

Q35 – For each of the following activities, how often does collective action influence your behavior? *Activities presented randomly.

	Always	Most of the time	About half of the time	Sometimes	Never
Bill (co)sponsorship	○	○	○	○	○
Vote on legislation or bill	○	○	○	○	○
Public statement or speech	○	○	○	○	○
Join or engage in collective action	○	○	○	○	○

Other, please specify: _____

Q36 – When (or why) is collective action more likely to influence your behavior?

_____

_____

_____

_____

Q37 – Discuss any memorable collective action event(s).

_____

_____

_____

_____

Q38 – Why were those collective action events memorable?

_____

_____

_____

_____

Q39 – How did you respond to the collective action events?

_____

_____

_____

_____

Q40 – What things make you more likely to respond to collective action?

_____

_____

_____

_____

Q41 – Are you ever concerned or conflicted about whether or how to respond to collective action?

o   Never (1)
o   Sometimes (2)
o   About half the time (3)
o   Most of the time (4)
o   Always (5)

If concerned or conflicted about whether or how to respond to collective action, Q42 – Why are you concerned or conflicted about whether or how to respond to collective action?

_____

_____

_____

_____

If NOT concerned or conflicted about whether or how to respond to collective action, Q43 – Why are you NOT concerned or conflicted about whether or how to respond to collective action?

_____

_____

_____

_____

Q44 – Is there any other information that you would like to share? If so, enter that information below.

_____

_____

_____

_____

If Former Elected Official, Q45–55

Q45 – Now we'd like to ask you a series of questions about collective action, which includes anything from people calling their legislators or signing petitions to boycotts, marches, and acts of civil disobedience. Other examples include letter-writing campaigns, advocacy, strikes, media appeals, marches, and riots. These don't have to target an elected official.

Q46 – For each of the following activities, how often did collective action influence your behavior? *Activities presented randomly.

	Always	Most of the time	About half of the time	Sometimes	Never
Bill (co)sponsorship	○	○	○	○	○
Vote on legislation or bill	○	○	○	○	○
Public statement or speech	○	○	○	○	○
Join or engage in collective action	○	○	○	○	○

Other, please specify: _____

Q47 – When (or why) was collective action more likely to influence your behavior?

_____

_____

_____

_____

Q48 – Discuss any memorable collective action event(s).

_____
_____
_____
_____

Q49 – Why were those collective action events memorable?

_____
_____
_____
_____

Q50 – How did you respond to the collective action events?

_____
_____
_____
_____

Q51– What things make you more likely to respond to collective action?

_____
_____
_____
_____

Q52 – Were you ever concerned or conflicted about whether or how to respond to collective action?

o   Never (1)
o   Sometimes (2)
o   About half the time (3)
o   Most of the time (4)
o   Always (5)

If concerned or conflicted about whether or how to respond to collective action, Q53 – Why were you concerned or conflicted about whether or how to respond to collective action?

_____
_____
_____
_____

If NOT concerned or conflicted about whether or how to respond to collective action, Q54 – Why were you NOT concerned or conflicted about whether or how to respond to collective action?

_____

_____

_____

_____

Q55 – Is there any other information that you would like to share? If so, enter that information below.

_____

_____

_____

_____

If Current Staffer, Q56–66

Q56 – Now we'd like to ask you a series of questions about *collective action*, which includes anything from people calling their legislators or signing petitions to boycotts, marches, and acts of civil disobedience. Other examples include letter-writing campaigns, advocacy, strikes, media appeals, marches, and riots. These don't have to target an elected official.

Q57 – For each of the following activities, how often does collective action influence the behavior of the elected official you work for? *Activities presented randomly.

	Always	Most of the time	About half of the time	Sometimes	Never
Bill (co)sponsorship	○	○	○	○	○
Vote on legislation or bill	○	○	○	○	○
Public statement or speech	○	○	○	○	○
Join or engage in collective action	○	○	○	○	○

Other, please specify: _____

Q58 – When (or why) is collective action more likely to influence the behavior of the elected official you work for?

_____

_____

_____

_____

Q59 – Discuss any memorable collective action event(s).

_____

_____

_____

_____

Q60 – Why were those collective action events memorable?

_____

_____

_____

_____

Q61 – How did your elected office respond to the collective action events?

_____

_____

_____

_____

Q62 – What things make your elected office more likely to respond to collective action?

_____

_____

_____

_____

Q63 – Are you ever concerned or conflicted about whether or how your elected office should respond to collective action?

o   Never (1)
o   Sometimes (2)

o   About half the time (3)
o   Most of the time (4)
o   Always (5)

If concerned or conflicted about whether or how to respond to collective action, Q64 – Why are you concerned or conflicted about whether or how your elected office should respond to collective action?

_____
_____
_____
_____

If NOT concerned or conflicted about whether or how to respond to collective action, Q65 – Why are you NOT concerned or conflicted about whether or how your elected office should respond to collective action?

_____
_____
_____
_____

Q66 – Is there any other information that you would like to share? If so, enter that information below.

_____
_____
_____
_____

If Former Staffer, Q67–77

Q67 – Now we'd like to ask you a series of questions about collective action, which includes anything from people calling their legislators or signing petitions to boycotts, marches, and acts of civil disobedience. Other examples include letter-writing campaigns, advocacy, strikes, media appeals, marches, and riots. These don't have to target an elected official.

Q68 – For each of the following activities, how often does collective action influence the behavior of the elected official you worked for? *Activities presented randomly.

	Always	Most of the time	About half of the time	Sometimes	Never
Bill (co)sponsorship	○	○	○	○	○
Vote on legislation or bill	○	○	○	○	○
Public statement or speech	○	○	○	○	○
Join or engage in collective action	○	○	○	○	○

Other, please specify: _____

Q69 – When (or why) is collective action more likely to influence the behavior of the elected official you work for?

_____
_____
_____
_____

Q70 – Discuss any memorable collective action event(s).

_____
_____
_____
_____

Q71 – Why were those collective action events memorable?

_____
_____
_____
_____

Q72 – How did your elected office respond to the collective action events?

_____
_____
_____
_____

Q73 – What things made your elected office more likely to respond to collective action?

_____

_____

_____

_____

Q74 – Were you ever concerned or conflicted about whether or how your elected office should respond to collective action?

o   Never (1)
o   Sometimes (2)
o   About half the time (3)
o   Most of the time (4)
o   Always (5)

If concerned or conflicted about whether or how to respond to collective action, Q75 – Why were you concerned or conflicted about whether or how your elected office should respond to collective action?

_____

_____

_____

_____

If NOT concerned or conflicted about whether or how to respond to collective action, Q76 – Why were you NOT concerned or conflicted about whether or how your elected office should respond to collective action?

_____

_____

_____

_____

Q77 – Is there any other information that you would like to share? If so, enter that information below.

_____

_____

_____

_____

8.3 CHAPTER 4 APPENDIX

American National Election Study (ANES) Survey Questions

Feminist or Women's Movement Issues

1992 ANES

VAR 923801: Recently there has been a lot of talk about women's rights. Some people feel that women should have an equal role with men in running business, industry, and government. Others feel that women's place is in the home.

1994 ANES

VAR 940928: Recently there has been a lot of talk about women's rights. Some people feel that women should have an equal role with men in running business, industry, and government. Others feel that women's place is in the home.

1996 ANES

VAR 960543: Recently there has been a lot of talk about women's rights. Some people feel that women should have an equal role with men in running business, industry, and government. Others feel that women's place is in the home.

LGBT Civil Rights Issues

1992 ANES

VAR 925923: Do you favor or oppose laws to protect homosexuals against job discrimination?
VAR 925925: Do you think homosexuals should be allowed to serve in the United States Armed Forces or don't you think so?

1994 ANES

No LGBT Civil Rights issue area questions.

1996 ANES

VAR 961193: Do you favor or oppose laws to protect homosexuals against job discrimination?
VAR 961195: Do you think homosexuals should be allowed to serve in the United States Armed Forces or don't you think so?

Senior Civil Rights Issues

1992 ANES

VAR 923811: Here are some more questions about federal spending. If you had a say in making up the federal budget this year, for which of the following programs would you like to see spending increased and for which would you like to see spending decreased . . . Social Security

1994 ANES

VAR 940819: If you had a say in making up the federal budget this year, for which of the following programs would you like to see spending increased and for which would you like to see spending decreased . . . Social Security

1996 ANES

VAR 960560: Here are some more questions about federal spending. If you had a say in making up the federal budget this year, for which of the following programs would you like to see spending increased and for which would you like to see spending decreased . . . Social Security

Abortion Issue Area

1992 ANES

VAR 923732: There has been some discussion about abortion during recent years. Which one of the opinions on this page best agrees with your view?

1. By law, abortion should never be permitted.
2. The law should permit abortion <u>only</u> in case of rape, incest or when the woman's life is in danger.
3. The law should permit abortion for reasons <u>other than</u> rape, incest, or danger to the woman's life, but only after the need for the abortion has been clearly established.
4. By law, a woman should always be able to obtain an abortion as a matter of personal choice.
7. Other, specify:
8. Don't know

1994 ANES

VAR 941014: There has been some discussion about abortion during recent years. Which one of the opinions on this page best agrees with your view?

1. By law, abortion should never be permitted.
2. The law should permit abortion <u>only</u> in case of rape, incest or when the woman's life is in danger.

3. The law should permit abortion for reasons <u>other than</u> rape, incest, or danger to the woman's life, but only after the need for the abortion has been clearly established.
4. By law, a woman should always be able to obtain an abortion as a matter of personal choice.
7. Other, specify:
8. Don't know

1996 ANES

VAR 960503: There has been some discussion about abortion during recent years. Which one of the opinions on this page best agrees with your view?

1. By law, abortion should never be permitted.
2. The law should permit abortion <u>only</u> in case of rape, incest or when the woman's life is in <u>danger</u>.
3. The law should permit abortion for reasons <u>other than</u> rape, incest, or danger to the woman's life, but only after the need for the abortion has been clearly established.
4. By law, a woman should always be able to obtain an abortion as a matter of personal choice.
7. Other, specify:
8. Don't know

African American Civil Rights Issues

1992 ANES

VAR 923724: Some people feel that the government should make every effort to improve the social and economic position of blacks. Others feel that the government should not make any effort to help blacks because they should help themselves.
VAR 925935: Some people say that because of past discrimination, blacks should be given preference in hiring and promotion. Others say that such preference in hiring and promotion of blacks is wrong because it gives blacks advantages they haven't earned. What about your opinion – are you <u>for</u> or <u>against</u> preferential hiring and promotion of blacks?

1994 ANES

VAR 940936: Some people feel that the government should make every effort to improve the social and economic position of blacks. Others feel that the government should not make any effort to help blacks because they should help themselves. VAR 941001: Some people say that because of past discrimination, blacks should be given preference in hiring and promotion. Others say that such preference in hiring and promotion of blacks is wrong because it gives blacks advantages they haven't earned. What about your opinion – are you <u>for</u> or <u>against</u> preferential hiring and promotion of blacks?

1996 ANES

VAR 960487: Some people feel that the government should make every effort to improve the social and economic position of blacks. Others feel that the government should not make any effort to help blacks because they should help themselves. VAR 961208: Some people say that because of past discrimination, blacks should be given preference in hiring and promotion. Others say that such preference in hiring and promotion of blacks is wrong because it gives blacks advantages they haven't earned. What about your opinion – are you <u>for</u> or <u>against</u> preferential hiring and promotion of blacks?

Pan-Latino, Asian American, Mexican American Civil Rights Issues

1992 ANES

VAR 926235: Do you think the number of immigrants from foreign countries who are permitted to come to the United States to live should be 1. Increased a lot, . . .

VAR 926242: Do you think that immigrants who come to the U.S. should be eligible as soon as they come here for government services such as Medicaid, Food Stamps, Welfare, or should they have to be here a year or more?

1994 ANES

VAR 941016: Do you think the number of immigrants from foreign countries who are permitted to come to the United States to live should be 1. Increased a lot, . . .

1996 ANES

VAR 961325: Do you think the number of immigrants from foreign countries who are permitted to come to the United States to live should be 1. Increased a lot, . . .

VAR 961326: Do you think that immigrants who come to the U.S. should be eligible as soon as they come here for government services such as Medicaid, Food Stamps, Welfare, or should they have to be here a year or more?

Social Issues

1992 ANES

VAR 923701: Some people think the government should provide fewer services, even in areas such as health and education in order to reduce spending. Suppose these people are at one end of the scale at point 1. Other people feel it is important for the government to provide many more services even if it means an increase in spending.

VAR 923718: Some people feel the government in Washington should see to it that every person has a job and a good standard of living. Others think government should just let each person get ahead on their own .... Where would you place yourself on this scale, or haven't you thought much about this?

VAR 923725: If you had a say in making up the federal budget this year, for which of the following programs would you like to see spending increased and for which would you like to see spending decreased .... Food stamps

VAR 923726: If you had a say in making up the federal budget this year, for which of the following programs would you like to see spending increased and for which would you like to see spending decreased .... Welfare programs

VAR 926115: The world is always changing and we should adjust our view of moral behavior to those changes.

VAR 926116: We should be more tolerant of people who choose to live according to their own moral standards even if they are very different from our own.

VAR 926117: This country would have many fewer problems if there were more emphasis on traditional family ties.

VAR 926118: The newer lifestyles are contributing to the breakdown of our society.

1994 ANES

VAR 940940: Some people think the government should provide fewer services, even in areas such as health and education in order to reduce spending. Suppose these people are at one end of the scale at point 1. Other people feel it is important for the government to provide many more services even if it means an increase in spending.

VAR 940930: Some people feel the government in Washington should see to it that every person has a job and a good standard of living. Others think government should just let each person get ahead on their own .... Where would you place yourself on this scale, or haven't you thought much about this?

VAR 940822: If you had a say in making up the federal budget this year, for which of the following programs would you like to see spending increased and for which would you like to see spending decreased .... Food stamps

VAR 940820: If you had a say in making up the federal budget this year, for which of the following programs would you like to see spending increased and for which would you like to see spending decreased .... Welfare programs

VAR 941030: The world is always changing and we should adjust our view of moral behavior to those changes.

VAR 941032: We should be more tolerant of people who choose to live according to their own moral standards even if they are very different from our own.

VAR 941031: This country would have many fewer problems if there were more emphasis on traditional family ties.

VAR 941029: The newer lifestyles are contributing to the breakdown of our society.

1996 ANES

VAR 960450: Some people think the government should provide fewer services, even in areas such as health and education in order to reduce spending. Suppose these people are at one end of the scale at point 1. Other people feel it is important for the government to provide many more services even if it means an increase in spending.

VAR 960483: Some people feel the government in Washington should see to it that every person has a job and a good standard of living. Others think government should just let each person get ahead on their own .... Where would you place yourself on this scale, or haven't you thought much about this?

VAR 960496: If you had a say in making up the federal budget this year, for which of the following programs would you like to see spending increased and for which would you like to see spending decreased .... Food stamps

VAR 960497: If you had a say in making up the federal budget this year, for which of the following programs would you like to see spending increased and for which would you like to see spending decreased .... Welfare programs

VAR 961248: The world is always changing and we should adjust our view of moral behavior to those changes.

VAR 961250: We should be more tolerant of people who choose to live according to their own moral standards even if they are very different from our own.

VAR 961249: This country would have many fewer problems if there were more emphasis on traditional family ties.

VAR 961247: The newer lifestyles are contributing to the breakdown of our society.

General Civil Rights, Minority Issues, Civil Liberties

1992 ANES

VAR 926024: Our society should do whatever is necessary to make sure that everyone has an equal opportunity to succeed.

VAR 926025: We have gone too far in pushing equal rights in this country.

VAR 926026: This country would be better off if we worried less about how equal people are.

VAR 926027: It is not really that big a problem if some people have more of a chance in life than others.

VAR 926028: If people were treated more equally in this country we would have many fewer problems.

VAR 926029: One of the big problems in this country is that we don't give everyone an equal chance

1994 ANES

VAR 940914: Our society should do whatever is necessary to make sure that everyone has an equal opportunity to succeed.

VAR 940915: We have gone too far in pushing equal rights in this country.

VAR 940917: This country would be better off if we worried less about how equal people are.

VAR 940918: It is not really that big a problem if some people have more of a chance in life than others.

VAR 940919: If people were treated more equally in this country we would have many fewer problems.

VAR 940916: One of the big problems in this country is that we don't give everyone an equal chance

1996 ANES

VAR 961229: Our society should do whatever is necessary to make sure that everyone has an equal opportunity to succeed.

VAR 961230: We have gone too far in pushing equal rights in this country.

VAR 961232: This country would be better off if we worried less about how equal people are.

VAR 961233: It is not really that big a problem if some people have more of a chance in life than others.

VAR 961234: If people were treated more equally in this country we would have many fewer problems.

VAR 961231: One of the big problems in this country is that we don't give everyone an equal chance

Appendices

Tables

TABLE 8.1 *Constituents' preferences and legislative support (Liberal only)*

	Model I	Model II	Model III	Model IV	Model V	Model VI
Protest	0.293***					
	(0.0546)					
Black Protesters		2.357***				
		(0.302)				
Latino Protesters			2.720***			
			(0.438)			
Asian Descendant Protesters				3.889**		
				(1.518)		
Low-Income Protesters					1.699***	
					(0.552)	
No Formal Interest Group						0.165*
						(0.0910)
Public Salience	−0.00430	−0.743	−0.671	3.253	−0.640*	−0.704**
	(0.105)	(0.805)	(1.514)	(3.589)	(0.335)	(0.337)
Education	0.172	−2.377**	−2.794*	−17.07**	−0.259	−0.252
	(0.109)	(0.945)	(1.453)	(7.285)	(0.325)	(0.325)
Democratic Representative	0.530***	0.337	−0.160	−1.668	0.422***	0.437***
	(0.0315)	(0.406)	(0.647)	(1.609)	(0.149)	(0.150)
Length of Service	−0.0949	1.047	−0.458	5.476	0.130	0.0678
	(0.0897)	(1.125)	(1.908)	(4.854)	(0.412)	(0.415)
Democratic Vote Margin	0.350***	0.171	−0.484	−7.897	0.297	0.360
	(0.111)	(1.462)	(2.253)	(5.772)	(0.478)	(0.478)
Black Representative	−0.0944	−1.548***	−2.632***	−5.541**	−0.464**	−0.477**
	(0.0595)	(0.576)	(0.963)	(2.635)	(0.202)	(0.203)
Latino Representative	0.129	−1.119	−2.620**	−5.099*	−0.297	−0.318
	(0.0828)	(0.701)	(1.105)	(3.009)	(0.252)	(0.253)
Female Representative	0.158***	0.0268	0.595	0.607	0.202	0.196
	(0.0498)	(0.466)	(0.800)	(1.801)	(0.174)	(0.174)
Constant	−0.869***	−0.318	−0.171	7.999*	−0.320	−0.439
	(0.0886)	(1.049)	(1.673)	(4.779)	(0.355)	(0.361)
Congress Year Dummies	Yes	Yes	Yes	Yes	Yes	Yes
Variance Component Congressional District Level	0.0449***	1.105**	3.820**	26.79	0.177*	0.176*
	(0.00775)	(0.535)	(1.791)	(25.76)	(0.0919)	(0.0924)
Observations	29882	472	294	176	2301	2285
Groups	453	94	70	64	213	212
Log likelihood	−20262.4	−265.5	−138.6	−63.53	−1558.4	−1553.7
LR test Chi^2	69.51***	16.58***	33.05***	33.05***	10.41***	10.26***

For each model, the dependent variable, legislative support, is binary taking on a value of 0 or 1. In Model 1, non-protesting districts are the omitted category. In Models II through VII, high-resource protesters are the omitted category. All other variables are coded 0 to 1. Coefficients are Log Odds. Standard errors in parentheses. *$p < 0.10$, **$p < 0.05$, ***$p < 0.01$

TABLE 8.2 *Resources, salience (size) and legislative support*

	Model I	Model II	Model III	Model IV	Model V
Resources					
Black Protesters	2.201*** (0.425)				
Latino Protesters		2.625 (2.461)			
Asian Descendant Protesters			4.247* (1.732)		
Low-Income Participants				0.842 (0.616)	
No Organized Interest Group					0.0583 (0.195)
Salience (Size)					
Group	−0.886 (0.484)	−1.228 (0.690)	0.670 (1.027)	0.323* (0.129)	0.263 (0.216)
Large	−0.370 (0.386)	1.045 (2.453)	0 (.)	0.437** (0.153)	0.431 (0.232)
Hundreds	−1.136 (0.709)	−0.707 (0.984)	1.661 (1.752)	0.317* (0.129)	0.238 (0.215)
Thousands	0 (.)	−2.388 (2.512)	0 (.)	−0.256 (0.191)	−2.495*** (0.551)
Tens of Thousands	0 (.)	0 (.)	0 (.)	−1.959*** (0.408)	−1.529* (0.606)
Resources X Salience (Size)					
Black Protesters × Group	−0.00912 (0.658)				

TABLE 8.2 *(Continued)*

Black Protesters × Hundreds	0.982 (0.802)				
Latino Protesters × Group		0.292 (2.510)			
Latino Protesters × Hundreds		3.299 (2.705)			
No Organized Interest Group × Group					0.168 (0.265)
No Organized Interest Group × Large					0.152 (0.315)
No Organized Interest Group × Hundreds					0.0643 (0.268)
No Organized Interest Group × Thousands					2.969*** (0.595)
No Organized Interest Group × Tens of Thousands					-0.760 (0.818)
Constant	-0.0107 (1.089)	0.920 (2.119)	6.060 (5.040)	-0.574 (0.385)	-0.692 (0.415)
Controls	Yes	Yes	Yes	Yes	Yes
Congress Year Dummies	Yes	Yes	Yes	Yes	Yes
Variance Component Congressional District Level	1.122* (0.558)	6.722* (3.211)	36.37 (48.80)	0.300* (0.132)	0.276* (0.130)
Observations	458	293	173	2212	2208
Log likelihood	-258.2	-121.4	-62.08	-1473.7	-1445.8

The dependent variable, legislative support, is binary taking on a value of 0 or 1. Coefficients are Log Odds. All independent variables are coded 0 to 1. Standard errors in parentheses. $*p < 0.05$, $**p < 0.01$, $***p < 0.001$

TABLE 8.3 *Resources, salience (media coverage) and legislative support*

	Model I	Model II	Model III	Model IV	Model V
Resources					
Black Protesters	2.204***				
	(0.334)				
Latino Protesters		2.388***			
		(0.467)			
Asian Descendant Protesters			4.173*		
			(1.621)		
Low-Income Participants				1.662**	
				(0.552)	
No Organized Interest Group					0.0338
					(0.0984)
Salience (Media Coverage)					
Multiple Articles	−0.285	−0.769	0.569	−0.107	−0.631**
	(0.491)	(0.648)	(1.009)	(0.125)	(0.210)
Resources × Salience (Media Coverage):					
Black Protesters × Multiple Articles	1.763*				
	(0.759)				
Latino Protesters × Multiple Articles		2.378			
		(1.240)			
No Organized Interest Group × Multiple Articles					0.708**
					(0.263)
Constant	−0.272	0.123	7.966	−0.352	−0.409
	(1.066)	(1.761)	(4.722)	(0.356)	(0.362)
Controls	Yes	Yes	Yes	Yes	Yes
Congress Year Dummies	Yes	Yes	Yes	Yes	Yes
Variance Component					
Congressional District Level	1.230*	4.350*	26.01	0.174	0.169
	(0.587)	(2.084)	(24.16)	(0.0922)	(0.0919)
Observations	472	294	176	2287	2271
Log likelihood	−261.5	−136.3	−63.37	−1546.4	−1537.9

The dependent variable, legislative support, is binary taking on a value of 0 or 1. Coefficients are Log Odds. All independent variables are coded 0 to 1. Standard errors in parentheses. $^*p < 0.05$, $^{**}p < 0.01$, $^{***}p < 0.001$

TABLE 8.4 *Resources, salience (disruptiveness) and legislative support*

	Model I	Model II	Model III	Model IV	Model V
Resources					
Black Protesters	1.864*** (0.358)				
Latino Protesters		1.495** (0.497)			
Asian Descendant Protesters			2.179 (1.923)		
Low-Income Participants				1.669** (0.553)	
No Organized Interest Group					0.218* (0.104)
Salience (Disruptiveness)					
Disruptive	−1.044* (0.448)	−1.758* (0.713)	−1.988 (1.562)	−0.0828 (0.0984)	−0.110 (0.191)
Resources x Salience (Disruptiveness):					
Black Protesters × Disruptive	1.046 (0.552)				
Latino Protesters × Disruptive		4.519*** (1.197)			
No Organized Interest Group × Disruptive					−0.0959 (0.224)
Constant	0.118 (1.084)	1.143 (1.886)	8.841 (4.996)	−0.295 (0.356)	−0.418 (0.363)
Controls	Yes	Yes	Yes	Yes	Yes
Congress Year Dummies	Yes	Yes	Yes	Yes	Yes
Variance Component					
Congressional District Level	1.103* (0.535)	4.330* (2.113)	31.80 (35.58)	0.176 (0.0916)	0.177 (0.0927)
Observations	472	294	176	2301	2285
Log likelihood	−262.7	−128.0	−62.56	−1558.0	−1552.0

The dependent variable, legislative support, is binary taking on a value of 0 or 1. Coefficients are Log Odds. All independent variables are coded 0 to 1. Standard errors in parentheses. $*p < 0.05$, $**p < 0.01$, $***p < 0.001$

TABLE 8.5 *General legislative support (minority roll-call votes) and constituent preferences (Liberal only)*

	Model I	Model II	Model III	Model IV	Model V	Model VI
Protest	0.0118*** (0.00199)					
Black Protesters		0.00121 (0.00468)				
Latino Protesters			0.0101* (0.00538)			
Asian Descendant Protesters				0.00700 (0.00894)		
Low-Income Protesters					0.00384 (0.00772)	
Informal Interest Group						0.000341 (0.00194)
Public Salience	−0.0417*** (0.00840)	−0.380*** (0.0377)	−0.311*** (0.0447)	−0.296*** (0.0483)	−0.419*** (0.0193)	−0.422*** (0.0194)
Education	0.0711*** (0.00722)	0.259*** (0.0195)	0.242*** (0.0237)	0.250*** (0.0267)	0.263*** (0.00892)	0.265*** (0.00898)
Democratic Representative	0.390*** (0.00191)	0.394*** (0.0110)	0.373*** (0.0139)	0.360*** (0.0161)	0.387*** (0.00494)	0.386*** (0.00498)
Length of Service	0.0404*** (0.00484)	0.129*** (0.0252)	0.118*** (0.0320)	0.118*** (0.0362)	0.138*** (0.0117)	0.141*** (0.0119)

TABLE 8.5 (Continued)

	Model I	Model II	Model III	Model IV	Model V	Model VI
Democratic Vote Margin	0.157***	0.163***	0.299***	0.260***	0.258***	0.258***
	(0.00489)	(0.0295)	(0.0391)	(0.0450)	(0.0134)	(0.0134)
Black Representative	0.142***	0.137***	0.119***	0.132***	0.124***	0.124***
	(0.00379)	(0.0134)	(0.0171)	(0.0191)	(0.00632)	(0.00634)
Latino Representative	0.122***	0.196***	0.175***	0.186***	0.192***	0.193***
	(0.00564)	(0.0156)	(0.0195)	(0.0221)	(0.00757)	(0.00761)
Female Representative	-0.0162***	0.00128	0.0121	0.00343	0.0168***	0.0170***
	(0.00297)	(0.0121)	(0.0153)	(0.0175)	(0.00563)	(0.00565)
Constant	0.124***	0.211***	0.142***	0.183***	0.105***	0.105***
	(0.00670)	(0.0261)	(0.0327)	(0.0362)	(0.0148)	(0.0149)
Congress Year Dummies	Yes	Yes	Yes	Yes	Yes	Yes
Variance Component						
Congressional District Level Constant	0.0123***	0.0243***	0.0229***	0.0211***	0.0283***	0.0286***
	(0.000827)	(0.00376)	(0.00433)	(0.00423)	(0.00283)	(0.00287)
Congressional District Level Residual	0.00612***	0.00238***	0.00213***	0.00151***	0.00244***	0.00244***
	(0.0000473)	(0.000138)	(0.000175)	(0.000176)	(0.0000642)	(0.0000645)
Observations	33929	722	401	238	3126	3110
Groups	453	110	82	71	228	227
Log likelihood	37197.9	967.1	522.7	311.0	4535.9	4508.8
LR test Chi²	31106.75***	705.56***	334.97***	224.84***	3695.19***	3674.65***

Estimates for Minority Roll Call Votes figure. For each model, the dependent variable, legislative support, is coded 0 to 1 and measures a legislator's political ideology based on their roll-call voting behavior relative to other members in the same Congress on roll call votes relating to minority issue areas. In Model 1, non-protesting districts are the omitted category. In Models II through VII, high-resource protesters are the omitted category. All other variables are coded 0 to 1. Coefficients are Log Odds. Standard errors in parentheses.

$*p < 0.10$, $**p < 0.05$, $***p < 0.01$

TABLE 8.6 *General legislative support (via all roll-call votes) and constituent preferences (Liberal only)*

	Model I	Model II	Model III	Model IV	Model V	Model VI
Protest	0.00560***					
	(0.00139)					
Black Protesters		−0.00220				
		(0.00336)				
Latino Protesters			−0.00449			
			(0.0383)			
Asian Descendant Protesters				−0.00227		
				(0.00730)		
Low-Income Protesters					−0.00183	
					(0.00541)	
Informal Interest Group						0.0000330
						(0.00136)
Public Salience	0.0254***	0.0149	−0.00306	−0.0326	−0.0959***	−0.0945***
	(0.00590)	(0.0259)	(0.0303)	(0.0338)	(0.0133)	(0.0134)
Education	0.0531***	0.134***	0.149***	0.150***	0.146***	0.145***
	(0.00503)	(0.0139)	(0.0167)	(0.0212)	(0.00620)	(0.00624)
Democratic Representative	0.440***	0.483***	0.459***	0.480***	0.459***	0.460***
	(0.00133)	(0.00775)	(0.00967)	(0.0122)	(0.00343)	(0.00346)
Length of Service	0.114***	−0.0497***	−0.0367	−0.0499*	0.0187**	0.0162*
	(0.00336)	(0.0179)	(0.0226)	(0.0287)	(0.00819)	(0.00828)
Democratic Vote Margin	0.00624*	0.0406*	0.113***	0.123***	0.0864***	0.0858***
	(0.00341)	(0.0210)	(0.0276)	(0.0355)	(0.00933)	(0.00938)
Black Representative	0.131***	0.107***	0.101***	0.0961***	0.0863***	0.0860***
	(0.00265)	(0.00949)	(0.0120)	(0.0149)	(0.00441)	(0.00443)

TABLE 8.6 (Continued)

	Model I	Model II	Model III	Model IV	Model V	Model VI
Latino Representative	0.134***	0.127***	0.131***	0.128***	0.128***	0.127***
	(0.00395)	(0.0112)	(0.0137)	(0.0176)	(0.00529)	(0.00531)
Female Representative	0.00615***	0.0122	0.0242**	0.0385***	0.0245***	0.0244***
	(0.00207)	(0.00859)	(0.0107)	(0.0135)	(0.00392)	(0.00394)
Constant	0.267***	0.284***	0.256***	0.254***	0.253***	0.254***
	(0.00520)	(0.0177)	(0.0223)	(0.0270)	(0.00947)	(0.00955)
Congress Year Dummies	Yes	Yes	Yes	Yes	Yes	Yes
Variance Component						
Congressional District Level Constant	0.00834***	0.00890***	0.00851***	0.00670***	0.0101***	0.0101***
	(0.000558)	(0.00133)	(0.00149)	(0.00126)	(0.00101)	(0.00101)
Congressional District Level Residual	0.00297***	0.00123***	0.00108***	0.00102***	0.00120***	0.00120***
	(0.0000229)	(0.0000708)	(0.0000870)	(0.000113)	(0.0000315)	(0.0000317)
Observations	34001	722	401	238	3128	3112
Groups	453	110	82	71	228	227
Log likelihood	49489.8	1223.2	670.2	382.7	5685.2	5652.2
LR test Chi²	40931.69***	727.74***	350.21***	181.88***	3592.10***	3561.91***

Estimates for All Roll Call Votes figure. For each model, the dependent variable, legislative support, is coded 0 to 1 and measures a legislator's political ideology based on their roll-call voting behavior relative to other members in the same Congress on all roll call votes. In Model 1, non-protesting districts are the omitted category. In Models II through VII, high-resource protesters are the omitted category. All other variables are coded 0 to 1. Coefficients are Log Odds. Standard errors in parentheses. $^{*}p < 0.10$, $^{**}p < 0.05$, $^{***}p < 0.01$

8.4 CHAPTER 5 APPENDIX

Figures and Tables

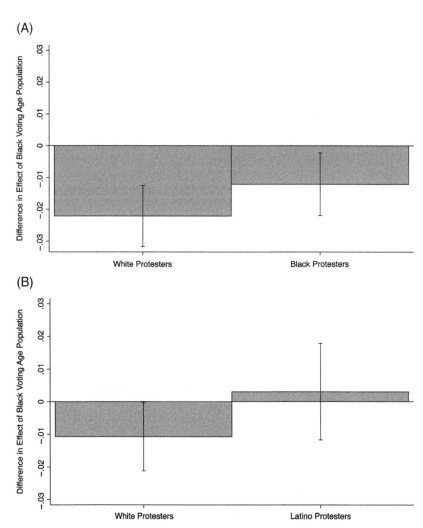

FIGURE 8.1 Effect of district's Black voting age population on legislator's voting behavior by protesters' resources

Note: Differences in the effect of a district's Black voting age population on the legislator's predicted probability of legislative support of protesters' concerns. All covariates are held at their means.

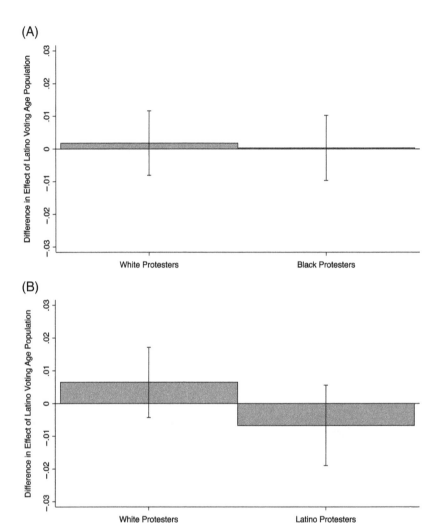

FIGURE 8.2 Effect of district's Latino voting-age population on legislator's
voting behavior by protesters' resources

Note: Differences in the effect of a district's Latino voting age population on the
legislator's predicted probability of legislative support of protesters' concerns.
All-covariates are held at their means.

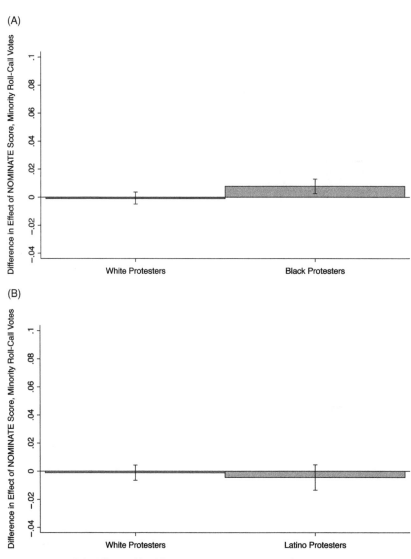

FIGURE 8.3 Effect of legislator's minority NOMINATE score on voting behavior by protesters' resources

Note: Differences in the effect of a legislator's voting behavior on minority roll-call votes on the legislator's predicted probability of legislative support of protesters' concerns. All covariates are held at their means.

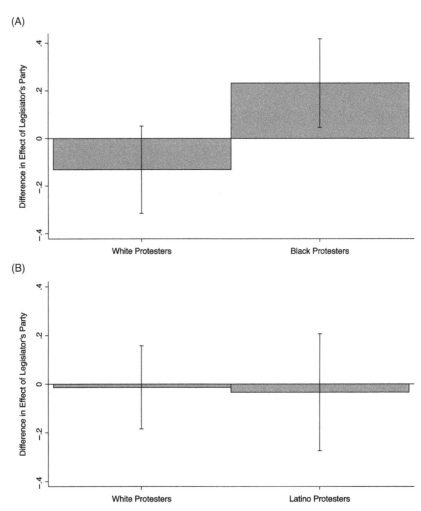

FIGURE 8.4 Effect of legislator's party on voting behavior by protesters' resources

Note: Differences in the effect of a legislator's party affiliation on minority roll-call votes on the legislator's predicted probability of legislative support of protesters' concerns. All covariates are held at their means.

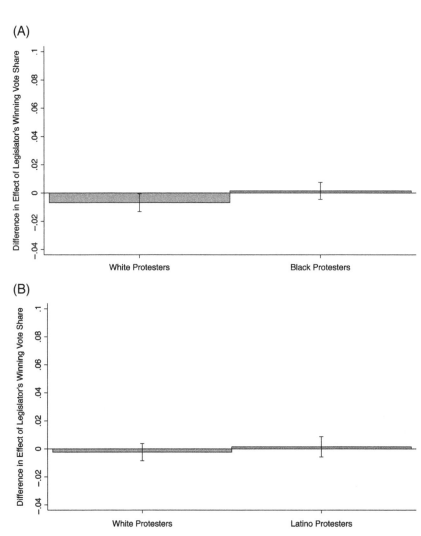

FIGURE 8.5 Effect of legislator's margin of victory on voting behavior by protesters' resources

Note: Differences in the effect of a legislator's winning vote share in the previous election on the legislator's predicted probability of legislative support of protesters' concerns. All covariates are held at their means.

TABLE 8.7 *Percent Black voting-age population and legislative support of protesters*

	Model I	Model II
Black Protesters	1.537***	
	(0.383)	
Latino Protesters		1.484**
		(0.543)
Percentage Black Voting-Age Population	−0.160***	−0.109
	(0.0423)	(0.0605)
Black Protesters × Percentage Black Voting-Age Population	0.0974**	
	(0.0339)	
Latino Protesters × Percentage Black Voting-Age Population		0.130**
		(0.0494)
Public Salience	−1.711*	−1.073
	(0.857)	(1.574)
Education	−2.362**	−2.713
	(0.910)	(1.468)
Democratic Representative	0.656	0.113
	(0.399)	(0.662)
Length of Service	0.277	−1.034
	(1.131)	(1.945)
Democratic Vote Margin	0.475	−0.799
	(1.432)	(2.304)
Black Representative	0.831	−2.177
	(0.896)	(1.758)
Latino Representative	−0.505	−2.123
	(0.669)	(1.114)
Female Representative	−0.524	0.251
	(0.467)	(0.809)
Constant	0.733	0.637
	(1.040)	(1.702)
Congress Year Dummies	Yes	Yes
Variance Component Congressional District Level	0.839	3.535*
	(0.433)	(1.785)
Observations	472	294
Log likelihood	−255.2***	−132.5***

Estimates informing Figure 5.2. The dependent variable, legislative support, is binary taking on a value of 0 or 1. Coefficients are Log Odds. All control variables are coded 0 to 1. Standard errors in parentheses. $*p < 0.05$, $**p < 0.01$, $***p < 0.001$

TABLE 8.8 *Latino voting-age population and legislative support of protesters*

	Model I	Model II
Black Protesters	2.481*** (0.449)	
Latino Protesters		4.481*** (0.766)
Percent Latino Voting-Age Population	0.0107 (0.0305)	0.0576 (0.0486)
Black Protesters × Percentage Latino Voting-Age Population	−0.00906 (0.0235)	
Latino Protesters × Percentage Latino Voting-Age Population		−0.107** (0.0326)
Public Salience	−0.812 (0.921)	−0.765 (1.712)
Education	−2.375* (1.024)	−3.197 (1.638)
Democratic Representative	0.336 (0.408)	−0.291 (0.696)
Length of Service	1.019 (1.136)	−0.926 (1.987)
Democratic Vote Margin	0.132 (1.507)	−0.427 (2.428)
Black Representative	−1.582** (0.585)	−2.848** (1.027)
Latino Representative	−1.230 (0.895)	−2.663 (1.576)
Female Representative	0.0217 (0.478)	0.711 (0.859)
Constant	−0.383 (1.073)	−0.698 (1.787)
Congress Year Dummies	Yes	Yes
Variance Component Congressional District Level	1.113* (0.539)	4.384* (2.010)
Observations	472	294
Log likelihood	−265.5***	−132.9***

Estimates informing Figure 5.3. The dependent variable, legislative support, is binary taking on a value of 0 or 1. Coefficients are Log Odds. All control variables are coded 0 to 1. Standard errors in parentheses. $*p < 0.05$, $**p < 0.01$, $***p < 0.001$

TABLE 8.9 *Minority NOMINATE score and legislative support of protesters*

	Model I	Model II
Black Protesters	−0.737	
	(0.789)	
Latino Protesters		4.319**
		(1.644)
Liberal Voting Behavior	−0.00399	−0.00934
	(0.0143)	(0.0229)
Black Protesters × Liberal Voting Behavior	0.0481***	
	(0.0120)	
Latino Protesters × Liberal Voting Behavior		−0.0218
		(0.0212)
Public Salience	−0.471	−0.758
	(0.854)	(1.530)
Education	−2.804**	−2.484
	(1.016)	(1.534)
Democratic Representative	−0.582	0.470
	(0.715)	(1.178)
Length of Service	0.585	−0.455
	(1.226)	(1.906)
Democratic Vote Margin	−0.0736	−0.0577
	(1.535)	(2.319)
Black Representative	−2.015**	−2.361*
	(0.662)	(1.003)
Latino Representative	−1.674*	−2.349*
	(0.820)	(1.182)
Female Representative	−0.0462	0.554
	(0.506)	(0.801)
Constant	1.090	−0.379
	(1.200)	(1.751)
Congress Year Dummies	Yes	Yes
Variance Component Congressional District Level	1.386*	3.744*
	(0.622)	(1.805)
Observations	472	294
Log likelihood	−255.8***	−138.0***

Estimates informing Figure 5.4. The dependent variable, legislative support, is binary taking on a value of 0 or 1. Coefficients are Log Odds. All control variables are coded 0 to 1. Standard errors in parentheses. $*p < 0.05$, $**p < 0.01$, $***p < 0.001$

TABLE 8.10 *Legislator's party and legislative support of protesters*

	Model I	Model II
Black Protesters	0.975*	
	(0.512)	
Latino Protesters		2.817***
		(0.862)
Democrat	−0.783	−0.114
	(0.536)	(0.739)
Black Protesters × Democrat	2.005***	
	(0.645)	
Latino Protesters × Democrat		−0.123
		(0.938)
Public Salience	−0.629	−0.671
	(0.831)	(1.521)
Education	−2.521***	−2.803*
	(0.956)	(1.459)
Length of Service	0.668	−0.472
	(1.170)	(1.915)
Democratic Vote Margin	0.287	−0.491
	(1.531)	(2.256)
Black Representative	−1.728***	−2.628***
	(0.608)	(0.965)
Latino Representative	−1.319*	−2.629**
	(0.735)	(1.110)
Female Representative	−0.0282	0.596
	(0.486)	(0.803)
Constant	0.605	−0.200
	(1.120)	(1.689)
Congress Year Dummies	Yes	Yes
Variance Component Congressional District Level	1.257**	3.867**
	(0.588)	(1.843)
Observations	472	294
Log likelihood	−260.5***	−138.6***

Estimates informing Figure 5.5. The dependent variable, legislative support, is binary taking on a value of 0 or 1. Coefficients are Log Odds. All control variables are coded 0 to 1. Standard errors in parentheses. $^*p < 0.05$, $^{**}p < 0.01$, $^{***}p < 0.001$

TABLE 8.11 *Legislator's race, ethnicity, and party and legislative support of protesters*

	Model I	Model II
Black Protesters	4.538***	
	(1.090)	
Latino Protesters		5.102***
		(1.398)
Mexican American Democrat	4.054***	5.757***
	(1.478)	(2.190)
Puerto Rican Democrat	−0.251	2.622
	(0.803)	(2.077)
White Democrat	3.299***	4.824***
	(1.170)	(1.576)
White Republican	3.952***	4.929***
	(1.213)	(1.641)
Black Protesters		
× Mexican American Democrat	−3.366**	
	(1.509)	
× Puerto Rican Democrat	0	
	(.)	
× White Democrat	−1.918*	
	(1.159)	
× White Republican	−3.481***	
	(1.199)	
Latino Protesters		
× Mexican American Democrat		−10.19***
		(2.682)
× Puerto Rican Democrat		0
		(.)
× White Democrat		−2.370
		(1.513)
× White Republican		−1.656
		(1.632)
Public Salience	−0.729	−0.885
	(0.786)	(1.794)
Education	−2.329**	−2.742
	(0.940)	(1.715)
Length of Service	0.117	−2.050
	(1.181)	(2.312)
Democratic Vote Margin	0.682	0.517
	(1.522)	(2.642)
Female Representative	−0.161	0.761
	(0.473)	(0.998)
Constant	−3.551**	−6.003**
	(1.704)	(2.808)

TABLE 8.11 (*Continued*)

	Model I	Model II
Congress Year Dummies	Yes	Yes
Variance Component Congressional District Level	0.979** (0.492)	5.432** (2.669)
Observations	462	277
Log likelihood	−254.4***	−119.7***

Estimates informing Figure 5.6. The dependent variable, legislative support, is binary taking on a value of 0 or 1. Coefficients are Log Odds. All control variables are coded 0 to 1. Standard errors in parentheses. $^*p < 0.05$, $^{**}p < 0.01$, $^{***}p < 0.001$

TABLE 8.12 *Legislator's gender and party and legislative support of protesters*

	Model I	Model II
Black Protesters	2.114** (0.943)	
Latino Protesters		3.697*** (1.363)
Male Democrat	−1.113 (1.038)	−0.805 (1.339)
Female Republican	−1.997 (1.579)	−1.582 (1.897)
Male Republican	0.161 (1.057)	−0.120 (1.349)
Black Protesters		
× Male Democrat	1.023 (1.014)	
× Female Republican	0.573 (1.685)	
× Male Republican	−1.484 (1.104)	
Latino Protesters		
× Male Democrat		−1.254 (1.435)
× Female Republican		−0.948 (2.203)
× Male Republican		−0.655 (1.651)

TABLE 8.12 *(Continued)*

	Model I	Model II
Public Salience	−0.629	−1.025
	(0.843)	(1.543)
Education	−3.080***	−3.664**
	(1.033)	(1.641)
Length of Service	0.688	−0.273
	(1.186)	(1.916)
Democratic Vote Margin	0.376	−0.438
	(1.548)	(2.238)
Black Representative	−1.823***	−2.504***
	(0.620)	(0.960)
Latino Representative	−1.489**	−2.641**
	(0.751)	(1.144)
Constant	1.017	0.738
	(1.478)	(2.083)
Congress Year Dummies	Yes	Yes
Variance Component Congressional District Level	1.293**	3.724**
	(0.594)	(1.833)
Observations	472	294
Log likelihood	−258.5***	−136.0***

Estimates informing Figure 5.7. The dependent variable, legislative support, is binary taking on a value of 0 or 1. Coefficients are Log Odds. All control variables are coded 0 to 1. Standard errors in parentheses. $^*p < 0.05$, $^{**}p < 0.01$, $^{***}p < 0.001$

TABLE 8.13 *Voting-age population and legislative support of protesters*

	Model I	Model II
Black Protesters	−1.121	
	(1.449)	
Latino Protesters		0.534
		(1.997)
Democratic Vote Margin	−0.0442**	−0.0207
	(0.0215)	(0.0277)
Black Protesters × Democratic Vote Margin	0.0520**	
	(0.0214)	
Latino Protesters × Democratic Vote Margin		0.0309
		(0.0281)
Public Salience	−0.752	−0.659
	(0.806)	(1.507)
Education	−2.243**	−2.666*
	(0.953)	(1.439)
Democratic Representative	0.484	−0.0969
	(0.413)	(0.643)
Length of Service	1.013	−0.367
	(1.145)	(1.915)
Black Representative	−1.511**	−2.730***
	(0.597)	(0.983)
Latino Representative	−1.051	−2.597**
	(0.723)	(1.102)
Female Representative	−0.0480	0.609
	(0.476)	(0.798)
Constant	2.725*	0.744
	(1.467)	(1.922)
Congress Year Dummies	Yes	Yes
Variance Component Congressional District Level	1.136**	3.767**
	(0.551)	(1.782)
Observations	471	294
Log likelihood	−259.6***	−138.0***

Estimates informing Figure 5.8. The dependent variable, legislative support, is binary taking on a value of 0 or 1. Coefficients are Log Odds. All control variables are coded 0 to 1. Standard errors in parentheses. *$p < 0.05$, **$p < 0.01$, ***$p < 0.001$

TABLE 8.14 *Years of service and legislative support of protesters*

	Model I	Model II
Black Protesters	2.368***	
	(0.453)	
Latino Protesters		3.485***
		(0.676)
Years of Service	0.0217	0.0347
	(0.0324)	(0.0448)
Black Protesters × Years of Service	−0.00133	
	(0.0373)	
Latino Protesters × Years of Service		−0.0900
		(0.0563)
Public Salience	−0.748	−0.817
	(0.806)	(1.473)
Education	−2.377**	−2.816*
	(0.945)	(1.464)
Democratic Representative	0.331	−0.178
	(0.407)	(0.638)
Democratic Vote Margin	0.163	−0.766
	(1.464)	(2.227)
Black Representative	−1.546***	−2.435**
	(0.577)	(0.949)
Latino Representative	−1.107	−2.733**
	(0.703)	(1.087)
Female Representative	0.0260	0.488
	(0.471)	(0.795)
Constant	−0.318	−0.325
	(1.060)	(1.655)
Congress Year Dummies	Yes	Yes
Variance Component Congressional District Level	1.099**	3.434**
	(0.533)	(1.634)
Observations	472	294
Log likelihood	−265.5*	−137.4*

Estimates informing Figure 5.9. The dependent variable, legislative support, is binary taking on a value of 0 or 1. Coefficients are Log Odds. All control variables are coded 0 to 1. Standard errors in parentheses. $*p < 0.05$, $**p < 0.01$, $***p < 0.001$

8.5 CHAPTER 6 APPENDIX

2012 Data Collection

The DCA codebook meticulously details the data collection and coding process that generated the 1960–1995 data. I use this information as a guide for the collection and coding of collective action events for 2012. In generating the initial data, coders manually searched the *New York Times* for instances of and information concerning collective action events. The new data are founded using a boolean search of Factiva, an online newspaper archive. Accordingly, there is some dissimilarity in the coding procedures.

The first step in the data collection process was to gather all newspaper articles from 2012 potentially relating to collective action. This was done by conducting a comprehensive Factiva boolean search. In developing the boolean search, I scanned the DCA codebook and data for all code words relevant to collective action events. I paid most attention to the title of the articles, the type of collective action listed, and characteristics of the event (e.g., violence, brutality, multiple arrests). The goal was to be as inclusive as possible to avoid excluding appropriate articles. I then tested the search on Factiva for a period covered by the DCA data. I found that around 90 percent of the articles present in the DCA were identical to those found by the Factiva boolean search. The majority of collective action events not found by the boolean search were reported in the other newspapers (i.e., not the *New York Times*).

The abundance of terms used to create the effective boolean search also produced many false positives including obituaries, recipes, and other articles fitting the search terms but irrelevant to the definition of collective action for the target year, 2012. For example, an article may mention the 1963 March on Washington or the 300 student-athletes recognized in a March edition of a newspaper. The former should be excluded from the sample since it does not fall within the date range. The latter should be excluded because while "March" is a relevant collective action term, the usage of the word refers to a date and not a collective action event. Accordingly, research assistants skimmed each article obtained by the search to exclude false positives.

Finally, research assistants coded each article following the DCA coding manual, which collects data on seventy-six variables. The coding produces rich information on the time, date, and location of the event; the demographics of participants; the specific type of event; the amount and type of violence, arrest, and police action associated with the event; the target; the purpose or impetus for the activity; and a multitude of other information. Additionally, research assistants code for whether the event occurred online.

Three research assistants coded the dependent variable, legislative support. For each collective action event uncovered in the newspapers, two research assistants used information from the newspaper articles to describe the grievance expressed during the protest. They then searched www.govtrack.us for the first final passage roll-call vote in the US House of Representatives relating to the grievance. For the bill to be recorded, it must have occurred after the event but before the end of the congressional term. If the two research assistants recorded two different roll-call bills, I or a third research assistant selected the bill that best fit the aforementioned requirements: the bill addressed the grievance raised during collective action and the vote was non-procedural, was not a voice vote, occurred after the protest, and took place before the end of the congressional session.

Empirical Model Specifications

As in previous chapters, I evaluate whether a legislator supports the interests of protesters in their district based on the resource capacity of the group protesting. For the dependent variable, *Support*, research assistants search www.govtrack.us for the first final-passage roll-call vote occurring after a protest and before the end of the congressional term. A relevant roll-call vote relates to the issue indicated in the protest data as motivating the collective action.

The dependent variable is a dichotomous variable indicating whether a member of the US House of Representatives voted in support of a grievance expressed during collective action by their constituents. Because the dependent variable is binary, each of the empirical models is a logistic regression. There were 89 unique collective action events in 2012 with a relevant roll-call vote within the Civil Rights, Minority Issue, and Civil Liberties major topics issue area classification. However, there were 10,765 observations available for analyses due to the presence of collective action events that occur red across geographic locations. Consider once again the Trayvon Martin collective action that occurred in places including Sanford, Florida, where he was killed; Chicago, Illinois, where Congressman Bobby Rush is a representative; and in physical and virtual communities across the United States.

Since the analyses seek to assess how legislators respond to collective action by their constituents, all congressional districts and their respective representatives representing the city in which a protest occurred are included as observations for each collective action event. To help address the possibility that a protest may be included multiple times in the analyses, the logistic regressions include congressional district random effects. This also helps account for atypical congressional districts that could bias the results.[1]

The primary independent variables relate to the resource capacity of collective action participants. Protesters' resource capacity is measured using the characteristics of protesting groups. The first independent variable, *Offline Protest*, is a dichotomous measure that takes on a value of 1 if the event took place in a physical space and 0 if it took place online, in a virtual forum. The *Black Participants* variable takes on a value of 1 if the participants are African American and 0 if the participants are coded as being White protesters,[2] or if the race or ethnicity of the protesters is not mentioned in the article. Similarly, the *Latino Participants* variable takes on a value of 1 if the participants are identified as being Mexican, Chicano, Central American, South American, Puerto Rican, Cuban, or Undifferentiated Hispanic. The *Latino Participants* takes on a value of 0 if the participants are coded as being White protesters or if the race or ethnicity of the protesters is not mentioned in the article. Finally, organizational capacity is measured with a binary variable that indicates whether a formal interest group is present at the event, where *No Formal Interest Group* is the low-resource group.[3]

The empirical models also include observational data on legislators and their congressional districts to help assess how factors typically known to influence legislative voting behavior compare with the influence of protest and protesters' resource capacities on legislative behavior. *Education* is a variable found using the American Fact Finder tool from the US Census Bureau (2011). It measures the percentage of the 25-year

---

[1] A Hausman test and a variable addition test (Wu 1973) suggest that a random effects model is more appropriate than a fixed effects model specification. Likewise, a likelihood ratio test reveals that both effects model specifications are more appropriate than a pooled logistic regression model. Even so, the primary independent variables are robust to alternative model specifications.

[2] White protesters are identified as belonging to undifferentiated White, Jewish, or European ethnic groups.

[3] This measure is from the DCA variable indicating the presence of a social movement organization.

and older population in a district that has a college education. The legislator's party affiliation, gender, race, and ethnicity are obtained from the University of Washington's Center for American Politics and Public Policy (Center for American Politics and Public Policy 2014). The legislator's length of service in Congress is obtained from the Office of the Clerk of the US House of Representatives (2012). Finally, the legislator's margin of victory in the previous election is obtained from CQ Press's voting and elections collection (CQ Press 2015).

Tables and Figures

TABLE 8.15 *Offline vs. online liberal protests, resources, and legislative support*

	Model I	Model II	Model III	Model IV
Offline Protest	0.491***	0.455***	0.530***	1.276***
	(0.0480)	(0.0645)	(0.0700)	(0.137)
Black Protesters		1.123***		
		(0.0969)		
Latino Protesters			6.206***	
			(0.897)	
No Formal Interest Group				−0.0860
				(0.0943)
Black Participants × Offline Protest		−0.807***		
		(0.123)		
Latino Participants × Offline Protest			0	
			(.)	
No Formal Interest Group × Offline Protest				−0.882***
				(0.146)
Education	−0.326	−0.308	−0.0860	−0.334
	(0.353)	(0.406)	(0.722)	(0.356)
Democratic Representative	1.517***	1.917***	2.961***	1.529***
	(0.123)	(0.142)	(0.262)	(0.124)
Length of Service	−0.0882	−0.101	−0.0635	−0.0927
	(0.331)	(0.380)	(0.677)	(0.334)
Democratic Vote Margin	−0.0352	−0.223	−1.221	−0.0716
	(0.453)	(0.525)	(0.961)	(0.458)
Black Representative	−0.0685	−0.0548	0.0408	−0.0700
	(0.201)	(0.230)	(0.403)	(0.203)
Latino Representative	0.152	0.150	0.384	0.148
	(0.229)	(0.263)	(0.466)	(0.231)
Female Representative	−0.0154	−0.00365	0.0190	−0.0154
	(0.141)	(0.161)	(0.285)	(0.142)
Constant	−1.486***	−1.804***	−2.215***	−1.392***
	(0.325)	(0.375)	(0.674)	(0.338)
Variance Component Congressional District Level	0.687***	0.933***	3.090***	0.702***
	(0.0740)	(0.0982)	(0.379)	(0.0754)
Observations	9551	9152	6674	9551
Groups	359	359	359	359
Log likelihood	−5483.1	−4933.2	−3182.5	−5443.8
Likelihood Ratio test χ^2	571.71***	694.83***	1007.10***	582.34***

The dependent variable, legislative support, is binary taking on a value of 0 or 1. In Model 1, online protests are the omitted category. In Models II through V, high-resource protesters are the omitted category for the protesters variables. All other variables are coded 0 to 1. Coefficients are Log Odds. Standard errors in parentheses. $^*p < 0.10$, $^{**}p < 0.05$, $^{***}p < 0.01$

Bibliography

Abrajano, Marisa A. and R. Michael Alvarez. 2010. *New Faces, New Voices: The Hispanic Electorate in America*. Princeton, NJ: Princeton University Press.

Agnone, Jon. 2007. "Amplifying Public Opinion: The Policy Impact of the U.S. Environmental Movement." *Social Forces* 85(4):1593–1620.

Alesina, Alberto, Edward Glaeser, and Bruce Sacerdote. 2001. "Why Doesn't the US Have a European-Style Welfare State?" *Brookings Papers on Economic Activity* 2:1–66.

Alexander, Michelle. 2012. *The New Jim Crow: Mass Incarceration in the Age of Colorblindness*. New York: The New Press. https://books.google.com/books?id=CNOFDwAAQBAJ

Andrews, Kenneth T. 2001. "Social Movements and Policy Implementation: The Mississippi Civil Rights Movement and the War on Poverty, 1965–1971." *American Sociological Review* 66:71–95.

Ansolabehere, Stephen, David Brady and Morris Fiorina. 1992. "The Vanishing Marginals and Electoral Responsiveness." *British Journal of Political Science* 22(1):21–38.

Ansolabehere, Stephen and Philip Edward Jones. 2010. "Constituents' Responses to Congressional Roll-Call Voting." *American Journal of Political Science* 54(3):583–597.

Arnold, R. Douglas. 1990. *The Logic of Congressional Action*. New Haven, CT: Yale University Press.

Arora, Maneesh, Davin L. Phoenix and Archie Delshad. 2019. "Framing police and Protesters: Assessing Volume and Framing of News Coverage post-Ferguson, and Corresponding Impacts on Legislative Activity." *Politics, Groups, and Identities* 7(1):151–164.

Bade, Rachael. 2015. "Pressure Builds on GOP for Police, Criminal Justice Reforms." www.politico.com/story/2015/05/police-reforms-republican-party-117742

Bailey, Michael A., Jonathan Mummolo, and Hans Noel. 2012. "Tea Party Influence: A Story of Activists and Elites." *American Politics Research* 40(5):769–804.

Banks, Antoine J., Ismail K. White, and Brian D. McKenzie. 2018. "Black Politics: How Anger Influences the Political Actions Blacks Pursue to Reduce Racial Inequality." *Political Behavior* 41:1–27.

Bartels, Larry M. 1991. "Constituency Opinion and Congressional Policy-Making: The Reagan Defense Build-Up." *American Political Science Review* 85(2):457–474.

Bartels, Larry M. 2008. *Unequal Democracy: The Political Economy of the New Gilded Age*. New York: Russell Sage Foundation and Princeton, NJ: Princeton University Press.

Baumgartner, Frank R., Jeffrey M. Berry, Marie Hojnacki, David C. Kimball, and Beth L. Leech. 2009. *Lobbying and Policy Change: Who Wins, Who Loses, and Why*. Chicago: University of Chicago Press.

Benkler, Yochai. 2006. *The Wealth of Networks: How Social Production Transforms Markets and Freedom*. New Haven, CT: Yale University Press.

Bennett, W. Lance and Alexandra Segerberg. 2013. *The Logic of Connective Action: Digital Media and the Personalization of Contentious Politics*. New York: Cambridge University Press.

Berlin, Ira. 1998. *Many Thousands Gone: The First Two Centuries of Slavery in North America*. Cambridge, MA: Harvard University Press.

Best, Samuel and Brian Krueger. 2005. "Analyzing the Representativeness of Internet Political Participation." *Political Behavior* 27(2):183–216.

Bimber, Bruce. 2001. "Information and Political Engagement in America: The Search for Effects of Information Technology at the Individual Level." *Political Research Quarterly* 54(1):53–67.

Bimber, Bruce, Andrew J. Flanagin, and Cynthia Stohl. 2005. "Reconceptualizing Collective Action in the Contemporary Media Environment." *Communication Theory* 15(4):365–388.

Bimber, Bruce, Andrew J. Flanagin, and Cynthia Stohl. 2012. *Collective Action in Organizations: Interaction and Engagement in an Era of Technological Change*. New York: Cambridge University Press.

Bobo, Lawrence and Franklin Gilliam. 1990. "Race, Sociopolitical Participation, and Black Empowerment." *American Political Science Review* 84(2): 377–394.

Borge, Rosa and Ana S. Cardenal. 2011. "Surfing the Net: A Pathway to Participation for the Politically Uninterested?" *Policy & Internet* 3(1):1–29.

Bowen, Daniel C. and Christopher J. Clark. 2014. "Revisiting Descriptive Representation in Congress: Assessing the Effect of Race on the Constituent-Legislator Relationship." *Political Research Quarterly* 67(3):695–707.

Brader, Ted, Nicholas Valentino, and Elizabeth Suahy. 2008. "What Triggers Public Opposition to Immigration? Anxiety, Group Cues, and Immigration Threat." *American Journal of Political Science* 52(4):959–978.

Broockman, David E. 2013. "Black Politicians Are More Intrinsically Motivated to Advance Blacks' Interests: A Field Experiment Manipulating Political Incentives." *American Journal of Political Science* 57(3):521–536.

Broockman, David E. and Christopher Skovron. 2018. "Bias in Perceptions of Public Opinion among Political Elites." *American Political Science Review* 112(3):542–563.

Browning, Rufus P., Dale Rogers Marshall, and David H. Tabb. 1984. *Protest Is Not Enough: The Struggle of Blacks and Hispanics for Equality in Urban Politics*. Berkeley: University of California Press.

Brumfield, Ben. 2012. "Eat Mor Chikin: Chick-fil-A's Stance on Same-Sex Marriage Faces Test." www.cnn.com/2012/08/01/us/us-chick-fil-a-controversy/index.html

Burch, Tracy. 2013. *Trading Democracy for Justice: Criminal Convictions and the Decline of Neighborhood Political Participation*. Chicago: University of Chicago Press.

Burstein, Paul. 1998. *Discrimination, Jobs, and Politics: The Struggle for Equal Employment Opportunity in the United States since the New Deal*. Chicago: University of Chicago Press.

Butler, Daniel M. and David E. Broockman. 2011. "Do Politicians Racially Discriminate Against Constituents? A Field Experiment on State Legislators." *American Journal of Political Science* 55(3):463–477.

Canes-Wrone, Brandice. 2001. "The President's Legislative Influence from Public Appeals." *American Journal of Political Science* 45(2):313–329.

Canes-Wrone, Brandice, William Minozzi, and Jessica Bonney Reveley. 2011. "Issue Accountability and the Mass Public." *Legislative Studies Quarterly* 36(1):5–35.

Carnes, Nicholas. 2012. "Does the Numerical Underrepresentation of the Working Class in Congress Matter?" *Legislative Studies Quarterly* 37(1):5–34.

Carnes, Nicholas. 2013. *White-Collar Government: The Hidden Role of Class in Economic Policy Making*. Chicago Studies in American Politics. Chicago: University of Chicago Press.

Carp, Benjamin L. 2010. *Defiance of the Patriots: The Boston Tea Party and the Making of America*. New Haven, CT: Yale University Press.

Carpenter, Daniel. 2016. "Recruitment by Petition: American Antislavery, French Protestantism, English Suppression." *Perspectives on Politics* 14(3):700–723.

Carpenter, Daniel and Colin D. Moore. 2014. "When Canvassers Became Activists: Antislavery Petitioning and the Political Mobilization of American Women." *American Political Science Review* 108(3):479–498.

Carpenter, Daniel and Benjamin Schneer. 2015. "Party Formation through Petitions: The Whigs and the Bank War of 1832–1834." *Studies in American Political Development* 29:213–234.

Carrubba, Clifford, Matthew Gabel, and Simon Hug. 2008. "Legislative Voting Behavior, Seen and Unseen: A Theory of Roll-Call Vote Selection." *Legislative Studies Quarterly* 33(4):543–572.

Center for American Politics and Public Policy. 2014. "Legislative Explorer Dataset." http://cappp.org/index.php/data/

Chenoweth, Erica and Maria J. Stephan. 2011. *Why Civil Resistance Works: The Strategic Logic of Nonviolent Conflict*. Columbia Studies in Terrorism and Irregular Warfare. New York: Columbia University Press.

Chong, Dennis. 1991. *Collective Action and the Civil Rights Movement.* Chicago: University of Chicago Press.

Clerk of the US House of Representatives. 2012. "Seniority List of the United States House of Representatives 112th Congress." clerk.house.gov

Cohen, Cathy. 1999. *The Boundaries of Blackness.* Chicago: University of Chicago Press.

Congress and Police Reform: Current Law and Recent Proposals. 2020. CRS Legal Sidebar, Congressional Research Service. Updated June 25, 2020. https://crsreports.congress.gov/product/pdf/LSB/LSB10486

Corrigall-Brown, Catherine. 2010. Patterns of Protest: *Trajectories of Participation in Social Movements.* Stanford, CA: Stanford University Press.

Cox, Gary and Mathew McCubbins. 1993. *Legislative Leviathan: Party Government in the House.* Berkeley: University of California Press

Cox, Gary and Matthew McCubbins. 2005. *Setting the Agenda: Responsible Party Government in the U.S. House of Representatives.* New York: Cambridge University Press.

CQ Press. 2015. "CQ Press Voting and Elections Collection." http://library.cqpress.com/elections

Crespin, Michael H. 2010. "Serving Two Masters: Redistricting and Voting in the U.S. House of Representatives." *Political Research Quarterly* 63(4):850–859.

Cress, Daniel M. and David A. Snow. 2000. "The Outcomes of Homeless Mobilization: The Influence of Organization, Disruption, Political Mediation, and Framing." *American Journal of Sociology* 105:1063–1104.

Davenport, Christian. 2010. *Media Bias, Perspective, and State Repression: The Black Panther Party.* New York: Cambridge University Press.

Davenport, Christian, Rose McDermott and David Armstrong. 2018. "Protest and Police Abuse: Racial Limits on Perceived Accountability." In *Police Abuse in Contemporary Democracies*, pp. 165–192. New York: Palgrave Macmillan.

Davenport, Christian, Sarah A. Soule and David A. Armstrong. 2011. "Protesting While Black? The Differential Policing of American Activism, 1960 to 1990." *American Sociological Review* 76(1):152–178.

Dawson, Michael C. 1994. *Behind the Mule: Race and Class in African-American Politics.* Princeton, NJ: Princeton University Press.

DiGrazia, Josepf. 2014. "Individual Protest Participation in the United States: Conventional and Unconventional Activism." *Social Science Quarterly* 95(1):111–131.

Earl, Jennifer and Katrina Kimport. 2011. *Digitally Enabled Social Change: Activism in the Internet Age.* Cambridge, MA: MIT Press.

Ellis, Christopher. 2012. "Understanding Economic Biases in Representation: Income, Resources, and Policy Representation in the 110th House." *Political Research Quarterly* 65(4):938–951.

Fenno, Richard. 1973. *Congressmen in Committees.* Boston, MA: Little, Brown.

Fenno, Richard. 1978. *Home Style: House Members in Their Districts.* New York: Longman.

Fiorina, Morris P. 1973. "Electoral Margins, Constituency Influence, and Policy Moderation: A Critical Assessment." *American Politics Quarterly* 1(4):479–498.

Fiorina, Morris P. 1974. *Representatives, Roll Calls and Constituencies*. Lexington, MA: Lexington Books.

Fiorina, Morris P. 1977. *Congress: Keystone of the Washington Establishment*. New Haven, CT: Yale University Press.

Fish, Sandra. 2014. "Americans for Prosperity: Koch Brothers' Advocacy Gets Local." http://america.aljazeera.com/articles/2014/8/12/colorado-kochtopusamerican sprosperity.html

Fisher, Samuel H. and Rebekah Herrick. 2013. "Old versus New: The Comparative Efficiency of Mail and Internet Surveys of State Legislators." *State Politics & Policy Quarterly* 13(2):147–163.

Francis, Megan Ming. 2014. *Civil Rights and the Making of the Modern American State*. New York: Cambridge University Press.

Francis, Megan Ming. 2018. "The Strange Fruit of American Political Development." *Politics, Groups, and Identities* 6(1):128–137.

Frymer, Paul. 2008. *Black and Blue: African Americans, the Labor Movement, and the Decline of the Democratic Party*. Princeton, NJ: Princeton University Press.

Gamson, William A. 1975. *The Strategy of Social Protest*. Homewood, IL: Dorsey Press.

Gamson, William A. 1990. *The Strategy of Social Protest*. 2nd ed. Belmont, CA: Wadsworth.

Garrow, David. 1978. *Protest at Selma* New Haven, CT: Yale University Press.

Gates Jr, Henry Louis and Donald Yacovone. 2013. *The African Americans: Many Rivers to Cross*. New York: SmileBooks

Gay Claudine. 2002. "Spirals of Trust? The Effect of Descriptive Representation on the Relationship between Citizens and Their Government." *American Journal of Political Science* 46(4):717–732.

Gay Claudine. 2007. "Legislating Without Constraints: The Effect of Minority Districting on Legislators' Responsiveness to Constituency Preferences." *Journal of Politics* 69(2):442–456.

Gerber, Elisabeth and Jeffrey B. Lewis. 2004. "Beyond the Median: Voter Preferences, District Heterogeneity, and Political Representation." *Journal of Political Economy* 112(6):1364–1383.

Gilens, Martin. 1999. *Why Americans Hate Welfare Race, Media, and the Politics of Antipoverty Policy*. Chicago: University of Chicago Press.

Gilens, Martin. 2005. "Inequality and Democratic Responsiveness." *Public Opinion Quarterly* 69:778–796.

Gilens, Martin. 2012. *Affluence and Influence: Economic Inequality and Political Power in America*. New York: Russell Sage Foundation and Princeton, NJ: Princeton University Press.

Gilliam, Franklin D. and Shanto Iyengar. 2000. "Prime Suspects: The Influence of Local Television News on the Viewing Public." *American Journal of Political Science* 44(3):560–573.

Gillion, Daniel Q. 2013. *The Political Power of Protest: Minority Activism and Shifts in Public Policy*. New York: Cambridge University Press.

Gillion, Daniel Q. 2020. *The Loud Minority: Why Protests Matter in American Democracy*. Princeton, NJ: Princeton University Press.

Giugni, Marco G. 2004. *Social Protest and Policy Change*. Oxford: Rowman & Littlefield

Goldstein, Kenneth. 2002. "Getting in the Door: Sampling and Completing Elite Interviews." *PS: Political Science & Politics* 35(4):669–672.

Greene, William H. 2008. *Econometric Analysis*. 6th ed. Upper Saddle River, NJ: Pearson/Prentice Hall.

Griffin, John D. 2006. "Electoral Competition and Democratic Responsiveness: A Defense of the Marginality Hypothesis." *Journal of Politics* 68(4):911–921.

Griffin, John D. and Brian Newman. 2007. "The Unequal Representation of Latinos and Whites." *Journal of Politics* 69(4):1032–1046.

Gurr, Ted Robert. 1970. *Why Men Rebel*. Princeton, NJ: Princeton University Press.

Hahn, Heather. 2014. "Church Leaders Strive to Be Peacemakers in Ferguson." www.umnews.org/en/news/church-leaders-strive-to-be-peacemakers-in-ferguson

Hajnal, Zoltan L. and Taeku Lee. 2011. *Why Americans Don't Join the Party: Race, Immigration, and the Failure (of Political Parties) to Engage the Electorate*. Princeton, NJ: Princeton University Press.

Hall, Richard L. 1996. *Participation in Congress*. New Haven, CT: Yale University Press.

Hamlin, Alan and Colin Jennings. 2011. "Expressive Political Behaviour: Foundations, Scope and Implications." *British Journal of Political Science* 41(3):645–670.

Hawkesworth, Mary 2003. "Congressional Enactments of Race-Gender: Toward a Theory of Raced-Gendered Institutions." *American Political Science Review* 97(4):529–550.

Henderson, John and John Brooks. 2016. "Mediating the Electoral Connection: The Information Effects of Voter Signals on Legislative Behavior." *Journal of Politics* 78(3):653–669.

Hooker, Juliet. 2016. "Black Lives Matter and the Paradoxes of U.S. Black Politics: From Democratic Sacrifice to Democratic Repair." *Political Theory* 44(4):448–469.

Hutchings, Vincent L. 1998. "Issue Salience and Support for Civil Rights Legislation Among Southern Democrats." *Legislative Studies Quarterly* 23:521–544.

Hutchings, Vincent L. 2003. *Public Opinion and Democratic Accountability: How Citizens Learn about Politics* Princeton, NJ: Princeton University Press.

Jefferson, Hakeem, Fabian G. Neuner and Josh Pasek. 2020. "Seeing Blue in Black and White: Race and Perceptions of Officer-Involved Shootings." *Perspectives on Politics*, 1–19. Published Online December 4, 2020.

Jenkins, Jeffery A., Michael A. Crespin and Jamie L. Carson. 2005. "Parties as Procedural Coalitions in Congress: An Examination of Differing Career Tracks." *Legislative Studies Quarterly* 30(3):365–89.

Jennings, M. Kent and Vicki Zeitner. 2003. "Internet Use and Civic Engagement." *Public Opinion Quarterly* 67(3):311–334.

Johnston, Hank, Enrique Larana and Joseph R. Gusfield. *1994. New Social Movements: From Ideology to Identity*. Philadelphia, PA: Temple University Press pp. 3–35.

Kenski, Kate and Natalie Jomini Stroud. 2006. "Connections Between Internet Use and Political Efficacy Knowledge, and Participation." *Journal of Broadcasting & Electronic Media* 50(2):173–192.

Kim, Claire Jean. 2000. *Bitter Fruit: The Politics of Black-Korean Conflict in New York City*. New Haven, CT: Yale University Press.

Kingdon, John. 1977. "Models of Legislative Voting." *Journal of Politics* 39:563–595.

Klandermans, Bert. 1984. "Mobilization and Participation: Social-Psychological Expansions of Resource Mobilization Theory." *American Sociological Review* 49:583–600.

Kochhar, Rakesh and Anthony Cilluffo. 2018. Income Inequality in the U.S. Is Rising Most Rapidly Among Asians. Technical report Pew Research Center. www.pewsocialtrends.org/2018/07/12/income-inequality-in-the-u-s-is-rising-most-rapidly-among-asians/

Kollman, Ken. 1998. *Outside Lobbying: Public Opinion and Interest Group Strategies*. Princeton, NJ: Princeton University Press.

Koopmans, Ruud 2008. "Protest in Time and Space: The Evolution of Waves of Contention." In the *Blackwell Companion to Social Movements*, edited by David A. Snow, Sarah A. Soule, and Hanspeter Kriesi, pp. 19–46. Malden, MA: Blackwell Publishing Ltd.

Krueger, Brian. 2002. "Assessing the Potential of Internet Political Participation in the United States: A Resource Approach." *American Politics Research* 30(5):476–498.

Krueger, Brian. 2006. "A Comparison of Conventional and Internet Political Mobilization." *American Politics Research* 34(6):759–776.

Lax, Jeffrey and Justin Phillips. 2009. "How Should We Estimate Public Opinion in the States?" *American Journal of Political Science* 53(1):107–21.

Lee, David S., Enrico Moretti and Matthew J. Butler. 2004. "Do Voters Affect or Elect Policies? Evidence from the U.S. House." *Quarterly Journal of Economics* 119(3):807–859.

Lee, Taeku. 2002. *Mobilizing Public Opinion: Black Insurgency and Racial Attitudes in the Civil Rights Era* Chicago: University of Chicago Press.

Lee, Woojin and John E. Roemer. 2006. "Racism and Redistribution in the United States: A Solution to the Problem of American Exceptionalism." *Journal of Public Economics* 90(6):1027–1052.

Leighley Jan E. and Christina Wolbrecht. 2005. "Race, Ethnicity, and Electoral Mobilization: Where's the Party?" In *Politics of Democratic Inclusion*, edited by Christina Wolbrecht, Rodney E. Hero. Peri E. Arnold, and Alvin B. Tillery, pp. 143–162. Philadelphia, PA: Temple University Press.

Leighley Jan E. and Jonathan Nagler. 2014. *Who Votes Now? Demographics, Issues, Inequality, and Turnout in the United States*. Princeton, NJ: Princeton University Press.

Lipsky Michael. 1968. "Protest as a Political Resource." *American Political Science Review* 62(4):1144–1158.

Lipsky Michael. 1970. *Protest in City Politics: Rent Strikes, Housing, and the Power of the Poor*. Chicago: Rand McNally

Lipsky Michael. 1980. *Street Level Bureaucracy: Dilemmas of the Individual in Public Services*. New York: Russell Sage Foundation.

Lipsky Michael and David J. Olson. 1977. *Commission Politics: The Processing of Racial Crisis in America*. New Brunswick, NJ: Transaction Books.

Lohmann, Susanne. 1993. "A Signaling Model of Informative and Manipulative Political Action." *American Political Science Review* 87(2):319–333.

Lublin, David. 1997. *The Paradox of Representation*. Princeton, NJ: Princeton University Press.

Lupia, Arthur and Gisela Sin. 2003. "Which Public Goods Are Endangered: How Evolving Communication Technologies Affect 'The Logic of Collective Action.'" *Public Choice* 117(4):315–331.

Lupo, Lindsey 2010. *Flak-Catchers: One Hundred Years of Riot Commission Politics in America*. Lanham, MD: Lexington Books.

Luttmer, Erzo F. P 2001. "Group Loyalty and the Taste for Redistribution." Journal of *Political Economy* 109(3):500–528.

Mansbridge, Jane. 1999. "Should Blacks Represent Blacks and Women Represent Women? A Contingent 'Yes.'" *Journal of Politics* 61(3):628–657.

Margetts, Helen, Peter John, Scott A. Hale and Taha Yasseri. 2016. *Political Turbulence: How Social Media Shape Collective Action*. Princeton, NJ: Princeton University Press.

Marwell, Gerald and Pamela E. Oliver. 1993. *The Critical Mass in Collective Action: A Micro-Social Theory*. New York: Cambridge University Press.

Masuoka, Natalie and Jane Junn. 2013. *The Politics of Belonging: Race, Public Opinion, and Immigration*. Chicago Studies in American Politics. Chicago: University of Chicago Press.

Mayhew, David R. 1974. Congress: The Electoral Connection. New Haven, CT: Yale University Press.

Mazumder, Soumyajit. 2018. "The Persistent Effect of the U.S. Civil Rights Movement on Political Attitudes." *American Journal of Political Science* 62(4):922–935.

McAdam, Doug. 1982. *Political Process and the Development of Black Insurgency, 1930–1970*. Chicago: University of Chicago Press.

McAdam, Doug and Yang Su. 2002. "The War at Home: Antiwar Protests and Congressional Voting, 1965–1973." *American Sociological Review* 67:696–721.

McCall, Leslie and Jeff Manza. 2011. "Class Differences in Social and Political Attitudes" In *Oxford Handbook of American Public Opinion and the Media*, edited by Lawrence Jacobs and Robert Shapiro, pp. 552-570. New York: Oxford University Press.

McCarthy John D. and Mayer N. Zald. 1973. *The Trend of Social Movements in America: Professionalization and Resource Mobilization*. Morristown, NJ: General Learning Press.

McCarthy John D. and Mayer N. Zald. 1977. "Resources Mobilization and Social Movements: A Partial Theory." *American Journal of Sociology* 82:1212–1239.

Mendelberg, Tali. 2001. *The Race Card Campaign Strategy, Implicit Messages, and the Norm of Equality*. Princeton, NJ: Princeton University Press.

Meyer, David. 2004. "Protest and Political Opportunities." *Annual Review of Sociology* 30:125–145.

Michener, Jamila. 2018. *Fragmented Democracy: Medicaid, Federalism, and Unequal Politics*. Cambridge: Cambridge University Press.

Miler, Kristina C. 2018. *Poor Representation: Congress and the Politics of Poverty in the United States*. Cambridge: Cambridge University Press.

Navarro, Bruno J. 2012. "Wearing Hoodie in Congress: Fair Protest or Disrespectful?" www.cnbc.com/id/46886308

NTIA. 2010. Digital Nation: 21st Century America's Progress Towards Universal Broadband Internet Access. Technical report. Washington, DC: US Department of Commerce. www.ntia.doc.gov/files/ntia/publications/ntia_internet_use_report_feb2010.pdf

Offe, Claus. 1985. "New Social Movements: Challenging the Boundaries of Institutional Politics." *Social Research* 52(4):817–868.

Olson, Mancur. 1965. *The Logic of Collective Action*. Cambridge, MA: Harvard University Press.

Orr, Shannon K. 2005. "New Technology and Research: An Analysis of Internet Survey Methodology in Political Science." *PS: Political Science and Politics* 38(2):263–267.

Page, Benjamin I., Larry M. Bartels and Jason Seawright. 2013. "Democracy and the Policy Preferences of Wealthy Americans." *Perspectives on Politics* 11(1):51–73.

Paquette, Danielle. 2020. "Kente Cloth Is Beloved in Ghana. Why Did Democrats Wear It?" *Washington Post*. www.washingtonpost.com/world/africa/democr ats-kente-cloth-ghana/2020/06/08/dc33bcc4-a9b5-11ea-a43b-be9f6494a87d_ story.html

Philpot, Tasha S. 2007. *Race, Republicans, and the Return of the Party of Lincoln*. Ann Arbor: University of Michigan Press.

Philpot, Tasha S., Daron R. Shaw and Ernest B. McGowen. 2009. "Winning the Race: Black Voter Turnout in the 2008 Presidential Election." *Public Opinion Quarterly* 73(5):995–1022.

Phoenix, Davin L. 2019. *The Anger Gap: How Race Shapes Emotion in Politics*. Cambridge: Cambridge University Press.

Piven, Frances and Richard Cloward. 1977. *Poor People's Movement: Why They Succeed, Why They Fail*. New York: Vintage.

Poggione, Sarah. 2004. "Exploring Gender Differences in State Legislators' Policy Preferences." *Political Research Quarterly* 57(2):305–314.

Poole, Keith and Howard Rosenthal. 1997. *Congress: A Political-Economic History of Roll-Call Voting*. New York: Oxford University Press.

Poole, Keith T. 2007. "Changing Minds? Not in Congress!" *Public Choice* 131(3–4):435–451.

Putnam, Lara, Erica Chenoweth and Jeremy Pressman. 2020. "The Floyd Protests Are the Broadest in US History – and Are Spreading to White, Small-Town America." *Washington Post Monkey Cage.* www.washingtonpost.com/politics/2020/06/06/floyd-protests-are-broadest-us-history-are-spreading-white-small-town-america/

Rainie, Lee. 2016. Digital Divides 2016. Technical report Pew Research Center. www.pewinternet.org/2016/07/14/digital-divides-2016/

Roediger, David R. 1999. *The Wages of Whiteness: Race and the Making of the American Working Class.* New York: Verso.

Rosenstone, Steven J. and John Mark Hansen. 1993. *Mobilization, Participation, and Democracy in America.* New York: Macmillan.

Sarmiento, Isabella Gomez. 2020. "Kente Cloth: From Royals to Graduation Ceremonies ... to Congress?" NPR. www.npr.org/sefrom-royals-to-gradua tion-ceremonies-to-congress

Schaeffer, Katherine. 2021. "The Changing Face of Congress in 7 Charts." www.pewresearch.org/fact-tank/2021/03/10/the-changing-face-of-congress/

Schattschneider, E. E. 1960. *The Semisovereign People: A Realist's View of Democracy in America.* New York: Holt, Rinehart and Winston.

Schlozman, Kay Lehman, Henry E. Brady and Sidney Verba. 2018. *Unequal and Unrepresented: Political Inequality and the People's Voice in the New Gilded Age.* Princeton, NJ: Princeton University Press.

Schlozman, Kay Lehman, Sidney Verba and Henry E. Brady 2010. "Weapon of the Strong? Participatory Inequality and the Internet." *Perspectives on Politics* 8(2):487–509.

Schwarz, Hunter. 2014. "Congress Decides to Get Serious about Tracking Police Shootings." www.washingtonpost.com/news/post-politics/wp/2014/12/11/con gress-decides-to-get-serious-about-tracking-police-shootings/?utm_term=.7ff4 6ee8f5fd.

Shipp, E. R. 1991. "Harlem Groups Try to Stop St. Luke's Growth." *New York Times.* www.nytimes.com/1991/04/14/nyregion/harlem-groups-try-to-stop-st-luke-s-growth.html

Shuit, Douglas P 1992. "Waters Focuses Her Rage at System." *Los Angeles Times.* http://articles.latimes.com/1992-05-10/news/mn-2503_1_maxine-waters.

Sneiderman, Phil. 1992. "Threats Against King Jurors Investigated: Simi Valley: The Warnings Appear to Be Concentrated in the City Where the Not-Guilty Verdicts Were Returned." *Los Angeles Times.* http://articles.latimes .com/1992-05-8/local/me-1708_1_simi-valley-police.

Sniderman, Paul M. and Edward G. Carmines. 1997. *Reaching Beyond Race.* Cambridge, MA: Harvard University Press.

Soss, Joe. 1999. "Lessons of Welfare: Policy Design, Political Learning, and Political Action." *American Political Science Review* 93(2):293–304.

Soule, Sarah A. and Susan Olzak. 2004. "When Do Movements Matter? The Politics of Contingency and the Equal Rights Amendment." *American Sociological Review* 69:473–497.

Stockdill, Brett C. 2003. *Activism Against AIDS: At the Intersection of Sexuality, Race, Gender, and Class.* Boulder, CO: Lynne Rienner Publishers.

Swain, Carol M. 1993. *Black Faces, Black Interests: The Representation of African Americans in Congress.* Cambridge, MA: Harvard University Press.

Tansey Oisín. 2007. "Process Tracing and Elite Interviewing: A Case for Non-Probability Sampling." *PS: Political Science & Politics* 40(4):765–772.

Tate, Katherine. 2004. *Black Faces in the Mirror: African-Americans and Their Representatives in the U.S. Congress.* Princeton, NJ: Princeton University Press.

Thomas, Sue. 2014. *Women and Elective Office: Past, Present, and Future.* New York: Oxford University Press, pp. 1–26.

Tillery Alvin B. 2019. "What Kind of Movement Is Black Lives Matter? The View from Twitter." *Journal of Race, Ethnicity and Politics* 4(2):297–323.

Tilly Charles. 1975 "Revolutions and Collective Violence." In *Macropolitical Theory, Volume III*, edited by Fred Greenstein and Nelson Polsby, pp. 483–555. Reading, MA: Addison-Wesley Publishing Company.

Tilly Charles. 1978. *From Mobilization to Revolution.* Reading, MA: Addison-Wesley Publishing Company.

Tolbert, Caroline J and Ramona S McNeal. 2003. "Unraveling the Effects of the Internet on Political Participation?" *Political Research Quarterly* 56(2):175–185.

Tolchin, Martin. 1989. "Retreat in Congress; The Catastrophic-Care Debacle – A Special Report; How the New Medicare Law Fell on Hard Times in a Hurry." www.nytimes.com/1989/10/09/us/retreat-congress-catastrophic-care-debacle-special-report-new-medicare-law-fell.html?pagewanted=all&src=pm

Turner, Trish. 2020. "Republicans Unveil 'Justice Act' Aimed at Policing Reform Propose FastTrack Action." ABC News. https://abcnews.go.com/Politics/republicans-unveil-justice-act-aimed-policing-reform-senate/story?id=71295669

U.S. Census Bureau. 2011. "2011 ACS 3-Year Estimates." http://factfinder2.census.gov

van der Linden, Sander. 2017. "The Nature of Viral Altruism and How to Make it Stick." *Nature Human Behavior* 1. http://dx.doi.org/10.1038/s41562-016-0041

Verba, Sidney, Kay Lehman Schlozman, and Henry E. Brady. 1995. *Voice and Equality: Civic voluntarism in American Politics.* Cambridge, MA: Harvard University Press.

Walker, Edward T. 2009. "Privatizing Participation: Civic Change and the Organizational Dynamics of Grassroots Lobbying Firms." *American Sociological Review* 74:83–105.

Wallace, Sophia J., Chris Zepeda-Millán, and Michael Jones-Correa. 2014. "Spatial and Temporal Proximity: Examining the Effects of Protests on Political Attitudes." *American Journal of Political Science* 58:433–448.

Warshaw, Christopher and Jonathan Rodden. 2012. "How Should We Measure District-Level Public Opinion on Individual Issues?" *Journal of Politics* 74(1):203–219.

Wasow, Omar. 2020. "Agenda Seeding: How 1960s Black Protests Moved Elites, Public Opinion and Voting." *American Political Science Review* 114(3):1–22.

Weaver, Vesla. 2007. "Frontlash: Race and the Development of Punitive Crime Policy." *Studies in American Political Development* 21:230–265.

Weber, Bruce. 1992. "Gay Irish Group Sues to March in Parade." *New York Times* www.nytimes.com/2015/01/19/us/in-ferguson-push-for-crim inal-justice-reform-draws-comparisons-to-60s-fight-for-civil-rights.html

Wemms, William and John Hodgson. 1824. The Trial of the British Soldiers, of the 29th Regiment of Foot: For the Murder of Crispus Attucks, Samuel Gray, Samuel Maverick, James Caldwell, and Patrick Carr, on Monday Evening, March 5, 1770, Before the Honorable Benjamin Lynde, John Cushing, Peter Oliver, and Edmund Trowbridge, Esquires, Justices of the Superior Court of Judicature, Court of Assize, and General Gaol Delivery, Held at Boston, by Adjournment, November 27, 1770. W. Emmons. https://books.google.com/books?id=uVZHAQAAMAAJ

Whitby Kenny J. 1997. *The Color of Representation: Congressional Behavior and Black Interests*. Ann Arbor: University of Michigan Press.

White, Ismail K and Chryl N. Laird. 2020. Steadfast Democrats: How Social Forces Shape Black Political Behavior Princeton, NJ: Princeton University Press.

Williams, Linda Faye. 2003. *The Constraint of Race: Legacies of White Skin Privilege*. University Park: Pennsylvania State University

Wouters, Ruud and Stefaan Walgrave. 2017. "Demonstrating Power: How Protest Persuades Political Representatives." *American Sociological Review* 82(2):361–383.

Wright, Matthew and Jack Citrin. 2011. "Saved by the Stars and Stripes? Images of Protest, Salience of Threat, and Immigration Attitudes." *American Politics Research* 39(2):323–343.

Wu, De-Min. 1973. "Alternative Tests of Independence between Stochastic Regressors and Disturbances." *Econometrica* 41(4):733–750.

Xenos, Michael and Patricia Moy 2007. "Direct and Differential Effects of the Internet on Political and Civic Engagement." *Journal of Communications* 57(4):704–716.

Yokley Eli. 2015*a*. "In Ferguson, Push for Criminal Justice Reform Draws Comparisons to '60s Fight for Civil Rights." *New York Times*. www .nytimes.com/2015/01/19/us/in-ferguson-push-for-criminal-justice-reform-draws-comparisons-to-60s-fight-for-civil-rights.html

Yokley Eli. 2015*b*. "In Missouri, a Ferguson Candidate Challenges the Establishment." *New York Times* www.rollcall.com/2015/11/06/in-miss ouri-a-ferguson-candidate-challenges-the-establishment/

Zepeda-Millán, Chris and Sophia J. Wallace. 2013. "Racialization in Times of Contention: How Social Movements Impact Latino Racial Identity." *Politics, Groups, and Identities* 1(4):510–27.

Index

Books in the Series (continued from page ii)

Doug McAdam and Hilary Boudet, *Putting Social Movements in Their Place: Explaining Opposition to Energy Projects in the United States, 2000–2005*

Doug McAdam, Sidney Tarrow, and Charles Tilly, *Dynamics of Contention*

Holly J. McCammon, *The U.S. Women's Jury Movements and Strategic Adaptation: A More Just Verdict*

Dana M. Moss *The Arab Spring Abroad: Diaspora Activism Against Authoritarian Regimes*

Shivaji Mukherjee *Colonial Institutions and Civil War: Indirect Rule and Maoist Insurgency in India*

Sharon Nepstad, *Religion and War Resistance and the Plowshares Movement*

Olena Nikolayenko, *Youth Movements and Elections in Eastern Europe*

Kevin J. O'Brien and Lianjiang Li, *Rightful Resistance in Rural China*

Eleonora Pasotti, *Resisting Redevelopment: Protest in Aspiring Global Cities*

Silvia Pedraza, *Political Disaffection in Cuba's Revolution and Exodus*

Marcos E. Pérez *Proletarian Lives: Routines, Identity and Culture in Contentious Politics*

Héctor Perla Jr., *Sandinista Nicaragua's Resistance to US Coercion*

Federico M. Rossi, *The Poor's Struggle for Political Incorporation: The Piquetero Movement in Argentina*

Chandra Russo, *Solidarity in Practice: Moral Protest and the US Security State*

Eduardo Silva, *Challenging Neoliberalism in Latin America*

Erica S. Simmons, *Meaningful Resistance: Market Reforms and the Roots of Social Protest in Latin America*

Sarah Soule, *Contention and Corporate Social Responsibility*

Suzanne Staggenborg, *Grassroots Environmentalism*

Sherrill Stroschein, *Ethnic Struggle, Coexistence, and Democratization in Eastern Europe*

Yang Su, *Collective Killings in Rural China during the Cultural Revolution*

Sidney Tarrow, *Movements and Parties: Critical Connections in American Political Development*

Sidney Tarrow, *The Language of Contention: Revolutions in Words, 1688–2012*

Sidney Tarrow, *The New Transnational Activism*

Wayne P. Te Brake, *Religious War and Religious Peace in Early Modern Europe*

Ralph A. Thaxton Jr., *Catastrophe and Contention in Rural China: Mao's Great Leap Forward Famine and the Origins of Righteous Resistance in Da Fo Village*

Ralph A. Thaxton Jr., *Force and Contention in Contemporary China: Memory and Resistance in the Long Shadow of the Catastrophic Past*

Charles Tilly, *Contention and Democracy in Europe, 1650–2000*

Charles Tilly, *Contentious Performances*

Charles Tilly, *The Politics of Collective Violence*

Marisa von Bülow, *Building Transnational Networks: Civil Society and the Politics of Trade in the Americas*

Lesley J. Wood, *Direct Action, Deliberation, and Diffusion: Collective Action after the WTO Protests in Seattle*

Stuart A. Wright, *Patriots, Politics, and the Oklahoma City Bombing*

Deborah Yashar, *Contesting Citizenship in Latin America: The Rise of Indigenous Movements and the Postliberal Challenge*

Andrew Yeo, *Activists, Alliances, and Anti-U.S. Base Protests*

CPSIA information can be obtained
at www.ICGtesting.com
Printed in the USA
LVHW040041221222
735706LV00003B/213

9 781009 074322